THIS IS PHILOSOPHY OF MIND

THIS IS PHILOSOPHY
Series editor: Steven D. Hales

Reading philosophy can be like trying to ride a bucking bronco—you hold on for dear life while "transcendental deduction" twists you to one side, "causa sui" throws you to the other, and a 300-word, 300-year-old sentence comes down on you like an iron-shod hoof the size of a dinner plate. *This Is Philosophy* is the riding academy that solves these problems. Each book in the series is written by an expert who knows how to gently guide students into the subject regardless of the reader's ability or previous level of knowledge. Their reader-friendly prose is designed to help students find their way into the fascinating, challenging ideas that compose philosophy without simply sticking the hapless novice on the back of the bronco, as so many texts do. All the books in the series provide ample pedagogical aids, including links to free online primary sources. When students are ready to take the next step in their philosophical education, *This Is Philosophy* is right there with them to help them along the way.

This Is Philosophy: An Introduction
Steven D. Hales

This Is Philosophy of Mind: An Introduction
Pete Mandik

Forthcoming:

This Is Metaphysics: An Introduction
Kristopher McDaniel

This Is Epistemology: An Introduction
Clayton Littlejohn

This Is Philosophy of Religion: An Introduction
Neil Manson

This Is Ethics: An Introduction
Jussi Suikkanen

This Is Modern Philosophy: An Introduction
Kurt Smith

This Is Political Philosophy: An Introduction
Alex Tuckness and Clark Wolf

This Is Bioethics: An Introduction
Udo Schuklenk

THIS IS
PHILOSOPHY
OF MIND
AN INTRODUCTION

PETE MANDIK

WILEY Blackwell

This edition first published 2014
© 2014 John Wiley & Sons, Inc.

Wiley-Blackwell is an imprint of John Wiley & Sons, formed by the merger of Wiley's global Scientific, Technical and Medical business with Blackwell Publishing.

Registered Office
John Wiley & Sons, Ltd, The Atrium, Southern Gate, Chichester, West Sussex, PO19 8SQ, UK

Editorial Offices
350 Main Street, Malden, MA 02148-5020, USA
9600 Garsington Road, Oxford, OX4 2DQ, UK
The Atrium, Southern Gate, Chichester, West Sussex, PO19 8SQ, UK

For details of our global editorial offices, for customer services, and for information about how to apply for permission to reuse the copyright material in this book please see our website at www.wiley.com/wiley-blackwell.

The right of Pete Mandik to be identified as the author of this work has been asserted in accordance with the UK Copyright, Designs and Patents Act 1988.

Library of Congress Cataloging-in-Publication Data
Mandik, Pete.
   This is philosophy of mind : an introduction / Pete Mandik.
      pages cm. – (This is philosophy ; 2996)
   Includes bibliographical references and index.
   ISBN 978-0-470-67447-5 (alk. paper) – ISBN 978-0-470-67450-5 (pbk. : alk. paper)   1. Philosophy of mind.   I. Title.
   BD418.3.M3535 2013
   128'.2–dc22
                                          2013006408

A catalogue record for this book is available from the British Library.

Cover design by www.cyandesign.co.uk

Set in 10.5/13 pt Minion by Toppan Best-set Premedia Limited

For Rachelle and Delia

CONTENTS

xiv   Contents

HOW TO USE THIS BOOK

Despite the enormous advances in understanding that humans have made about themselves and the world around them, many mysteries remain. Many of those mysteries have to do with the *mind*. This guide to philosophical approaches to the mind is intended to be useful both to students taking a course with a teacher and readers tackling the subject on their own. The book's 15 chapters were written with a typical 15-week university semester in mind, though it is not essential that all the chapters be read or read in precisely the order in which they are presented. Although there is cross-referencing between the chapters to aid those reading from beginning to end, the chapters can serve as stand-alone units, with each chapter ending with an annotated bibliography. As much as possible, the annotated bibliographies contain links to readings available on the Internet.

Here's another thing for Internet users to keep in mind: I encourage readers—both students and teachers—to consult the companion blog for this book, located at http://tipom.blogspot.com. The blog is a frequently updated online resource compiling relevant additional readings, videos, visual aids, pointers to relevant scientific work, and definitions of key terms. Teachers in particular are encouraged to start off on the blog at http://tipom.blogspot.com/p/teacher-tips.html, although students might get something out of looking at that part as well!

ACKNOWLEDGMENTS

For valuable comments on early versions of some of this material, I am grateful to Jeff Dean, Steven Hales, Chase Wrenn, and several anonymous referees. Very special thanks for highly thorough help goes to Helen Kemp, Josh Weisberg, and Tad Zawidzki.

For love, support, and advice based on a truly humbling grasp of English, I thank my wife, Rachelle Mandik.

1

MEET YOUR MIND

Unless you've lost your mind, or never had one in the first place, likely you'll 1.1
agree that your mind is a pretty special part of you. Maybe, even, your mind
is *all* that you are—maybe you're nothing but a mind. Maybe that's too
extreme, but you do have to admit that your mind is an excellent candidate
for your single most defining feature. It's certainly a much better candidate
for the seat of your you-ness than your foot, your liver, or your haircut. So
what is this special thing, this mind of yours? In this chapter we'll examine
some of the main aspects of the mind that philosophers have been interested in. We'll also look at some of the main philosophical problems concerning the mind.

Aspects of Mind

Because you have a mind, there are certain special things you can *do*. You 1.2
can think and perceive. You can enjoy and you can suffer. You can learn
from the past and plan for the future. You can make choices. You can spring
into action. You can dream.

Because you have a mind, there are special things that you *have*. You have 1.3
beliefs. You have feelings. You have mental images. You have memories. You
have the reasons for the way that you act.

Thought and experience

Stop and attend to your mind right now. What do you notice about your 1.4
own mind? What's in it that isn't in your foot, your liver, or your haircut?

This Is Philosophy of Mind: An Introduction, First Edition. Pete Mandik.
© 2014 John Wiley & Sons, Inc. Published 2014 by John Wiley & Sons, Inc.

One striking collection of items populating your mental landscape is your experiences, especially your *sensory* experiences. You see colors and shapes. You hear noises and melodies. You feel textures and temperatures. Further, you have experiences besides those that are straightforwardly sensory. You experience a faint twinge of anxiety or are overcome by an intense dread. These are your emotional experiences.

1.5   In addition to your experiences, when you attend to your mind you may notice various *thoughts* that you have. You are thinking when you *believe* that there are leftovers in the fridge, *wonder* whether the weather will be nice tomorrow, or *doubt* that you will win a million dollars. Beliefs, judgments, and doubts are kinds of thoughts.

1.6   Like philosophy in general, philosophy of mind is rife with controversy. One sort of controversy concerns the view that our mental states may be sorted into the experiences and the thoughts. Are these groups too few? Perhaps there is more to the mind than thoughts and experiences. Perhaps mental images or emotions are neither thoughts nor experiences. Another perspective is that sorting mental states into thoughts and experiences is to create *more* groups than there really are. Maybe all mental states are really a kind of experience. Or, instead, all are just thoughts. We will return to such controversies later. Suffice for now to say that the most widely held view on this matter is that there are both thoughts and experiences and there may be other sorts of mental states as well.

Conscious and unconscious

1.7   At least since the time of Freud, if not earlier, people have been familiar with the idea that some of our mental states occur unconsciously, while others occur consciously. Freudian psychologists sought to explain much human behavior in terms of unconscious desires such as the unconscious desire to kill one of your parents and have sex with the other one. Perhaps another example of the unconscious is the unconscious knowledge that guides an expert as they hit a tennis ball or play a musical instrument. They aren't consciously thinking of what they're doing, and when they do try to consciously attend to, for instance, what comes next in the music that they are performing, this act of consciousness makes them make a mistake.

1.8   In contrast to such unconscious mental states there are, of course, the conscious ones. Consider your experience of the words that you are reading right now. In attending deliberately to the words on the screen or page you consciously experience the way they look (or feel, if you are reading this in Braille).

Qualia

One fascinating aspect of our mental states, an aspect mostly associated 1.9 with our conscious sensory states, is something that philosophers call a quale (singular, pronounced KWAH-LAY) and qualia (plural, pronounced KWAH-LEE-AH). The word "qualia" comes from the Latin for "qualities," and philosophers of mind reserve the term for special qualities of mental states. One important phrase that helps philosophers of mind convey the idea of qualia is the phrase "what it's like." Consider the question of what it's like to see red as opposed to seeing blue. Imagine the difficulty in explaining to someone who has been blind their whole life what it's like to see red. Would it really suffice to describe it as like seeing something warm or seeing something that makes people hungry? Or instead must such descriptions necessarily leave something out? Consider the philosophers' puzzle of the inverted spectrum: Is it possible that what it's like for you to see red is the same as what it's like for me to see green and vice versa? These are difficult philosophical questions. Anyway, the main point for now is that insofar as you followed this brief discussion employing the phrase "what it's like" in connection with conscious sensory experiences, you have a feel for what qualia are. Qualia are the subjective aspects of experiences, the aspects of *what it's like* to have experiences.

Sensory perception

It's difficult to deny the importance of sensory perception. One old and 1.10 influential philosophical position, empiricism, even goes so far as to hold sensory perception to be the source of all our ideas and knowledge: Nothing gets in the mind without first getting in the senses.

Saying what makes sensory perceptions distinctive is an interesting phil- 1.11 osophical problem. What serves to distinguish, say, visually perceiving a cat from merely thinking about a cat? One sort of answer to this question is that in the case of perception there must be a direct sort of causal interaction between the perceiver and the thing perceived whereas there need not be such interaction between a thinker and the thing thought about. You can think about things that are too small or too far way to have noticeable effects on you, but noticeable effects are a requirement on the perception of perceptible objects.

Emotion

1.12 Emotions are a very interesting sort of mental state. Consider thinking, without having any emotional reaction one way or another, that there is a dog in the room. Now compare this to being angry or being happy that there is a dog in the room. What differentiates the mere thought from the anger or the happiness? In the case of anger we might be tempted to say there's something intrinsically negative in it, whereas the mere thought is neither positive nor negative. There's something to this suggestion, but it seems not enough. The fear that there's a dog in the room is negative too, but it doesn't seem to be exactly the same sort of thing as anger. So there must be more to these negative emotions than simply adding some negativity to otherwise neutral thoughts.

Imagery

1.13 Here's an exercise of imagination. Imagine a capital letter "J" and a capital letter "D." Now imagine that the letter "D" is rotated 90 degrees counterclockwise and placed on top of the "J." Now answer this question: What common object does the resulting figure resemble? If you answered "umbrella" you've thereby demonstrated the power of mental imagery. The word "imagery" is closely associated with things of a visual nature, but there can also be nonvisual mental imagery. It thus makes sense to talk about forming mental images of smells or imagining hearing certain sounds. One thing that's interesting about mental imagery is the way it seems to sit astride the contrast we drew earlier between thoughts and sensory experiences. Images are more similar to sense experiences in some ways and more similar to thoughts in others.

1.14   Let us note now a similarity that thoughts and images share that distinguishes each from sensory perception. We can exert a kind of *direct* control on our thoughts and images that we cannot exert on what we perceive. Suppose you see a red stop sign. While you can easily imagine or think about the stop sign as being some other color, you cannot simply choose to perceive the red stop sign as green. If you wanted to see it as green, you'd have to exert some indirect control on your perception, like painting the sign green.

Will and action

We have, so far, contrasted thoughts and experiences, conscious states and   1.15
unconscious states, perception and imagery. Here's another contrast of
special importance: It's the contrast between what happens to us and what
we do. Where perceptions and experiences are things that happen to us,
action and *will* clearly concerns what we *do*. One way in which some philosophers have sought to explain the difference between what we do and
what merely happens to us is by making reference to a special faculty of
will, a faculty by means of which events are caused that count as actions
we've performed instead mere happenings that occur.

Self

Consider the following questions that concern personal identity: Who are   1.16
you? What distinguishes you from other people? What sort of thing is a
person? What distinguishes people from mere objects?

Some have sought to answer such questions by referring to a certain kind   1.17
of entity—a *self*. What is a self? It's what makes you a somebody instead of
nobody at all, a person instead of a mere object. And it's what serves to
distinguish you from everybody else. Some philosophers have denied that
there is any such thing as a self. The philosopher David Hume, being an
empiricist, stressed the grounding of what we know in what we can perceive
with the senses. Some think of the self as the thing that has experiences, a
thing separate from the experiences themselves. But Hume invites us to pay
close attention to our experiences and notice that all we are able to attend
to are the experiences themselves, for instance, an experience of heat, of
color, or of shape. Try as we might, looking inward, we never catch a
glimpse of any entity doing the glimpsing—we find only what is glimpsed.
Perhaps, then, the self is nothing at all.

Propositional attitudes

One way in which philosophers think about certain mental states, especially   1.18
mental states such as beliefs and desires, is as what philosophers call "propositional attitudes." When a person has a propositional attitude, there is a
proposition—roughly, a declarative sentence, a sentence that may be either
true or false—toward which they bear an *attitude*, examples of which
include believing, doubting, wondering, judging, desiring, fearing, and

intending. Consider the following examples, and note that each attitude is in *italics* and the proposition toward which the attitude is directed is in **bold**.

1. Alice *believes* that **her team will win.**
2. Bruno *doubts* that **the rain will stop before dinner time.**
3. Carla *judges* that **there is more water in the container on the left.**
4. Dwayne *fears* that **his dog ate his 20 dollar bill.**

1.19   Other examples of propositional attitudes are not as obvious as 1–4, but nonetheless, we can identify the proposition toward which an attitude is directed. Consider these cases:

5. Eileen *intends* to go to the movies on Saturday.
6. Franklin *desires* to eat the biggest piece of pizza.

In 5 and 6, the attitudes are obvious: intending in the case of 5 and desiring in the case of 6. However, what are the propositions in question? We can answer that question by considering another: What proposition has to be true for Eileen to accomplish what she intends and what proposition has to be true for Franklin to obtain what he desires? The answer to that question is this: The two propositions that must be true are "Eileen goes to the movies on Saturday" and "Franklin eats the biggest piece of pizza." We can now take this information and assemble versions of 5 and 6 that more closely resemble 1–4. While it may sound a little weird to describe things in the following way, there's nothing strictly incorrect about 5* and 6*:

5*.   Eileen *intends* that **Eileen goes to the movies on Saturday.**
6*.   Franklin *desires* that **Franklin eats the biggest piece of pizza.**

Philosophical Problems

1.20 We've seen some of the main aspects of mind that have interested philosophers, but to see what *really* interests philosophers we need to look at the puzzles and problems that arise when we try to understand aspects of the mind. First and foremost among these problems is that old classic, the mind–body problem.

Mind–body problem

When we contemplate the various mental states and mental properties it   1.21
may strike us how very different they are from physical states and properties. But what makes something physical? First off, consider your own body.
Your body is a physical thing, and it has the sorts of properties—physical
properties—that are the proper study of physics and other physical sciences
like chemistry. Your body has mass, it takes up a certain volume of space,
it moves through space with a certain momentum, and it has various
chemical constituents (e.g., hydrogen, oxygen, and carbon). The human
body is not the only thing worth calling a "physical body." Tables and chairs
are physical bodies. So are rocks rolling down hills and apples falling out
of trees (as are the hills and the trees). So, anyway, minds and mental properties seem to be very different from physical bodies and physical properties. We are led, then, to wonder what sort of *relations* there can be between
mental things and properties on the one hand and physical things and
properties on the other.

   So, now that we have a bit of a feel for what minds and bodies are, what   1.22
is the mind–body problem? It's probably best to think of it as a cluster of
closely related problems. The main problems in this cluster are:

1.   The problem of explaining what the real difference is, if any, between
     the mental and the physical.
2.   The problem of explaining, if the mental and the physical are very dif-
     ferent, *how* they can possibly relate to each other in the ways we com-
     monly suppose them to relate. For example, how can minds have effects
     on bodies and vice versa?
3.   The problem of explaining, if minds are really just a kind of physical
     thing, *how* that can be. How can it really make sense to treat minds as
     just another physical thing in the universe?

   To help get a further feel for the mind–body problem, it helps to con-   1.23
template the ideas of the one philosopher who has been most central to
subsequent discussions of the mind–body problem, the philosopher René
Descartes. Descartes thought that the mind was radically different from
physical bodies. He held that minds were essentially thinking things that
didn't take up any space and that physical bodies were essentially unthinking things that did take up space. This is the essence of his *substance
dualism*, which we will discuss at much greater length in chapter 2.

1.24   Given how radically different minds and bodies are supposed to be, a puzzle arises about how they can ever interact. Call this the *problem of interaction*. We'll say a lot more about this problem in chapter 9, but for now let's look at a quick sketch. To see how this problem arises for Descartes' substance dualism (aka Cartesian substance dualism), let's take this in a series of steps. First, note that minds and bodies do seem to interact. In fact, there are two directions of interaction, one for perception and one for action. In the case of perception, something happens in the world that has a causal effect on our minds. A car explodes causing us to see a ball of fire and hear a loud BOOM! In the case of action, something happens in the mind that has a causal effect on the world. Suppose I wanted to blow up a car. I have, in my mind, an intention to make things go BOOM! Next, I formulate a plan in my mind to gather the required explosives. And eventually, in the world, there's a mighty explosion.

1.25   Let's go on now to the second step in seeing what's problematic about the problem of interaction for Cartesian substance dualism. Note what usually happens when one thing causes another. They must be at the same place at the same time. To light the fuse, the flame must be brought near it. To boil the water, the pot must be put on the stove. To heal the wound, the medicine must be put on it. Causation seems to require proximity. Even in cases that look like action at a distance, like when a remote is used to turn on a television, something crosses the space in between, in this case invisible radiation. However, in Cartesian substance dualism, while bodies take up space, minds do not. Taking up no amount of space, they therefore are nowhere. They simply aren't located in space. How, then, can anything happening in space affect or be affected by anything outside of it? And here's a related problem: How come things happening in your mind have a direct effect on your body but not on mine?

1.26   To avoid the problem of interaction, as well as other problems that arise for Cartesian substance dualism, many philosophers of mind have been driven to reject dualism and embrace some version or other of *monism*. If we describe dualism as the view that there are fundamentally two sorts of things in the universe, the mental and the physical, then we can describe monism as the view that there is only one sort of thing. Maybe, then, everything is mental. (That's an option we'll explore further in chapter 4.) Or, to take a more popular option, maybe everything, including your mind, is physical. How, though, can the mind be physical? Well, perhaps the right way to think of this is to just say that your mind is your brain (see chapter 6). This would certainly resolve the problems surrounding interaction, for, clearly, brains can have effects on and be affected by physical bodies. However, this sort of solution runs into other problems.

If the mind is a physical thing like a brain, it still seems that, in addition   1.27
to its physical properties, it also has distinctively mental properties. Take, for example, *qualia*. What it's like to see red or feel pain is something I know only from the inside. No amount of investigation of my brain from the outside seems sufficient to reveal the nature of my qualia. It has therefore seemed plausible to many philosophers that qualia are a kind of nonphysical mental property. This kind of thinking leads to a different kind of dualism than the dualism of Descartes. As we'll explore further in chapter 3, this is a dualism of properties instead of a dualism of substances.

Other problems

While the mind–body problem is perhaps the central problem in philoso-   1.28
phy of mind, there are other problems as well, and we'll take a very quick look at them in the remainder of this chapter. In particular, we will be looking at the following problems:

- the problem of perception
- the problem of other minds
- the problem of artificial intelligence
- the problem of consciousness
- the problem of intentionality
- the problem of free will
- the problem of personal identity

The problem of perception   The problem of perception involves a conflict   1.29
between two individually plausible ideas about the nature of perception. The first is that when we perceive, we are thereby in a direct sort of relation to some object in the world. When I open my eyes and see a red book on the table before me, I am thereby in a relation with that red book. The red book is there, and my perceiving it is a kind of openness to this object in the real world.

The second idea about perception is an idea that comes from philosophi-   1.30
cal reflection on misperceptions and hallucinations. Perhaps you seem to see a pink elephant in the room with you, but as a matter of fact you are really dreaming or hallucinating. Since there is no pink elephant in the

room with you, whatever you are perceptually aware of, it cannot be a pink elephant. Many philosophers have hypothesized that this *something* that you are thereby aware of while dreaming or hallucinating is a *mental* something. Let's call it a perceptual *idea*. In hallucinating a pink elephant, you aren't aware of any real pink elephant, you are aware of an *idea* of a pink elephant.

1.31   Viewed from the "inside," both an accurate perception of a real object and a false perception of a hallucinated object can seem just the same. Since they can seem the same, there has to be something in common between the two situations. One sort of view that some philosophers have found attractive is to say that what's common to both the accurate perceptual case and the false hallucinatory case is that what one is really directly aware of is an idea in one's mind. Thus, even when I accurately perceive a red book on the table, I'm only *indirectly* aware of the red book. What I'm directly aware of is the idea of the red book. So, both the accurate perception of a red book and the hallucination of a red book are something very similar, for both involve a direct awareness of an idea in my own mind. However, many philosophers have found this to be an unhappy result. If all we are ever directly aware of are the insides of our own minds, the so-called external world starts to sound like some extra stuff that might as well not be there anyway. The proposed irrelevance of the real world strikes many as a deeply disturbing idea. These sorts of ideas, and the philosophical responses to them, are going to be explored more thoroughly when we get to chapters 4 and 11.

1.32   *The problem of other minds*   Suppose you see someone acting as though they were in pain and it occurs to you that they are *only* acting. A very good actor can act convincingly as if they are in pain without actually being in pain. A good actor can do this for other mental states besides pain—they can act hungry, angry, confused, deranged, or enraged without actually being in those mental states. The very possibility of playacting helps to highlight the *contingent* relationships between our inner mental lives and our outward behaviors. (Sad behavior is related to sadness only *contingently* if it's possible to have sadness without the behavior or vice versa.) However, given the assumption that the relation between mind and behavior is contingent, the possibility arises that those other human bodies that you see everyday actually are moving and speaking without any inner mental lives at all. Now, if *that* is a genuine possibility—a possibility that you can't rule out simply by observing behaviors—then the following question arises: If you do know that others have minds, *how* do you know it? The problem of answering this question is the problem of other minds.

One sort of solution to the problem of other minds is to adopt a kind 1.33 of behaviorism. On this sort of view, what a mental state *is* is something closely tied to particular kinds of behaviors. And so, regardless of whether a mental state belongs to you or someone else, what ultimately grounds your knowledge of the mental state is knowledge about certain kinds of behavior. We will take up further discussion of both behaviorism and the problem of other minds in chapter 5.

The problem of artificial intelligence   The way we've talked about the 1.34 problem of other minds so far has been in connection with other *people* and to ask whether they have minds (and if they do, how we know that). Another sort of question we can ask is whether things that are very different from people can nonetheless have minds. What about, for example, computers and robots? In science fiction stories we are often presented with futuristic machines capable of thinking and behaving intelligently. Could there ever be, in real life, artificial forms of genuine intelligence? Can a machine think? Some philosophers answer "yes." They say that humans themselves are a kind of machine, and that our own brains are a kind of computer. This is a version of a view known as *functionalism*, to be explored further in chapters 7 and 8.

Now, if this latter kind of idea is correct, that humans themselves are 1.35 kinds of thinking machines, the question arises of how such machines— human machines—work in order to give rise to thoughts. If we are thinking machines, then what are the general mechanical requirements on being a thinking thing? What sorts of things would you have to build into a machine if you were going to give it the power to think?

One sort of proposal that has received a lot of attention from philoso- 1.36 phers is that thinking is essentially *linguistic* and that the general mechanical requirements on thinking can only be satisfied by a machine that implements a *language of thought*. This hypothetical language of thought is a system of symbols that are combined in various rule-governed ways to form the various thoughts—beliefs, desires, etc.—that we have. As will be discussed further in chapter 7, the language of thought hypothesis is highly controversial, and many of its opponents propose that mechanical minds will need to be much more explicitly brain-like, and be constructed as highly connected networks—artificial neural networks composed of parallel distributed processors.

1.37 *The problem of consciousness* Regardless of whether *thinking* is best explained mechanistically by reference to an inner symbol system, there are separate questions about how to explain other aspects of the mind, aspects beyond simply thinking. What about conscious sensations like a feeling of pain or a visual sensation of a bright shade of red? How can a mechanical or physical system have those aspects of mentality most distinctive of *consciousness*? Some philosophers have held that those aspects of consciousness, like the quale that goes along with seeing a bright shade of red, will never be explained by any kind of physical process. Some philosophers hold that there's an *explanatory gap*—no matter how much you may know about the physical processes in some creature's brain, you'll never be able to explain why there's a red sensation versus either a green sensation or no sensation at all. Other philosophers are far more optimistic about explaining consciousness, and we will examine, in chapter 14, proposed philosophical explanations of consciousness.

1.38 *The problem of intentionality* Let's leave aside conscious sensations for just a moment and go back to questions about thinking. Earlier we were wondering about the requirements of being able to think. We mentioned the problem of whether thinking requires the existence of a language of thought. But there's another sort of problem connected to thinking, and it's a problem that we might state in this way: What sort of *relation* is it that takes place between a thinker and the things the thinker thinks about? This problem is the problem of *intentionality*.

1.39 Another way of stating the problem is in terms of "aboutness." When we think, we think *about* things. I'm thinking about the planet Jupiter right now. Jupiter is one thing; my thought about it is another. But what is this "aboutness"? Is it a relation between Jupiter and me? If aboutness is a relation, then it looks like it's a very weird sort of relation. One thing that's really weird about "aboutness" is that I can think about things that don't even exist. I can think about unicorns—magical horses with horns—even though there really is no such thing. The problem of intentionality, the problem of explaining "aboutness," will be taken up in chapter 13.

1.40 *The problem of free will* It seems to be a pretty important part of our conception of ourselves that we take ourselves and others to do certain things *freely*. On the face of it, it looks like a pretty important part of deciding whether someone is *morally responsible* for something is to decide whether or not they did it of their own free will. However, perhaps the very idea of free will is mistaken. Perhaps everything that happens has to happen that way (it's all fated or predetermined) and thus there's really no such thing as a person acting of their own free will. Everything that a person does is actually something that they were made to do by a complicated network of causes involving both biological and societal factors. Or maybe not. The problem of free will, taken up in chapter 12, is the problem of whether there is any, and if so, what its nature is.

The problem of personal identity   So-called identical twins aren't truly 1.41 identical. The Olsen twins, Mary-Kate Olsen and Ashley Olsen, aren't truly identical, since they aren't one and the same person. They are merely similar. True identity has to do with the conditions under which something counts as one and the same.

Here's a general problem about identity: How much can a single thing 1.42 change without becoming a second thing? Suppose I take a precious wooden chair and burn it until it's a pile of ash. Many people would regard that as a second thing: I no longer have a chair, I have a pile of ash. Another series of changes I can introduce to the chair is to gradually replace parts of it. One day I replace one of the legs, another day I replace the seat, and so on, until each part has been replaced and the resulting chair has none of the original wood in it. Is the chair I have after making all these replacements one and the same as the chair I started with? Or have I instead gradually destroyed one chair while creating a second one?

These sorts of puzzles about identity can be applied to entities besides 1.43 chairs. From birth to adulthood, a person undergoes many changes. During their life, cells in their body die and are eliminated as waste, while new cells grow to replace them. This replenishment of materials is one of the main functions of the nutrition we take in through food and drink. Like the chair described earlier, a person has their parts (at molecular and cellular levels) replaced. An adult is no longer a baby. But is the adult one and the same person as the baby? Did you used to be a baby, or are you instead some other person who has replaced the baby?

One of the greatest changes that occurs to a person's body is that their 1.44 body will die. Many religious traditions hold that there is life after death— that a person can continue their existence despite the death of their body. Perhaps their life after death is a purely spiritual existence in a nonphysical heaven or hell, or perhaps they are reincarnated and live in a new body. Either way, different positions concerning the mind–body problem and personal identity have different things to say about whether and how life after death might be possible. A functionalist who rejects substance dualism can nonetheless embrace the possibility of life after death. On one such version of the view, the relation of mind and body is analogous to the relation, in computers, between software and hardware. Surviving death is fundamentally the running of an old piece of software on a new piece of hardware. We will further explore the questions of personal identity and life after death in chapter 15.

Conclusion

1.45 The mind is most certainly one of the strangest and most wonderful parts of existence, and surely plays a central role in what it means to exist as a person. However, so much about the mind is ill understood, and there are many controversies amongst philosophers about how best to tackle the various topics related to the mind, topics such as feeling, thinking, and acting. Some of these controversies concern the most vexing problems in all of philosophy. Such problems include the problem of free will, the problem of artificial intelligence, and the question of what, if anything, happens to us after we die.

Annotated Bibliography

Bourget, David and Chalmers, David (eds.) (2012) "Philosophy of Mind, General Works," *PhilPapers*, full text available at http://philpapers.org/browse/philosophy-of-mind-general-works, accessed February 5, 2013. This frequently updated online bibliography contains many entries with abstracts and links to the full text of articles.

Mandik, Pete (2010) *Key Terms in Philosophy of Mind* (London: Continuum). More than just a dictionary of philosophy-of-mind terminology, this book also contains entries on key texts and key thinkers in the philosophy of mind.

Mandik, Pete (ed.) (n.d.) "Further reading," in *This is Philosophy of Mind: The Blog*, http://tipom.blogspot.com/search/label/Further%20reading. A frequently updated collection of additional readings on various topics in the philosophy of mind.

2

SUBSTANCE DUALISM

Consider, just for a moment, something horrible. Consider what would 2.1
happen to you if your body, including your brain, were totally destroyed.
Imagine your body falling into a vat of acid or a pit of lava, its molecules
violently and completely scattered in all directions. Question: Could you
survive such a horrible event? On one view, the answer is "yes." On this
view you are your mind and your mind is a completely distinct thing from
your physical body. Surviving death, then, is easy to do.

The idea that you are nonphysical and wholly distinct from your physical 2.2
body is found in many religious traditions. However, our concern here is
not with religious approaches to such an idea, but instead with philosophical ones. We will examine the main philosophical reasons in favor of and
against the view known as *substance dualism*.

Arguments for Substance Dualism

Philosophers are very interested in examining arguments, both pro and 2.3
con, for various positions. Philosophers of mind are no exception. Here
we'll take a look at three kinds of arguments for substance dualism. They
are (1) Leibniz's law arguments, (2) explanatory gap arguments, and (3)
modal arguments. Along the way we'll also look at some criticisms of these
arguments.

This Is Philosophy of Mind: An Introduction, First Edition. Pete Mandik.
© 2014 John Wiley & Sons, Inc. Published 2014 by John Wiley & Sons, Inc.

Leibniz's law arguments

2.4 At the heart of substance dualism is the idea that your mind and your brain are two distinct things, not one and the same thing. At the heart, then, is the idea of the nonidentity of two things. Central to the logic governing the ideas of identity and nonidentity is a principle of reasoning philosophers and logicians have come to call "Leibniz's law." For our purposes, we can represent Leibniz's law as *the indiscernibility of identicals*, the principle that if x and y are one and the same, then x and y must have all of their properties in common. And if there is some property that the one has and the other lacks, then x and y are distinct. They are two distinct things, not one and the same thing.

2.5 Leibniz's law is obviously relevant to substance dualism. If there are one or more properties that your mind has and your body lacks, or that your body has and your mind lacks, then it follows by Leibniz's law that your mind and your body are distinct. A similar kind of reasoning attempts to show that the mind is not identical to any physical thing—any physical body, object, or system. Crucial to such lines of reasoning is to identify some property that minds have and physical things lack, or vice versa.

2.6 There are several ways in which different approaches to substance dualism might try to characterize the very different natures of minds and physical bodies. We will turn now to look at five alleged differences between minds and physical bodies.

2.7 The first alleged difference between minds and physical bodies originates with Descartes. He holds that physical bodies are spatial and that minds are not. But what does this mean? Two important things it means is that they have spatial parts and that they have spatial location. Even physical bodies that might be too hard to actually cut nonetheless are conceivably divisible into spatially definable parts. A magically hard diamond that cannot be cut in half nonetheless has two spatially definable halves. This is what allows it to be, for instance, half in and half out of a box. Some substance dualists hold that, in contrast to physical bodies, it makes no sense at all to describe a mind as having spatial parts. Is your belief that the Eiffel Tower is in Paris in the left or right half of your mind? Is your sensation of pain in the top or the bottom half of your mind? Cartesian substance dualists reject such questions as nonsensical.

2.8 Of course, the belief is about something having a spatial location—it is, after all a belief about the Eiffel Tower's spatial location. But this undisputed fact concerning what the belief is about does not settle anything concerning where the belief itself is. And if you yourself aren't in Paris, what sense does it make to say that your belief about Paris is a belief spatially located in Paris?

Are things any different with a sensation of pain? If you injure your hand, don't you feel the pain in your hand? As many philosophers will point out, where we feel the pain to be (in a hand) does not settle the issue of where the sensation of pain itself is. A well-known phenomenon that occurs to amputees is that they will suffer phantom pains—it will feel as if they have an intense pain in a hand that was lost long ago (perhaps bitten off by a shark). So a pain can be felt in a hand that no longer exists (the shark digested it). 2.9

Of course, many physicalists will resist this dualist line of thought about spatial parts and spatial locations. They may hold that even though it is not apparent where your belief or sensation is, nonetheless, in reality, it does have a spatial location, perhaps in the cerebral cortex of your brain. We will have much more to say about physicalists in later chapters. 2.10

The second alleged contrast between mental and physical substances is another that we can trace back to Descartes. He holds that minds are thinking things and that physical objects are unthinking things. Thinking is a *rational* process or activity. It is the process or activity of *reasoning*. Descartes holds that only mental substances are capable of performing this activity or undergoing this process. According to Descartes, only a mental substance can be a thinking thing. In contrast, every physical object, no matter how fancy or complicated, is necessarily an unthinking thing. Of course, as we'll discuss in chapters 6 and 7, many proponents of neuroscience and artificial intelligence disagree with such a view. 2.11

A third alleged contrast between mental and physical substances has to do with the way that, when we think, we think *about* things. This property of "aboutness," also known as *intentionality*, is held by some dualists to be a property that only nonphysical things can have. Intentionality is a very unusual phenomenon. On the face of it, it appears to be a sort of relation—you think about things. You think about the Eiffel Tower, and this looks to be a relation between you and the Eiffel Tower. However, if thinking about is a relation, it looks to be a very strange relation. One sort of thing we seem to be able to think about are things that are so far away that not even light can have made the journey between us and those things. We can also think about things in the far future and the distant past. Perhaps strangest of all is our ability to think about things that do not even exist, things that happen not to exist, such as a 20-foot dog, and things that couldn't possibly 2.12

exist, such as four-sided triangles. Given how strange intentionality is, it is difficult to see how something that's purely physical, like a brain, can have it and thereby be related to things that don't exist in space and time.

2.13   A fourth alleged contrast between mental substances and physical substances is that only mental substances can bear properties that are "phenomenal." What are phenomenal properties? We can get an especially strong feel for phenomenal properties when we attend to the qualities of conscious sensory experiences, such as the painfulness of stubbing a toe and the tanginess of biting into a lemon. There is something it is like to be a conscious human being biting into a lemon. The tanginess of the sensation seems not to be a property of the lemon itself—the lemon doesn't taste itself. The tanginess doesn't even need the lemon to exist, since we can have hallucinatory taste sensations. Similarly, as mentioned in connection with phantom limbs, we can have hallucinatory pain sensations. Where do such phenomenal properties reside? A substance dualist offers that such properties cannot reside in merely physical objects.

2.14   A fifth alleged contrast between mental and physical substances is a difference in how they are known. Physical bodies seem to be known via the senses. However, the senses can be deceived, and, thus, sometimes something that seems to exist really doesn't. If it is *possible* that you are wrong in believing something, then you can't be sure that you're right. Even if you are right, granting the mere possibility that you might be wrong means that you don't know that you're right with absolute certainty.

2.15   Arguably, while you *can* be wrong about the existence of physical objects, you *can't* be wrong about the existence of your own mind. If you think that you are thinking, you are guaranteed to be correct. And if you are thinking, then your mind must exist. According to this line of thought, your mind is known with certainty to exist even though no physical object is known with certainty to exist.

2.16   Now that we have examined the five alleged differences between minds and bodies, we can return to the discussion of Leibniz's law. We can take any one of the five differences, combine it with Leibniz's law, and create an argument for substance dualism. Take, for example, the distinction having to do with spatial parts and spatial locations. A substance dualist can argue that bodies, but not minds, have spatial properties, and thus a mind must be distinct from every physical body.

2.17   Consider another Leibniz's law argument for substance dualism. Recall the claim that minds but not bodies have the special epistemological feature of being known for certain to exist. Arguably, one knows for certain that one's mind exists, but one does not know for certain that any physical bodies exist. Perhaps you know of their existence, but not with absolute certainty. So the mind has the property of being known with certainty to exist, while every physical body lacks that property. It would seem to follow by Leibniz's law that the mind must be distinct from every physical body.

Criticism of Leibniz's law arguments: Intensional fallacy

The problem of the intensional fallacy arises for certain uses of Leibniz's 2.18 law. Some Leibniz's law arguments for dualism commit this fallacy. Recall, for instance, a version of a Leibniz's law argument that goes like this:

Premise 1: I know with absolute certainty that my mind exists.
Premise 2: I don't know with absolute certainty that any physical thing exists.
Conclusion: For any given physical thing, my mind cannot be identical to it; my mind must be some distinct and nonphysical thing.

We can state the argument in a way that makes the appeal to Leibniz's law even more apparent:

Premise 1: My mind has the property of being known with certainty.
Premise 2: No physical thing has that property.
Premise 3: By Leibniz's law, if my mind has a property that no physical thing has, then my mind is not identical to any physical thing.
Conclusion: My mind is not identical to any physical thing.

So, what is the problem with this sort of argument? What is the problem 2.19 that we are calling the *intensional fallacy*? This problem can be spelled out in terms of the following analogy:

Recall the story about the comic-book superhero, Superman. As anyone 2.20 who has read a Superman comic book or seen a Superman movie knows, Superman and Clark Kent are one and the same person. However, as all fans of these stories know, the character Lois Lane *doesn't know* that Clark Kent and Superman are one and the same. Consider the following bad argument about Superman, an argument that abuses Leibniz's Law:

Premise 1: Superman has the property of being believed by Lois to be bulletproof.

Premise 2: Clark Kent lacks the property of being believed by Lois to be bulletproof.

Premise 3: If Superman has a property that Clark Kent lacks then, by Leibniz's law, Clark and Superman are two distinct people.

Conclusion: Clark and Superman are two distinct people.

Why is the above argument an *abuse* of Leibniz's law? In order for Leibniz's law to be used correctly, the relevant properties have to be properties of the things we are seeking to identify or distinguish. However, what Lois believes about Superman isn't really a property of Superman. She can believe he is a great guy and later change her mind and believe that he is a jerk without anything thereby changing *in Superman*. Similarly, Lois's belief that Clark isn't bulletproof isn't a property of Clark.

2.21   This bad form of reasoning is known as the *intensional fallacy*. Note that we are here spelling "intensional" with an "s"—it is not to be confused with "intentional" spelled with a "t." Without getting too deep into the technical details, we can describe the intensional fallacy as involving a confusion between, on the one hand, properties that something *really* has, with, on the other hand, properties it has only *under some description*. What we think about something may be very different from what really truly is going on with that thing. Such a difference is important to keep in mind, especially as we turn to other sorts of arguments for substance dualism.

Explanatory gap arguments

2.22   Explanatory gap arguments identify some aspect of the mind that cannot be explained in terms of physical substances and then conclude that this aspect of the mind must be due to the mind's being a nonphysical, wholly mental substance.

2.23   Take, for example, an explanatory gap argument of Descartes' concerning language. One important thing that you use your mind for is to produce and understand language. Descartes thinks that such an ability could never be explained in terms of the functioning of a purely physical system—no machine, no matter how elaborate, could engage in an intelligent conversation with an adult human. Even if a machine made sounds that superficially seemed like speech, it couldn't understand anything it said. According to Descartes, nonhuman animals are mere machines that therefore can't use language. The question of whether there can be genuinely intelligent machines is one that we'll explore a lot more in chapter 7. But suffice it for now to say that maybe Descartes would have been a bit more optimistic about the prospects of thinking machines if he could have traveled to our time and see the amazing things that computers and robots can do. For our present purposes, we can see Descartes as saying that there is an explanatory gap between physical substances and the intelligent use of language. Further, we see him concluding from the *explanatory* gap that there must be a *substantial* gap—that there is a distinction here between two distinct things. On the one hand are mental things, which are the proper basis for the understanding of language, and on the other hand are physical things, which cannot themselves engage in intelligent conversation.

The intelligent use of language is not the only thing that a dualist 2.24 can appeal to in attempting an explanatory gap argument. They may instead focus on the phenomenal aspects of our mental lives, especially as they arise in connection with conscious sensory perception. In a famous argument of Leibniz's, he attacks the physicalist presumption that a physical system such as a brain might suffice to give rise to genuine perceptions such as the visual perception of a bright red rose. Central to Leibniz's argument is a thought experiment in which he imagines being shrunk down small enough that he can walk around inside of a brain the way one might walk around inside of a factory. According to Leibniz, upon such a close examination of a physical system, one will find many parts working together according to mechanical principles, but nothing that will serve to explain perception.

It should be noted that Leibniz's ultimate view isn't really a form of 2.25 substance dualism, but instead a kind of idealism (a topic we'll examine further in chapter 4). Nonetheless, Leibniz can agree with the substance dualist that there is an explanatory gap that threatens any physicalist view of perception.

Criticisms of explanatory gap arguments

Explanatory gap arguments can be viewed as making a kind of prediction, 2.26 a prediction about what will never happen at any future date. Different versions of explanatory gap arguments make different predictions. One version predicts that we will never be able to explain language as something that a purely mechanical system can accomplish. Another version predicts that an explanation given in purely physical terms will never suffice to explain perception. However, insofar as explanatory gap arguments are making predictions, they can be called into doubt.

2.27   One basis for calling them into doubt is a general principle concerning how we can never be absolutely certain about what the future will bring. Perhaps the future will bring a currently unforeseen breakthrough in artificial intelligence and robotics resulting in conclusive demonstrations of purely mechanical systems that understand language and perceive the world around them.

2.28   Another basis for doubting the predictions at the heart of explanatory gap arguments is to look at past cases of scientific ignorance that were followed by breakthroughs and then draw an analogy between those past episodes and our current situation. Long ago, before the formulation of the Darwinian theory of evolution and the discovery of DNA, many aspects of the functioning of life were regarded as complete mysteries. There was a time in which people postulated the existence of a special substance, known as the *élan vital*, the presence of which accounted for the life in a living thing and served to distinguish living from nonliving things. We can easily imagine someone from long ago formulating an explanatory gap argument for the existence of this *élan vital*. Such a gap argument would make the prediction that descriptions of mere arrangements of molecules would never be able to explain biological processes such as growth and reproduction, and conclude that such processes must instead be due to the presence of a special nonphysical substance. In retrospect, such an argument would seem silly, for we currently possess a large and powerful body of knowledge concerning how biological processes are simply special and complicated collections of chemical processes. By analogy, just as no *élan vital* was necessary for explaining life, no distinctively mental, nonphysical substance is necessary for explaining the mind.

Modal arguments

2.29   One especially prominent sort of argument for dualism is what philosophers have called a *modal* argument, for it hinges on the notion of *possibility*, and philosophers refer to possibility and necessity as *modalities* and study them by using *modal logic*. Crucial to a modal argument for substance dualism is a premise concerning the *possibility* of a mind existing without any body existing. Clearly, if it is indeed possible for your mind to exist without your body existing, then the mind must be something other than your body. However, this invites the question of how it could be shown that this indeed is a real possibility.

2.30   One often discussed way of attempting to establish this as a real possibility is by starting with a premise about what can be conceived or imagined, or, in Descartes' terminology, what one can have "a clear and distinct idea" of. So, one way we might try to formulate a modal argument for substance dualism is like this:

Premise 1: I can conceive of my mind existing without any physical body existing.
Premise 2: If I can conceive of something, it must therefore be possible.
Premise 3: It is possible for my mind to exist without any physical body existing.
Premise 4: If it is possible for my mind to exist without any physical body existing, then my mind is not identical to any physical body.
Conclusion: My mind is a thing distinct from any physical body.

Here's another way to formulate a modal argument for substance dualism, this time using a phrase famously associated with Descartes, the phrase "clear and distinct idea": 2.31

Premise 1: I can form a clear and distinct idea of my mind existing without any physical thing existing.
Premise 2: Whatever I can form a clear and distinct idea of happening, is something that can possibly happen.
Premise 3: If it is possible for one thing to exist apart from another, they cannot be one and the same thing, but must be two distinct things.
Conclusion: My mind is a thing distinct from any physical body.

Criticism of the modal arguments: Does conceivability really entail possibility?

Moving from conceivability to real possibility is a crucial part of modal arguments. In the arguments formulated in the previous section, this crucial role is played by premise 2. But this part is also the most controversial part of such arguments. Why should it follow from the mere fact that I can conceive of something that it really is possible? Maybe I am merely mistaken in my conceptions! 2.32

Consider some complex mathematical proposition. Being mathematical, if it is true, it is necessarily true. (And if it is false, its negation is necessarily true.) But since the proposition is complex I can conceive of the proposition being true, since I'm no mathematician, and it isn't obviously false. (And I can equally well conceive of its negation being true.) But it shouldn't follow from my conceiving that truth that it should be possible. It may very 2.33

well be, unbeknownst to me, impossible. So in this case at least, conceivability seems to be a poor guide to possibility.

2.34   While many critics of modal arguments think that the move from conceivability to possibility can never be justified, many fans of the modal arguments try to defend such a move. One such a defense says that if the conceiving is done by an ideal conceiver—maybe not someone as smart as God is supposed to be, but still someone pretty reliable in their conceptions—then if they conceive something as happening, it must really be possible for it to happen. But this sort of defense invites the further question of how to decide whether someone is conceiving things in a way that an ideal conceiver would. Also: Couldn't even an ideal conceiver make mistakes about what's really possible? The issues involved are quite complex, and go far beyond this introductory discussion of philosophy of mind.

2.35   We have been focusing on criticisms of *arguments* for dualism, but there have also been criticisms of dualism *itself*. One of the main lines of complaint has to do with dualism's seeming ineptitude in dealing with one of the central problems of philosophy of mind, the *problem of interaction* (a major focus of chapter 9).

Mind–Body Interaction as a Problem for Substance Dualism

2.36 One of the most famous examples of substance dualism is Descartes' (aka Cartesian) dualism. In addition to holding that mind and body belong in different categories of substance, Cartesian dualism also holds that these separate kinds of substance are able to interact causally. One can have causal effects on the other, and vice versa. (A little bit later we'll consider non-Cartesian versions of substance dualism, versions that deny that there's any interaction between minds and physical bodies.)

2.37   According to common sense, there are causal interactions between your mind and items in the physical world. It's also part of common sense that the flow of causation between mind and world goes both ways. The main examples of things in the physical world having effects on the mind occur in perception. There's a loud bang and a powerful stink and you hear the one and smell the other. And if the big stinky explosion hurts you, you might learn not to stand so close when the chemistry teacher mixes those chemicals together. The main examples of the mind having causal effects on physical things occur in intention and action. You form an intention to paint your room and when you put this intention into action, all sort of physical events ensue, including the motions of your limbs and the application of paint to the walls.

Descartes attempts to accommodate these aspects of common sense into his dualistic theory. He affirms that there are indeed casual interactions from mind to physical world and back again. Further, Descartes holds that the location of the interface between your mind and the body is a singular structure in the human brain known as the pineal gland. Not only was Descartes a philosopher and a mathematician, he had a keen interest in anatomy and physiology. The reasoning that led Descartes to single out the pineal gland seems to be the following. Like most of the rest of the body, the different parts of the brain generally come in twos. Just as you have two hands and two eyes, so does the brain have, for instance, two cerebral hemispheres, and so on. However, the pineal gland struck Descartes as unique among brain structures. Unlike all of the parts of the nervous system that come in twos, each person has only one pineal gland. 2.38

Now, there's something a little odd about all of this, and it isn't merely that the pineal gland is a poor choice for a location of the mind–body interface. The problem has more to do with the fact that the pineal gland, like physical entities in general, has a location. Why is this a problem for Cartesian substance dualism? We'll see in just a moment. 2.39

Princess Elisabeth's objection

One of the most influential objections raised against Descartes' dualism was by Princess Elisabeth of Bohemia (1618–1680), who had a philosophical correspondence with Descartes. The letters between Descartes and Elisabeth have been preserved (Bennett, 2010). Elisabeth's objection has to do with causal interactions between minds and bodies. 2.40

According to Cartesian substance dualism, thinking is something that can only be done by nonmaterial mental substances, and having spatial properties like size, shape, and location is something that can only be done by nonmental material substances. We might summarize, then, by saying that only material substances can be spatial. But here's where this starts to make the problem of interaction seem like a really big problem for the Cartesian substance dualist. It looks to be very problematic to hold that something that is nonspatial can have effects on and be affected by something that is spatial. 2.41

2.42   Consider how causal interaction takes place between physical objects. One example of an interaction is a collision in which one ball knocks into and moves a second ball. In this case, the first ball moves to the location of the second and, upon making contact, pushes it out of the way. Note that, in order for this to take place, both objects must be spatial objects. It's difficult, perhaps impossible, to understand how the first ball can make the second change location without the first moving to the spatial location of the second. Even cases that might superficially look like action at a distance, like magnetism, are really cases that involve things occupying the intervening space. In such cases waves of energy or microscopic particles traverse the distance between the two objects. Physical causation looks to depend crucially, then, on the spatial relations between the interacting entities. It is thus utterly opaque how a nonspatial entity can affect or be affected by a spatial one.

The dualistic alternatives to Cartesian interactionism

2.43   One option explored by substance dualists is to deny that there is any mind–body interaction. From the point of view of common sense, the denial of mind–body interaction is downright disturbing. It looks like, on such a proposal, your intention to raise your hand has no effect on whether your hand gets raised. That you have control over your body would then be a kind of illusion. (The closely related idea that free will is an illusion is something we'll explore further in chapter 12). What is happening, on this view, when it seems like we've perceived some physical event in the world? On this view, our perceptual state is *not* caused by the event in the world it is a perception of. If you stub your toe and then feel an intense pain, the pain is *not* caused by the damage to the toe. Clearly this is highly contrary to common sense!

2.44   Note, however, that a substance dualist who denies causal interaction does not have to affirm that it is a mere coincidence that certain mental happenings are synchronized with certain physical happenings. Historically, there have been two developments of the idea that there is no causal interaction between mind and body, both of which don't make it a mere coincidence that there's an ordered pattern of relationships between mental events and physical events. These two views are known as *occasionalism* and *parallelism*. The most famous versions of these views, the version of occasionalism proposed by Malebranche and the version of parallelism proposed by Leibniz, bring God into the picture.

The role that God is hypothesized to play is that he's responsible for the   2.45
ordered relationship between the mental events and the physical events. In
the case of occasionalism, God is hypothesized to intervene at each step
in a version of continual creation. When, for instance, you form an intention to raise your hand, God steps in and makes your hand go up. And
when a heavy object falls on your toe, God steps in to make sure that you
suffer a pain.

In the case of Leibniz's parallelism, God does not step in at every moment,   2.46
but instead sets up two parallel streams of events from the beginning of
the universe. When he created the universe, he created a physical stream
and a mental stream that run in parallel. The ordered relationships between
the two are predetermined. Like two synchronized clocks, the two streams
unfold without interacting. The relation between the two is a *preestablished
harmony*.

There are several striking and unappealing features of these key versions   2.47
of occasionalism and parallelism. First, insofar as they give a major role to
God, they inherit any doubts one might raise about whether God actually
exists. Whether God exists is no small controversy, so we'll here leave it
aside. Other problems for these views are ones that survive even on the
assumption that God does indeed exist. That everything is predetermined,
as hypothesized in Leibnizian parallelism, does violence to the idea that we
have free will and are thus morally responsible for our actions. A similar
problem about moral responsibility arises in connection with Malebranche's
occasionalism. If God intervenes to execute the physical consequences of
mental decisions, then God is a moral accomplice in various evil actions.
Suppose, for instance, a person plans a murder and intends to shoot their
victim to death. In Malebranche's occasionalism, the person with the murderous intent is not as directly responsible for the pulling of the gun's
trigger as God is. God steps in to make sure the trigger is pulled in accordance with the murderous intent of the shooter!

We will leave aside for now further questions that arise for substance   2.48
dualism about the problem of interaction and other problems involving
mental causation. We will return to such issues in chapter 9.

Conclusion

At first glance, substance dualism may seem like a very natural and highly   2.49
plausible view. The proposition that a person's mind and body are two

distinct things capable of existing independently of one another has a certain appeal. It comforts us that there's something special about us, perhaps something so special that it can even survive the death of the body. However, the view runs into serious problems. The main problems concern mental causation, especially the mind's causal effects on physical bodies.

Annotated Bibliography

Bennett, Jonathan (ed.) (2010) "Correspondence between René Descartes and Princess Elisabeth of Bohemia," full text available at http://www.earlymoderntexts.com/pdf/descelis.pdf, accessed February 5, 2013. One of the main things that Elisabeth famously gives Descartes a hard time about is the problem of mental causation, especially as it arises for substance dualism.

Descartes, René (1641) *Meditations on First Philosophy*, full text available at http://www.earlymoderntexts.com/de.html, accessed February 5, 2013. Descartes' classic argument for his version of substance dualism appears in the last of his six meditations, but the second meditation is important also.

Descartes, René (1649) *The Passions of the Soul*, full text available at http://www.earlymoderntexts.com/despas.html, accessed February 5, 2013. See especially Part I for Descartes' exposition of the interaction between the soul and the body, and how the site of interface is located in the pineal gland of the brain.

Leibniz, Gottfried (1714) *The Monadology*, full text available at http://www.earlymoderntexts.com/pdf/leibmona.pdf, accessed February 5, 2013. Although Leibniz's view is a form of idealism, not a substance dualism, he shares with the substance dualists a hostility toward physicalism. Section 17 of his *Monadology* contains one of the earliest explanatory gap arguments. Section 7 contains an expression of Leibniz's doctrine of pre-established harmony.

Malebranche, Nicolas (1688) *Dialogues on Metaphysics*, full text available at http://www.earlymoderntexts.com/f_maleb.html, accessed February 5, 2013. For a taste of the occasionalism for which Malebranche is famous, see especially the fourth dialogue.

Mandik, Pete (ed.) (n.d.) "Dualism," in *This Is Philosophy of Mind: The Blog*, http://tipom.blogspot.com/search/label/Dualism. A frequently updated collection items from around the Internet concerning substance dualism as well as property dualism.

3

PROPERTY DUALISM

Introducing Property Dualism: Qualia and the Brain

The previous chapter was concerned with the view that minds and physical 3.1
bodies are two distinct kinds of things. In the present chapter, the focus is
not so much on things, but instead on the properties or qualities of things.
More specifically, we will be concerned with the relations between a person's mental properties and their physical properties. Perhaps a person
is just one "thing" but has two very different sorts of properties. *Property
dualism* holds that mental properties are a distinct kind of property, a
kind of property not identical to or "reducible" to any kind of physical
property.

   To get the feel of what property dualism is all about, it helps to focus on 3.2
two key ideas in philosophy of mind, and notice an apparent tension
between them. The first idea is the idea of mental properties known col-
lectively as *qualia*. The second idea is a simple kind of physicalism that we
can express simply as the view that all properties are physical properties.
On this simple physicalism, even mental properties are really just a kind of
physical property. For simplicity of the present discussion, let's focus on a
particular version of this simple physicalism, one that says that mental
properties are just a special kind of brain property. This simple physicalism
includes the proposal that the pleasantness of pleasure as well as the painfulness of pain just are a certain kind of property of the brain, a brainy
property perhaps best understood as a complex pattern of electrochemical
activity distributed across various multicellular circuits in the higher parts

This Is Philosophy of Mind: An Introduction, First Edition. Pete Mandik.
© 2014 John Wiley & Sons, Inc. Published 2014 by John Wiley & Sons, Inc.

of the central nervous system. (This mind-as-brain view is the main focus of chapter 6.)

3.3   Many philosophers of mind have thought that whatever plausibility this physicalist view of mind as brain may have, it stumbles badly on qualia. It is difficult for many to see how qualia themselves could just be a pattern of electrochemical signals in the brain. We may be reminded here of Leibniz's thought experiment about shrinking down and walking through the brain. As shrunken explorers we may see various physical processes— exchanges of chemicals across cellular membranes—but nothing that looks like it could explain qualia. To further get a feel for the motivations of property dualism let's turn to two other thought experiments—the inverted spectrum thought experiment and the zombie thought experiment. These thought experiments are closely associated with versions of the modal argument for property dualism.

The Inverted Spectrum

3.4   Before we jump in and conduct the inverted spectrum thought experiment, let's first conduct a real experiment. This is a simple experiment that you can conduct yourself and requires little more than having two eyes. Cover just one of your eyes for 30–60 seconds. Afterwards, alternate looking out of just one eye and then just out of the other. While doing this, make note of the way things look out of each eye. Look at a white piece of paper out of one eye and then out of the other. What are some of the differences you notice? Do things look a little darker out of one and lighter out of the other? Is there a slight shift in the colors? Perhaps things look a little pinker or more orange out of the one eye and just a bit bluer out of the other?

3.5   The differences in the appearance of the paper are due neither to changes in the paper itself nor to changes in the lighting conditions. Due to changes inside of you, you have a different experience connected with the view from each eye, and the difference between the experiences is a difference in what *quale* each has. There are different *qualia* associated with the two experiences, and these different qualia help make up the subjective differences in the way the white paper looks through the two different eyes.

3.6   Let us move now from this real experiment to a thought experiment— the inverted spectrum thought experiment. Imagine two different people— Ingrid and Norma—who see colors in very different ways. Whereas Norma sees colors in the normal way, Ingrid sees them in the opposite way. Ingrid sees red the way Norma sees green, and vice versa, and so on for all the colors. If you've ever seen a photographic negative, then you have some idea of what color opposites are. Do you know what a hue circle is? An example of a hue circle is samples of six colors—red, orange, yellow, green, blue, and purple—arranged in a circle. Imagine taking one hue circle, rotating it 180 degrees, and plopping it on top of another one. This gives you a sense of the systematic way in which Ingrid's color qualia are inverted with respect to Norma's.

Imagine that, despite the subjective differences between the way colors 3.7 appear to Norma and Ingrid, the two women are nonetheless objectively similar with respect to their color-related behaviors, including their verbal behaviors. If we held up a ripe tomato and asked what color it was, *both* Norma and Ingrid would answer "red." If we presented them with a lime, both would answer "green." If we showed them three paint chips of slightly different shades, A, B, and C, and asked them whether A was more similar to B than to C, they would both give the same answer.

Perhaps you are now wondering how Norma and Ingrid could be behav- 3.8 iorally identical even though they see colors in ways opposite from each other. Why wouldn't Ingrid, the one with inverted qualia, say instead that the lime is red? To understand this, imagine that the way colors look to both Norma the normal and Ingrid the invert were like that since birth. So, before they were taught color words, the way the colors looked to one of them was the opposite of the way the colors looked to the other. We can imagine that they were taught color words under the following sort of conditions: Each of their parents would hold up a lime and say "green," then hold up some broccoli, and again say "green," and so on. Regardless of what the internal subjective reaction to such presentations is—that is, regardless of whether the quale in question is inverted or normal—the child will learn to call the color of limes and broccoli "green."

To continue the thought experiment, let us imagine that Norma and 3.9 Ingrid are not just similar with respect to their observable behaviors, but further that they are similar with respect to all of the properties that can be observed by some third person. This includes observations of the insides of their bodies that can be made using scientific instruments. Imagine that the detailed structure of their brains is the same in Ingrid and Norma while they see colors they would both call "green." Imagine that, despite these physical similarities, Ingrid and Norma are still different with respect to their qualia.

3.10   If what we've imagined is indeed possible, then it is possible for two people to be the same with respect to their physical properties yet different with respect to their qualia. And if this is indeed possible, then qualia cannot be identical to any physical properties. Qualia must instead be nonphysical properties.

3.11   The inverted spectrum thought experiment is often discussed in philosophy of mind in connection with *modal arguments* for property dualism. One way we can spell out such an argument is like this:

Premise 1: Inverted spectra are conceivable. That is, it is conceivable for there to be a being that has all of my physical properties but has different qualia.

Premise 2: If it is conceivable for a being to have all of my physical properties while having different qualia, then it is possible for there to be such a being.

Premise 3: If it is possible for there to be a being that has all my physical properties while having different qualia, then qualia are not physical properties.

Conclusion: Qualia are not physical properties.

3.12   Of course, if you tend to lean toward physicalism, you may very well find that there's something very suspicious about the inverted spectrum thought experiment and the related modal argument. We will address concerns like this a bit later. But first, let us turn to another thought experiment—the *zombie* experiment—and a related modal argument.

Attack of the Zombies

3.13   In the philosophy of mind, when people talk about zombies, they aren't talking about undead monsters from horror movies. The word "zombie" in philosophical contexts is a technical term. The philosopher's zombie is a person who has no qualia, but is nonetheless similar to normal people in various ways. For instance, zombies are sometimes hypothesized to lack qualia while nonetheless behaving just like normal humans. (The question, "How do you know other people are not zombies?" is a version of the problem of other minds, a problem that we will explore in greater depth in chapter 5.)

We can adapt the story about Norma and Ingrid to illustrate the notion 3.14 of zombies. We can change the thought experiment from being an inverted spectrum thought experiment to being a zombie thought experiment. So, imagine that Norma has the normal range of qualia. But for Ingrid, instead of imagining her as having inverted qualia, imagine her having no qualia whatsoever, while still being behaviorally just like Norma. What is it like to be Ingrid? There's *nothing* it is like to be Ingrid, just as there's nothing it is like to be a rock or a piece of wood.

In order to connect the idea of a zombie to property dualism, we need 3.15 to do more than just imagine that Ingrid the zombie is *behaviorally* similar to Norma. We have to imagine that Ingrid is similar to Norma with respect to internal physical properties as well. If we used a brain scanner and examined the functioning brains of both Norma and Ingrid while they looked at a lime, we would notice no difference in the functioning of their brains, even though, by hypothesis, Norma has green qualia when she sees a lime and Ingrid has no qualia whatsoever. Further, Ingrid's lack of qualia in no way prevents her from acting the way Norma does. Like Norma, when shown a lime and asked its color, Ingrid will reply "green."

Maybe this is hard to imagine, but here are some considerations that 3.16 certain kinds of information processing can take place without there being any qualia: Consider, for example, the creation and maintenance of unconscious memories. Consider also the information processing that takes place in a calculator or in a laptop computer. Information can be stored and processed in machines and living brains without thereby giving rise to conscious experiences and their associated qualia. Much of what guides intelligent behavior can be done unconsciously. Conceivably, then, perhaps all of it can.

Of course, if you have physicalist leanings, you may resist the idea that 3.17 Norma and Ingrid can have the same internal structure and outward behavior while only one of them has qualia. In contrast, if you think that the story of Norma and zombie-Ingrid describes a coherent possibility, you may find yourself tempted towards property dualism about qualia. On this view, it's possible for Ingrid to lack qualia while being *physically* just like Norma because qualia aren't physical properties. Qualia are a kind of non-physical property.

Like the inverted spectrum thought experiment, the zombie thought 3.18 experiment is often discussed in philosophy of mind in connection with various *modal arguments* for property dualism. One way we can spell out such an argument is like this:

Premise 1: Zombies are conceivable. That is, it is conceivable for there to be a being that has all my physical properties but lacks my qualia.

Premise 2: If it is conceivable for a being to have all of my physical properties while lacking my qualia, then it is possible for there to be such a being.

Premise 3: If it is possible for there to be a being that has all my physical properties while lacking qualia, then qualia are not physical properties.

Conclusion: Qualia are not physical properties.

3.19   Let us turn now to examine another famous line of thought in favor of property dualism, the knowledge argument.

The Knowledge Argument

3.20 Just as in the modal arguments for property dualism, a thought experiment plays a central role in discussions of the knowledge argument. The central character of this thought experiment is a character created by the philosopher Frank Jackson. This character is Mary, a brilliant futuristic neuroscientist who knows everything there is to know about the physical properties of brains, especially the parts of brains involved in color vision. Further, Mary knows all of the relevant physical facts concerning light and the surfaces of objects that light is reflected off. As far as the strictly physical facts are concerned, Mary knows everything there is to know about what is involved in human color perception. She knows, in extraordinary detail, precisely what happens in a person's brain when they see red things. However, Mary has acquired her vast scientific knowledge under unusual conditions. Mary has only ever seen things in black, white, and shades of gray. In one version of the thought experiment, Mary is confined to a room in which everything is painted black, white, or some shade of grey. Special dyes are injected into her body so that when she looks at herself, she sees only black, white, and gray. Her education about science is acquired through books and videos that are entirely in black, white, and gray. In another version of the thought experiment, instead of being confined in a black and white room, Mary has surgery, resulting in her vision consisting solely of black, white, and shades of gray. The surgery occurs prior to her ever seeing anything red. The exact details of how Mary came to gain so much physical knowledge without ever having seen red are inconsequential. What matters for the thought experiment is that Mary can have, in her capacity as a super-scientist, knowledge of all the physical properties involved in human color vision, including the vision of red objects, even though she herself has never undergone a visual experience of anything red.

The next stage in the thought experiment is to contemplate whether 3.21 Mary's knowledge of color vision while in her black and white captivity is complete. Is there anything that, in never having had an experience of red, Mary doesn't know? Many people who contemplate this question say that of course there is something Mary doesn't know—Mary doesn't know what it is like to see red. This claim about Mary can be used in an argument against physicalism and in favor of property dualism. This is the knowledge argument, which we can state as follows:

Premise 1: If physicalism is true, that is, if all properties are physical prop-
    erties, then, Mary knows everything there is to know about color vision.
Premise 2: Mary does not know everything there is to know about color
    vision (she doesn't know what it is like to see red).
Conclusion: Physicalism is false. Not all properties are physical properties.
    There is at least one nonphysical property (a red quale).

The knowledge argument receives much of its force from a widely held 3.22 view about how we know about our own qualia, namely, that they cannot be known by description but only by acquaintance. To get a feel for the description/acquaintance distinction, let us look at some examples. First, consider an example of knowledge by description. Imagine that there are two people, Yvonne and Hiro, having a conversation. Suppose that it comes out in the conversation that Yvonne has never seen the Japanese flag before and that she doesn't know what it looks like. Suppose further, that Hiro does know what it looks like. Is this something that Hiro can explain to Yvonne? Yes, of course. Hiro can describe the flag to Yvonne as a white rectangle with a red circle on it. If, after receiving this description, we showed Yvonne pictures of several flags that she had never seen before, she could pick out which one is the Japanese flag. Yvonne gained knowledge of what the Japanese flag looked like from the description that Hiro gave her. Yvonne has acquired *knowledge by description*.

Let us turn, now, to an example of *knowledge by acquaintance*. Suppose 3.23 that Yvonne has a sister, Helen, and Helen has not only never seen the Japanese flag, she has never seen a white rectangle or a red circle. How can this be? Helen is blind, and has been blind since birth. Could Hiro explain to Helen what red looked like? Suppose he tried. Would any description allow her to pick out which color is red if she is ever given the gift of sight? Many people, including philosophers of mind, would be inclined to say that no amount of description can convey what it is like to see red. What it is like is "ineffable"—it cannot be put into words. We can come to know what it is like, but only by undergoing the experience ourselves. Thus, we know it only by acquaintance. It should be noted that this view, while popular, is not entirely uncontroversial. The controversial nature of the view will come out more clearly as we go deeper into the knowledge argument and see the controversies that emerge in connection with it.

3.24   One sort of complaint that philosophers of mind have made about the knowledge argument concerns its first premise. We can describe the first premise as depending on the idea that if one knows all the *factual* knowledge about some domain, then one has *all* of the knowledge that pertains to that domain. Another way of putting this idea is that all knowledge is knowledge of facts, or, in other words, all knowing is *knowing-that*. Some philosophers have sought to deny this premise and put forward the idea that some knowledge is not knowledge of facts, and further, this is the sort of knowledge that Mary lacks during her imprisonment. But what sort of knowledge might Mary lack besides factual knowledge? One sort of suggestion is that Mary lacks procedural knowledge or know-how. In lacking know-how, one lacks the knowledge that makes one able to do something. But what isn't Mary able to do? Perhaps she is not able to recognize or imagine red.

3.25   Another sort of suggestion along these lines concerns a notion of *knowledge by acquaintance* that is allegedly distinct from knowledge of facts. If you know some facts about Barack Obama, but you have never met him in person, we might say: "You know about him, but you don't *know him*." If knowledge by acquaintance is a genuinely distinct form of knowledge, then it is logically possible to know all of the facts about a person without "knowing" that person in the acquaintance sense of the term. Perhaps a similar sort of thing applies to knowledge of qualia.

3.26   Part of the point of the know-how response as well as the acquaintance response to the knowledge argument is to show how it may be possible for Mary to be ignorant of what it is like to see red without falsifying physicalism. These responses target the first premise of the knowledge argument.

3.27   Another kind of response targets the second premise of the argument and denies that imprisoned Mary is ignorant in any interesting sense. According to philosophers attracted to this second response, Mary's neuroscientific knowledge does suffice for her to know what it's like to have experiences of red even though she hasn't yet undergone those experiences.

This may be difficult for us to imagine, but this difficulty may simply be due to our lack of understanding of the relevant neuroscience. Such a completed neuroscience may be very far in our future, and our impoverished imagination about how it will explain conscious experience is comparable to an ancient Greek trying to imagine what Einstein meant by saying that $E = mc^2$.

The Explanatory Gap Argument

We've already encountered explanatory gap arguments in connection with substance dualism. There's very little that's different in applying explanatory gap arguments to property dualism. It might help, however, to say a little bit more about properties and explanation. Consider the following example of a scientific explanation: Many readers of this book will have taken a class on chemistry, perhaps at the high school level, and are familiar with the standard scientific explanation of why heating a gas increases the pressure it exerts against the sides of its container. The explanation goes something like this: The sample of gas just is a collection of molecules that are moving around. The heat of the sample is the average kinetic energy of those molecules in motion. The pressure the gas exerts against the sides of the container is the cumulative transfer of momentum from the moving particles to the container sides. Raising the temperature of the gas is one and the same as increasing the average kinetic energy of the molecules, which in turn results in the molecules hitting the sides of the container harder, since the molecules are moving faster. 3.28

We can break this explanation down into three components: (1) the target phenomenon, (2) the explaining theory, and (3) the identification of items from the target with items in the theory in a way that closes an explanatory gap. 3.29

First, there is the target phenomenon, the thing that needs to be explained. In this case the target phenomenon is the fact that increasing a gas's temperature increases its pressure. We can describe this in terms of key properties and relations between them. One property of a gas is its temperature, another it its pressure, and part of what we want explained is why increasing the one increases the other. 3.30

Second, there is the explaining theory. It is spelled out in terms of the kinetic energy of molecules, which also involves properties. In this case, there is the property of a collection of molecules having a certain average 3.31

kinetic energy. There is also the property of conferring a certain amount of momentum to the sides of the container.

3.32   Third, there is the closing of an explanatory gap. In the explanation, the properties of the target phenomenon are identified with properties in the explaining theory. For example, temperature is identified with average molecular kinetic energy. Finally, once we see how all the parts fit together, the explanation makes sense. We see why increasing heat would result in more pressure (instead of less pressure or no pressure change). Thus, the gap between the target and the theory is closed.

3.33   Now let's imagine a possible explanation of qualia in terms of physical properties such as the physical properties of brains and the neurons of which brains are composed. An example target phenomenon might be to explain why I have a red quale when I look at a ripe tomato. The key property in the target phenomenon is the red quale. What needs to be explained is why I have *that* quale instead of, say, a green quale or no qualia at all. Why am I not a spectrum invert or a zombie?

3.34   We can imagine a proposed physical explanation of the target. We might imagine that the gist of such an explanation will be along the following lines: When light of such-and-such wavelength stimulates the so-and-so neurons in the eyes, this results in such-and-such patterns of activity in the blankity-blank region of the cerebral cortex. For shorthand we can say that the explanation is that having a red quale is having Z-fiber activation in one's brain.

3.35   So here's a proposed identification: Having a red quale is just having Z-fiber activation. Does this explain the target? Does this close the gap? Many philosophers of mind have felt that such an explanation must always fall short. They would say that we'll always leave unanswered *why* Z-fiber activation should go along with having a red quale as opposed to either a green quale or no quale at all. The various kinds of properties that Z-fibers or anything physical can have, properties having to do with mass, momentum, electrical charge, etc., seem like they could never suffice to explain why what it's like to see red is like *that* and not some other way (or no way at all). It looks, then, that there will always be an *explanatory gap* between physical properties and qualia.

3.36   One way we might summarize the general form of the property dualist argument based on the explanatory gap is as follows.

Premise 1: If qualia are identical to any physical properties, then there can be a scientific theory that explains qualia solely in terms of physical properties.

Premise 2: There can never be a scientific theory that explains qualia solely in terms of physical properties.

Conclusion: Qualia are not identical to any physical properties—they are a kind of nonphysical property.

Let's turn to a thought experiment to make the second premise seem 3.37 plausible. Here we can plug in a modification of Leibniz's thought experiment. Imagine being shrunk down and exploring a brain. Nothing you would observe would suffice to explain qualia. Even if you were a gifted scientist who had an amazing memory and powers of observation, this would not help you explain qualia. It would help you predict the activities of the various neural events that you observe, the various electrochemical events that constitute the main activities of the neurons that make up the human brain. Nonetheless, you would be entirely in the dark about *why* any of this gives rise to consciousness and *how* it does so. You would be powerless to explain qualia because you would be powerless to answer the relevant "why" and "how" questions.

Does Property Dualism Lead to Epiphenomenalism?

One kind of worry that philosophers have raised against property dualism 3.38 is that it seems to give rise to an unacceptable form of epiphenomenalism. Briefly, epiphenomenalism about qualia is the view that qualia do not count among the causally efficacious properties of people (or anything). In short, the epiphenomenalist thinks that qualia don't *do* anything. This worry about property dualism is similar to a worry about substance dualism we discussed in the previous chapter: the problem of interaction. We'll have a lot more to say about such problems in chapter 9, so we will be relatively brief here.

In order to further understand epiphenomenalism, it will help to examine 3.39 the distinction between properties that are causally efficacious and properties that are not. Supposed you throw a baseball at a window and the window breaks. Which properties of the baseball are most directly responsible for the window breaking? The baseball has many properties—it has a certain mass, a certain shape, a certain color. Another of its properties is the property of having been signed by a famous baseball player. Which properties are important in explaining why the baseball caused the window to break? It probably matters what the mass is. If the ball were as light as a feather, it's unlikely you could throw it hard enough to break a window.

Does it matter that a famous baseball player signed it? Probably not. The ball would have done just as much damage if the player wasn't famous or didn't even sign it. Similarly irrelevant is the baseball's color. You could have painted it bright pink and that would be unlikely to make it safe for throwing directly at glass windows.

3.40   What we've just illustrated in terms of the baseball is a distinction between properties that are causally efficacious and properties that are not causally efficacious (with respect to the breaking of the glass). The baseball broke the glass in virtue of being a certain mass and traveling at a certain speed in a certain direction. The baseball did not break the glass because it was a certain color or signed by a certain player.

3.41   We can use the idea of causally efficacious properties to understand the debate over epiphenomenalism about qualia. What's epiphenomenalism about qualia? It is the view that qualia are not causally efficacious properties. For instance, the painful quale associated with stubbing your toe is not the reason you cry or cuss. What causes those behaviors are certain nerve impulses leading to the relevant muscles, and the causally efficacious properties are physical properties like the mass and charge of the particles that make up those nerves and their electrochemical signals. The painful quale—the very painfulness of the painful experience—is irrelevant in causing your various behaviors.

3.42   How does property dualism lead to epiphenomenalism? The basic thought here is that scientific explanations of various events can supply fully physical explanations—explanations that mention only physical properties. There's no causal work to do, then, for any properties that are nonphysical. If qualia are nonphysical, they can't help make anything physical happen.

3.43   One way we can spell out how property dualism leads to epiphenomenalism is in terms of zombies. If it is possible for a creature to be just like you physically and behave just like you in response to physical stimuli without any qualia, then none of your qualia are causally responsible for your responses to physical stimuli. Since your zombie twin responds in the same way, it's natural to suppose that whatever the causally efficacious properties are, they are the ones you share with your zombie twin. But, by hypothesis, that leaves only physical properties, since those are the only kinds of properties that you share with your zombie twin.

3.44   The idea that qualia are epiphenomenal has seemed to a lot of philosophers to be much too contrary to common sense. To many philosophers, it seems contrary to common sense to hold that grimacing or swearing when you stub your toe is not caused by a pain quale—the *painfulness* of a pain experience. Such philosophers thus find property dualism to be contrary to common sense. Epiphenomenalism also leads to another problem, one concerning knowledge.

How Do You Know You're Not a Zombie?

Another complaint that some philosophers have raised against property 3.45 dualism is that it seems to make certain aspects of our self-knowledge especially problematic. Of course, there are all sorts of problems concerning knowledge of minds. Take, for instance this question: How do you know other people aren't zombies? This question is a version of the problem of other minds, a problem we will focus on quite a bit in chapter 5. But consider a related question, a question concerning yourself. Do you know that you are not a zombie?

One of the most disturbing consequences of property dualism about 3.46 qualia, at least according to some philosophers (especially the philosopher Daniel Dennett in his book, *Consciousness Explained*, 1991), is that not only does it thereby seem impossible to know whether anyone else is not a zombie, you can't even be sure of yourself that you aren't a zombie. To appreciate this point will require several steps. We've already seen the first step, and it's the idea that property dualism about qualia leads to doubts about whether others are zombies, since they would behave in all the same ways regardless of whether or not they have qualia.

The next step is to appreciate that, by being property dualists about just 3.47 qualia, such dualists leave open the possibility that zombies can have lots of other aspects of mentality, aspects such as thought, judgment, and belief. Further, there are several positive reasons for thinking that such aspects are fully physical, and so can be possessed by a zombie lacking nonphysical qualia. One such reason is that one can have such mental states without being conscious at the time. Consider your knowledge of what color ripe tomatoes usually are. Prior to considering that question right now, you probably weren't consciously thinking about, or consciously forming mental images of, tomatoes. Nonetheless, the information needed to answer the question was stored away, as an unconscious state, in your memory. Further, the storage of information in memory is relatively easy to see as something that a purely physical system can do. The manipulation and storage of information are the primary tasks that computers perform, and there's little doubt that computers are fully physical systems. (We'll have a lot more to say about the relevance of computers to understanding the human mind when we get to chapter 7.)

3.48   Now we are in a position to appreciate the idea that, if qualia are non-physical and distinct from mental states such as judgments, beliefs, and thoughts, then I can't know that I'm not a zombie. Right now, as I'm typing this, I'm looking at my computer screen. It seems to me like I have a conscious perception of the color of the screen. I judge that I am enjoying a visual quale right now. However, since judgments are physical and separate from qualia, it is possible to have the very same judgment without having any qualia at all. Another way to put the crucial point is like this: I judge that I am not a zombie, but it may very well be the case that I am a zombie. All of my thoughts and judgments to the contrary may very well be false. And if it is possible that they are false, then I can't really know that they are true. Therefore, if the assumptions we made above are correct, then I can't know whether or not I'm a zombie. However, the proposition that I can't know of myself whether I am a zombie is absurd. And if property dualism and its accompanying epiphenomenalism lead to this, then they are absurd. Or so argue some philosophers.

Conclusion

3.49   Property dualism is more popular than substance dualism in contemporary philosophy of mind. Most of the discussions of property dualism revolve around consciousness and qualia, which are especially difficult aspects of mind to understand. Part of what sustains the popularity of property dualism are the vivid and fanciful thought experiments concerning zombies, inverted spectra, and futuristic brain scientists. Despite the popularity and vividness of property dualism, many, if not most, philosophers of mind resist dualism in all its forms.

Annotated Bibliography

Alter, Torin (2002) "Knowledge Argument," in Marco Nani and Massimo Marraffa (eds.), *A Field Guide to the Philosophy of Mind*, full text available at http:// host.uniroma3.it/progetti/kant/field/ka.html, accessed February 5, 2013. An accessible overview of Jackson's Mary thought experiment, the knowledge argument based on it, and various responses to the argument.

Byrne, Alex (2010) "Inverted Qualia," in Edward N. Zalta (ed.), *The Stanford Encyclopedia of Philosophy (Spring 2010 Edition)*, full text available at http://plato.stanford.edu/archives/spr2010/entries/qualia-inverted/, accessed February 5, 2013. A very thorough overview of the issues surrounding the inverted qualia thought experiment. Contains many cool images of what various color inversions might look like.

Chalmers, D. (2003) "Consciousness and its Place in Nature," in S. Stich and F. Warfield, (eds.), *Blackwell Guide to Philosophy of Mind* (Oxford: Blackwell), full text available at http://consc.net/papers/nature.html, accessed February 5, 2013. Overview of the main issues regarding the naturalization of qualia, from one of the foremost contemporary critics of physicalism. Contains a nice framework for understanding the commonalities between the main anti-physicalist arguments—the knowledge argument, the explanatory gap argument, and the modal argument.

Dennett, Daniel (1991) *Consciousness Explained* (New York: Little, Brown). As rich and fascinating as it is controversial, it's a source of many excellent insights and arguments, including Dennett's "zimbo" argument.

Jackson, Frank (1982) "Epiphenomenal Qualia," *Philosophical Quarterly*, *32*(127), 127–136. The classic source of Jackson's knowledge argument and the Mary thought experiment. Also contains an underappreciated thought experiment about Fred, who sees more colors than normal humans.

Levine, Joe (1983) "Materialism and Qualia: The Explanatory Gap," *Pacific Philosophical Quarterly*, *64*, 354–361. The classic source of Levine's explanatory gap argument.

Nagel, Thomas (1974) "What's Is It Like to Be a Bat?," *Philosophical Review*, *83*, 435–450. This hugely influential article sets the agenda for much subsequent discussion of whether consciousness and qualia are physical. Nagel's line of thought serves as a precursor to Jackson's knowledge argument.

Polger, Tom (2002) "Zombies," in Marco Nani and Massimo Marraffa (eds.), *A Field Guide to the Philosophy of Mind*, full text available at http://host.uniroma3.it/progetti/kant/field/zombies.htm, accessed February 5, 2013. An accessible overview of the philosophical significance of zombies.

Robinson, William (2002) "Qualia Realism," in Marco Nani and Massimo Marraffa (eds.), *A Field Guide to the Philosophy of Mind*, full text available at http://host.uniroma3.it/progetti/kant/field/qr.htm, accessed February 5, 2013. Accessible overview of qualia by a prominent property dualist.

4

IDEALISM, SOLIPSISM, AND PANPSYCHISM

Here's something that might sound crazy, but is nonetheless taken seriously 4.1
by many philosophers: Not only do humans and other animals have minds,
but even plants and bacteria have minds. Further, even so-called inanimate
objects like grains of sand, droplets of water, and even individual atoms
each have their own minds. Maybe the mind of a grain of sand is simpler
than the mind of a human being, but it is a mind nonetheless. Everything
has its own mind. This is *panpsychism*.

Here's another crazy sounding idea that has been a topic of many serious 4.2
philosophical discussions: Suppose that the only thing that actually exists
is your own mind. Suppose that there aren't any other things in existence,
no other people and no other minds—and no material objects such as
rocks and trees. Everything that you take to be real is really just an idea in
your own mind, and your experience of this so-called reality is no different
from a very long and realistic dream. This is *solipsism*.

The solipsist and the panpsychist agree that everything has a mind. They 4.3
disagree about whether there is more than one mind. According to solipsism, there's only one.

Solipsism is a version of a more general view that we can call *idealism*. 4.4
According to idealism, everything is either a mind or something that
depends on a mind. Solipsistic versions of idealism hold that there is only
one mind. Nonsolipsistic versions of idealism hold that there are multiple
minds.

Panpsychists don't have to believe in idealism. Idealists say that every- 4.5
thing either is a mind or something that depends on a mind. Panpsychists

This Is Philosophy of Mind: An Introduction, First Edition. Pete Mandik.
© 2014 John Wiley & Sons, Inc. Published 2014 by John Wiley & Sons, Inc.

say instead that everything *has* a mind. Stated this way, panpsychism leaves open whether there might be nonmental physical properties of the things that have minds. So, in addition to having a mind with its various mental properties, perhaps a rock also has nonmental aspects. Maybe, says the panpsychist, the rock's mass or shape is a strictly mind-independent property. An idealist would disagree with such a view. According to the idealist, even the mass and the shape of the rock must depend on someone or other's mind.

Solipsism: Is It Just Me?

4.6   Try to imagine that you are the only thing that exists in the whole universe. Exactly one thing exists, and it is you. Perhaps this seems impossible. After all, you are a living being. As such, you require many things for your existence—air to breathe, water to drink, food to eat. Therefore, there cannot be just you, there must be these other things besides. Further, your body has parts, each of which is a thing. If you exist, then so do your hands, feet, heart, stomach, etc. So this idea that you are the only thing in existence seems like it is impossible. If you exist, then one way or another, many things exist.

4.7   Note however, these remarks about you needing air, water, and food, and about you having hands and a stomach, all are connected with the idea that you have a physical body. But imagine instead that this is incorrect. Imagine that you have no physical body. Of course, it *appears* that you have a body, and that this body is in a world filled with many other physical things. But maybe these appearances are just illusions. Perhaps they are just a kind of idea or perception in your mind.

4.8   Is this something that you can imagine? If so, then what you are imagining is that solipsism is true. Solipsism may strike you as a very odd philosophical theory. Maybe it even strikes you as disturbing or depressing. If solipsism is true, then you are truly alone, and all of your so-called friends are like imaginary friends or characters in a dream. You are the only person who is truly real.

4.9   Probably none of the great philosophers of history explicitly believed in solipsism. The reason solipsism gets discussed is that many have worried that solipsism is implicit in various views that certain philosophers have explicitly held. It becomes a criticism of a view if it leads to solipsism.

There is a cluster of views associated with the philosopher Descartes that   4.10
seems implicitly solipsistic. The main view in this cluster is the view that
the only thing that can be known with certainty is one's own mind. The
existence of anything else is open to doubt and thus not known with
certainty.

It should be noted that Descartes is not explicitly a solipsist. He argues   4.11
that he does indeed have knowledge of all sorts of objects existing in the
external world. However, Descartes' argument for knowledge of the external world depends on an appeal to God that many philosophers have found
unsatisfying. Descartes argues that since God exists, created Descartes, and
is a good God, then Descartes can trust that God wouldn't allow Descartes
to be stuck with a bunch of massively mistaken beliefs. Descartes' appeal
to God is largely regarded as circular. Descartes trusts his reasons for believing that God exists on the grounds that God gave Descartes a reasoning
capacity that is largely trustworthy. If we don't allow Descartes and his fol-
lowers an appeal to God or something else that can play a similar role in
guaranteeing the trustworthiness of beliefs about an external world, then
it looks like the Cartesian is led in the direction of a kind of solipsism.

So far we've been describing solipsism as something that might be   4.12
implicit in one or more philosophical views. However, it would be instruc-
tive to examine what it might look like to give an explicit argument for
solipsism. Here is one example:

Premise 1: The only things that exist are things that are known for certain
to exist.
Premise 2: The only thing that is known for certain to exist is my own
mind.
Conclusion: The only thing that exists is my own mind.

Note that the second premise is an idea we brought up in discussing
Descartes. Note also that such a premise is not alone capable of establishing
solipsism. By itself, it only undermines *knowledge* of a world external to my
mind. Possibly, such a world exists anyway, regardless of whether I know
so. The first premise is designed to block this possibility.

Here's another possible argument for solipsism. Central to this argument   4.13
is an appeal to something known as *Occam's razor*, which is often expressed
as the idea that simpler hypotheses are more likely to be true than complex
hypotheses. On one interpretation of Occam's razor, solipsism counts as
the simplest hypothesis since it hypothesizes the existence of only one

thing, namely *me*. How can we spell out this line of thought as an explicit argument for solipsism? One way to go is the following argument, which has as one of its premises a very strong statement of Occam's razor:

Premise 1: The simplest of any set of competing hypotheses is guaranteed to be true, and its competitors are guaranteed to be false.
Premise 2: Solipsism is the simplest hypothesis.
Conclusion: Solipsism is true; the only thing that exists is me.

This argument is perhaps too simple to convince anyone. However, it does help to illustrate the challenge of going straight from simplicity to solipsism. First, note that premise 1 is far too strong to be taken seriously. No version of Occam's razor stated in terms of a *guarantee* (as opposed to just an increase of probability) is worth taking seriously. Second, questions can be raised about premise 2. Is solipsism really the simplest hypothesis? What about the hypothesis that we can call a kind of *nihilism*, the hypothesis that nothing at all exists? Perhaps nihilism can be ruled out on the sorts of grounds we associate with Descartes: I know that at least I exist, because I can't doubt that I'm thinking, and so on. But this point helps spell out how more premises need to be added to an argument that hopes to prove solipsism by way of an appeal to simplicity.

4.14   In order to prove solipsism false, you'd need a proof that at least one thing besides your own mind exists. One sort of thing that may exist besides your own mind is the mind of one or more other people. Another sort of thing that may exist besides your mind is the various physical things that sensory perception seems to reveal all around us. Whether our senses give us knowledge of physical items in a world external to our mind is another big topic in philosophy, so big as to be largely regarded as separate from the philosophy of mind (and more properly thought of as belonging to the philosophical branch known as *epistemology*), so the remarks here will be largely concerned with the relation of that topic to philosophy of mind.

4.15   One argument against solipsism focuses on certain aspects of my experience and argues that the only possible *explanation* of those aspects is if they are caused by something external to me. One example of this line of thought focuses on certain patterns of regularity in experience. For instance, I repeatedly and regularly experience night following day, things rolling down hills instead of up them, and hot things leading to pains when pressed to my skin. What is the best explanation for this regularity in my experience? According to this line of thought, the experiences themselves can't explain it, because the resulting explanation is ultimately circular. What needs to be explained is why my experience is the way it is and not some other way. An appeal to something *in* experience won't give an explanation *of* experience.

Another argument along these lines appeals to the pattern of experience 4.16 often being contrary to my will. Often, my experiences are very unpleasant despite my best efforts. If what I experience is entirely in my mind the way a daydream is, then why can't I conjure up a series of experiences that is entirely pleasant, or at least not so unpleasant? One premise of this argument is the proposition that if something is entirely in my mind, then it ought to be entirely under the control of my will. Another premise says that some things aren't entirely under the control of my will. The conclusion is that at least one thing exists outside of my own mind.

One thing that should be noted about these sorts of arguments is that 4.17 perhaps they only serve to prove the existence of something external to our minds without specifying whether those external things are physical, mental, or something else entirely. For instance, maybe the idealist George Berkeley is right and multiple minds exist but the only things that exist are minds. Such a view is consistent with the line of thought that says that something external to my experience has to exist in order for there to be an explanation of certain patterns in my experience. So, by itself, an appeal to a need for an explanation will not be enough to get a dualistic or physicalistic antisolipsism as opposed to an idealistic antisolipsism.

What more can we add to this style of argument to help prove the exist- 4.18 ence of physical objects? One thing we can add is an appeal to the predictive success of scientific theories that are stated in terms of physical objects. For someone who has a certain amount of scientific education, part of what is in their experience is a grasp of scientific theories that describe physical objects, objects like planets and atoms. Further, such theories make highly accurate predictions about future experiences. One such prediction is that we will observe such-and-such planet located in the night sky on such-and-such date. Again we can raise a question about explanation. What's the best explanation of the predictive success of these physical theories? For philosophers attracted to this line of thought, the answer is clear—the best explanation is that the theories are *true*. There really are physical objects external to our minds.

Idealism: It's All in the Mind

4.19 The version of idealism that we are primarily interested in presently is a version that we can call a *universal* idealism. It is universal because it holds that *everything* that exists is either itself a mind or is some idea depending on a mind (or some other mentally dependent thing). The universal idealist denies that anything can exist without some mind existing. Universal idealism is not very popular these days, so it's likely that you don't believe it. However, there probably is a version of idealism that you do believe in, and we can call it a version of *limited* idealism. It's limited in holding that some (though not all) things are either minds or depend for their existence on minds.

4.20   What sorts of things depend for their existence on minds? Well, mental states themselves, perceptions and beliefs for example, pretty clearly depend on minds. But this is not as interesting an example of a limited idealism as some other examples. Consider, for example, idealism about *beauty*. Such a view is encoded in the saying "beauty is in the eye of the beholder." According to this view no one is beautiful unless someone perceives him or her as beautiful.

4.21   In contrast to the idealist is the *realist*. If a limited idealist believes of a thing that it is mind-*dependent*, then a limited realist about that thing believes that it is mind-*independent*. We can illustrate this in terms of our example about beauty. A realist about beauty would disagree with the saying, "beauty is in the eye of the beholder." The realist about beauty holds that things are beautiful independently of what anyone perceives, thinks, etc. Regardless of whether someone perceives or thinks about a beautiful object, it would be beautiful anyway.

4.22   We turn now to consider a philosopher who argues for a kind of universal idealism. The idealism of George Berkeley grew out of his commitment to empiricism. Briefly, empiricism is the view that all knowledge and all ideas arise from our sensory perception. Berkeley argues from empiricist premises to the conclusion that existence itself depends on sensory perception. His view can be summed up by the motto, *esse est percipi*, which can be translated as "to be is to be perceived."

4.23   Earlier, we contrasted idealism with realism. The version of realism that Berkeley explicitly argues against is something he calls *materialism*. In this context, materialism is the view that, in addition to the properties of our perceptions, there is an underlying nonmental substance that is the cause of those properties but is neither the property of any perception nor a property of a mind itself. Note that elsewhere in this book we use "materialism" as interchangeable with "physicalism" as denoting a kind of monism. In the context of Berkeley's arguments, "materialism" denotes a view that a dualist and a monist can agree on against Berkeley. It is the view that there are material substances that have properties independent of our perceptions of them.

Berkeley's view may seem quite odd, perhaps even startling. However, he 4.24 devised many highly clever arguments for his view. We will briefly examine a few of them here.

Berkeley's argument from pain

Consider the pain that you feel if you (accidentally!) burn yourself with a 4.25 candle flame or cut yourself with a knife. Ask yourself, when these painful things happen, *where* does the painfulness exist? Which of the following two choices seems more plausible?

1. The painfulness exists in the knife or the flame.
2. The painfulness exists in the mind of the person who suffers a cut or a burn.

You'll probably agree that the second option makes much more sense. It's very hard to believe that there is pain in a knife. That would mean that the knife is suffering! It's far more plausible that pain occurs in the person who is cut by the knife.

Now turn your attention to other perceptible properties, properties that 4.26 are sometimes so intense that they become painful. Such properties include brightness and temperature. If a bright light gets brighter and brighter, eventually it can become so bright that it's painful to look at. If painfulness exists in the mind, and very bright light is a kind of painfulness, then very bright light exists in the mind too. But if bright light exists in the mind, then, plausibly, dim light exists in the mind also.

Berkeley's argument from perceptual relativity: Berkeley's bucket

Suppose that there is a bucket filled with tepid or lukewarm water. Imagine 4.27 sticking both of your hands in the tepid water after first preparing them in the following way: Put your left hand is some very hot water for 30 seconds (not so hot as to be painful, though) and put your right hand in some very cold water. After soaking your hands in the waters of different temperatures for 30 seconds, place them both in the lukewarm water in the bucket. You will notice that the water in the bucket feels quite cool on your hand that was previously in hot water and at the same time it will feel quite warm on your hand that was previously in cold water. With which hand are you able to feel the temperature that the bucket's water actually has? The two experiences associated with the two hands cannot both be accurate, for it would be a contradiction for the water in the bucket to be very warm and not very warm at exactly the same time. And there's no basis for selecting only one of the experiences as accurately representing the temperature of the bucket, for neither seems a better candidate than the other. The idealistic conclusion, then, is that the felt temperature is a property of the experiences or sensory ideas, but not a property in the so-called material object, which in this case is the water in the bucket.

Berkeley's "Nothing but an idea can resemble an idea"

4.28   Berkeley holds that ideas represent by *resembling* what they represent. If your idea of a horse represents a horse, then your idea must itself resemble a horse. However, according to Berkeley, the only thing that an idea can resemble is another idea. An idea cannot resemble so-called material objects then. It follows that you cannot even coherently conceive of material objects, since you can form no idea that would resemble one and thus adequately represent one. It follows also that if you have an idea that represents a horse, the horse must itself be an idea.

Berkeley's master argument

4.29   The argument known as Berkeley's "master argument" is so called because Berkeley claimed that this is the argument he would be willing to stake his whole case on.

4.30   If realism is true, and idealism is false, then it ought to be possible for something like a tree to exist even if no mind exists. If realists are right about trees, then trees are mind-independent—they do not depend on minds for their existence. The gist of Berkeley's master argument is to try to show that we cannot even conceive of anything existing mind-independently.

Try this: Attempt to conceive of something that exists without any mind 4.31
existing. Conceive of a tree. Notice this, however: Any time that you conceive of a tree, your mind thereby exists. How else do you do the conceiving
if not with your mind? According to Berkeley this serves to show that we
cannot even form an idea of a tree existing independently of minds, for
any attempt to do so requires the existence of our own minds.

Why Berkeley is not a solipsist

So far, the arguments of Berkeley's at which we have looked are designed 4.32
to show that there are no material objects or substances. So-called material
things like rocks, trees, and horses are really just collections of ideas.
However, describing idealism that way is to describe a view that is fully
consistent with solipsism, since these collections of ideas may very well
just be *my* ideas. Perhaps there are no other minds or spiritual substances
besides my own. However, Berkeley argues that there must be minds other
than my own.

If you examine your own ideas you will notice that there is a pattern to 4.33
many of them. That pattern must be caused by something. Now, sometimes, in exercising my will, I am the cause of the pattern of ideas. However,
there are other times, especially in sensory perception, in which I am
passive but there is nonetheless a succession of ideas. Something must be
the cause. My mind cannot be the cause since this occurs passively. Berkeley
holds that the cause cannot itself be an idea. It follows, then, that the causes
must be mental substances distinct from my own. That is, other minds
besides my own must exist (or, at least, one other mind must exist).

Let us turn now from these arguments for idealism to consider how one 4.34
might argue against idealism.

Arguing against idealism

One sort of argument that can be given against idealism is very similar 4.35
to an argument we discussed in connection with solipsism. Such an argument notes that there is a pattern to our various ideas and that this presence
of a pattern cries out for an explanation. Why is it that multiple people
agree that there is such a material object as the moon? And why is it
that there is agreement between your own mental states across different
times concerning the moon? For instance, you look at it, you look away,
and when you look back again, the moon is still there. What accounts for

this agreement among your own mental states? The most natural explanation of such coherence across multiple mental states is that there is a common cause of those mental states—that there is something external that is causing them to agree. On one definition of a material object, a material object is something that is causally efficacious and is capable of existing mind-independently. According to this line of thought, then, the best explanation of the coordination of ideas and the coherence of our various mental states, is that there are material objects that cause this coordination and coherence.

Panpsychism: Mind Is Everywhere

4.36 Going just by the word "panpsychism" we can see that it is the view that mind (*psyche*) is everywhere (*pan*). Philosophically, the idea that mind is everywhere or that everything has a mind or mind-like aspect is indeed a crucial core idea of panpsychism. However, panpsychists often embrace additional theses besides the thesis of the ubiquity of mind. Another core idea of most versions of panpsychism is that mind is a *fundamental* aspect of reality.

4.37   As with many views in philosophy, we can understand this view by contrasting it with an opposing view. In this case, the opposed view is that mentality is not fundamental. Now, there are two ways in which mentality can fail to be fundamental. The first is if there is no mentality at all. This is a view known as *eliminativism* or *eliminative materialism* and we will postpone discussing it further until chapter 10. The other way in which mentality is interpreted to be not fundamental is a view we can call "emergentism," for it is the view that there are minds and that they arise out of or *emerge* from the more fundamental aspects of reality, aspects usually taken to be physical and not mental. For the purposes of the present discussion, we can call the crucial contrast a contrast between panpsychists and emergentists.

4.38   The various kinds of physicalist monism that we will examine in chapters 5 through 10 can all be regarded as versions of emergentism. They all take it upon themselves to explain how mentality can emerge out of certain organizations of material parts, parts that are individually not mental. This may seem like an especially daunting task, and, especially when it comes to consciousness, many philosophers have thought that there is a permanent explanatory gap. They hold that consciousness cannot be explained in terms of physical processes. Some philosophers have been moved by such a consideration to reject physicalist emergentism and embrace panpsychism.

We will examine three general sorts of arguments for panpsychism. The 4.39 first sort involves drawing analogies between humans, who clearly have minds, and nonhumans such as plants, to try to show that nonhumans behave in ways sufficiently like humans to justify treating them as having one or more aspects of mentality (e.g., perception, intelligence, memory, will). The second kind of argument appeals to a principle that "nothing can come from nothing." The basic idea here is that in asserting that mind can arise out of nonmind, the emergentist violates a general principle that the only thing that can arise from nothing is . . . *nothing!* The third kind of argument makes appeal to the idea, argued for by Darwin and others, that new organisms arise via a process of evolution by natural selection. According to this evolutionary argument for panpsychism, each new creature is a gradual modification of some previously existing creature, and there is no clear line in the evolution of creatures where we can draw a distinction between those with minds and those without minds. If there's no clear line—no reason for drawing the line at one point rather than another—then perhaps the most reasonable conclusion is to not draw any line between mind and nonmind.

The analogy argument

Like many people, you would probably kill an insect by stepping on it 4.40 without giving it a second thought. And, also like many people, you would be horrified at even the thought of killing a puppy, kitten, or baby human by stomping on it with your foot. But what's the difference that makes a difference here? All of these creatures are alive and use sensory organs to stay alive and avoid danger. According to the panpsychist, despite differences in size, all of these creatures are sufficiently analogous in their structure and behavior to regard as having minds. Perhaps they all have enough mentality to make them all equally deserving of not being killed by being stepped on!

What are the important analogies between humans and other animals 4.41 that make it appropriate to think that the other animals have minds? For starters, we can draw analogies in three areas of mentality (although there are likely analogies that can be drawn beyond these three areas): (1) perception, (2) memory, and (3) will. Like humans, other animals are (1) equipped with sensory organs that allow them to detect stimuli, some of which are beneficial to the organism, others of which are harmful. Like humans, other animals (2) can learn and store information in their memories for use at a later time. Like humans, other animals (3) can make decisions and act in ways based on sensed and remembered information.

4.42   Panpsychists extend such analogies beyond animals to include single-celled (unicellular) organisms and plants. Single-celled organisms such as bacteria have ways of sensing their environments and moving through them. Scientists have even demonstrated simple forms of learning in bacteria! Plants move on much slower timescales, but they move nonetheless. Their movements serve their needs—for example, bringing their leaves closer to sunlight and their roots closer to water and nutrients. Panpsychists view such movements as evidence for plant mentality.

4.43   So-called inanimate objects can even be brought into consideration under such analogies. A piece of metal reacts to being heated—it will change its size and even color. A panpsychist can view this as the metal's perceptual response to the hot stimulus. And a piece of metal can be bent or stamped with a certain shape that it will retain over time. This might be viewed as a kind of memory. Do nonliving things have a kind of will? The swerving movements of particles have been viewed by some panpsychists as the result of decisions, decisions flowing from the free will of the individual particles.

The nothing from nothing argument

4.44   The principle that nothing can come from nothing—in Latin, *ex nihilo nihil fit*—is a widely accepted principle. You yourself probably subscribe to it. If something comes to be, it cannot have come from nothing. Babies come from parents, apples come from trees, fire comes from fuel, oxygen, and heat. The idea that something could just pop into existence without having come from anything — something from nothing—strikes many people as utterly absurd.

4.45   Now consider the basic view of the relation of mind to the rest of the universe according to emergentism. Fundamentally, the universe is made of things that themselves have no mentality. Such things are the fundamental particles studied by physicists, particles like the protons, neutrons, and electrons that make up the chemicals in your brain and rest of your body. According to emergentists, each particle in your brain individually lacks consciousness. However, by being arranged in a special way, those particles thereby give rise to your consciousness. But, isn't this then a case of something—your consciousness—coming out of nothing? Your consciousness is not in any of the individual particles. And if we just threw the particles in a bucket all scrambled up, that wouldn't give rise to your consciousness either. So it looks like we have something very similar here, according to emergentism, to something from nothing. If emergence really happens, then we get mind from no-mind. But if this is an example of something from nothing, then we should reject emergentism and embrace panpsychism.

The evolutionary argument

One of the basic ideas of Darwinian evolution by natural selection is that 4.46 organisms change gradually over multiple generations. New traits are incremental modifications of the traits from a previous generation. The fossil record shows gradual changes in size and shape. If this gradual aspect of evolutionary change is a universal feature of the evolution of traits, then even human mental traits must have evolved gradually from predecessors that themselves had mental traits. However, unless mentality was always present in the history of evolution of life on earth, there has to have been some point where a creature with mentality originated from a creature without mentality. Another way to put this is that there has to be somewhere in this historical progression where we can "draw a line" separating the minded from the un-minded. However, there doesn't seem to be an obvious place anywhere in the history of evolving creatures where we can draw such a line. The panpsychist concludes that there is no line and that there's a continuity of mentality running through evolutionary history from our earliest unicellular ancestors to us. And if the emergence of life from nonliving matter was similarly a process of incremental change, then there is no line to be drawn between the living and the nonliving that would serve to distinguish the minded from the un-minded.

Arguing against panpsychism: The combination problem

To get a feel for what the combination problem is, it helps to first bring to 4.47 mind a criticism about explanation that panpsychists raise against emergentists. The gist of the criticism is that emergentists will never be able to explain how a bunch of atoms, each of which by itself does not have a mind, can combine to give rise to my mind.

4.48   Next, recall that certain panpsychists have sought to avoid the problems of emergentism by positing that minds can be found throughout physical nature, so that even the individual atoms that make up my body and brain each have their own consciousness, albeit a simpler form of consciousness than my own. But here's where the combination problem arises for this kind of panpsychism. Insofar as my atoms have a kind of consciousness different from my own, the panpsychist is in as much a need of an account of the emergence of my consciousness as is the physicalist emergentist. And if it is true that no such account will ever be possible for physical emergentism, it looks like no such account would be possible for this kind of panpsychist emergentism either.

4.49   Another way of viewing the combination problem for panpsychism is that it is a version of the "nothing from nothing" argument, but applied against panpsychism (instead of against physicalist emergentism). Suppose that my atoms have a different consciousness from my own. Call each of those minds a *not-Pete mind*. My own mind, the Pete mind, arises from the combination of not-Pete minds. But this is a case of something from nothing, because it looks like the Pete mind is emerging from a combination of not-Pete minds.

4.50   Of course, it should be noted that certain versions of panpsychism are immune to the combination problem. For instance, a solipsistic idealism according to which my mind is the only mind and so-called physical atoms are just ideas in my mind can't be argued against on the basis of combinations, since solipsism doesn't hold that my mind arises out of any combination. My mind is the only thing in existence, so there aren't multiple things to combine. Other kinds of idealism are similarly immune. Examples are the idealisms of Berkeley and Leibniz, whereby there are multiple minds, but each mind is simple, meaning that each mind is in no way composed of parts.

Conclusion

4.51   Idealism, solipsism, and panpsychism are united in seeing mind as a much more widespread phenomenon than common sense dictates. Indeed, solipsism sees the entirety of existence as restricted to a single mind. Despite their counterintuitive nature, these philosophical positions are highly intriguing, and their opponents have sometimes struggled to spell out exactly what might be wrong with them. Panpsychism, for instance, offers a special kind of challenge to those philosophers interested in the explanation of consciousness: Why isn't it true that everything has its own form of consciousness?

Annotated Bibliography

Berkeley, George (1713) *Three Dialogues between Hylas and Philonous in Opposition to Sceptics and Atheists*, full text available at http://www.earlymoderntexts.com/bd.html, accessed February 6, 2013. Berkeley lays out his defenses of idealism and immaterialism in these fun and highly readable dialogues.

Chalmers, David (2003) "The Matrix as Metaphysics," in Christopher Grau (ed.), *Philosophers Explore the Matrix* (Oxford: Oxford University Press), full text available at http://consc.net/papers/matrix.html, accessed February 6, 2013. Taking up themes from the Matrix movies, Chalmers explores the philosophical implications of possibilities like solipsism and that the world might be a computer simulation.

Nagel, Thomas (1979) "Panpsychism," in Thomas Nagel, *Mortal Questions* (Cambridge: Cambridge University Press). Discussion of links between emergentism and panpsychism.

Seager, William and Allen-Hermanson, Sean (2012) "Panpsychism," in Edward N. Zalta (ed.), *The Stanford Encyclopedia of Philosophy (Spring 2012 Edition)*, full text available at http://plato.stanford.edu/archives/spr2012/entries/panpsychism/, accessed February 6, 2013. A top-notch overview of the pros and cons of panpsychism.

Thornton, Stephen (2004) "Solipsism and the Problem of Other Minds," in *Internet Encyclopedia of Philosophy*, full text available at http://www.iep.utm.edu/solipsis/, accessed February 6, 2013. A fantastic discussion of solipsism and related themes, especially from the point of view of the philosophy of Ludwig Wittgenstein.

5

BEHAVIORISM AND OTHER MINDS

Behaviorism: Introduction and Overview

Behaviorism is the view that everything there is to know or say about 5.1
people with regard to their mental states can be known or said in terms of
their observable behaviors (including verbal behaviors). We might go even
further and say that, according to behaviorism, all there is to mental states
are certain patterns of behavior or certain dispositions toward certain
behaviors.

These simple statements of behaviorism can be broken down into three 5.2
claims about mental states. The first is a claim about how to gain *knowledge*
of mental states. The second is about the *meanings* of what we say when
we use terminology like "belief" and "desire." The third is about what
mental states *are*, that is, what their ultimate nature is. Philosophers describe
these three claims like this: The first claim is *epistemological*, the second is
semantic, and the third is *metaphysical*.

To illustrate these three claims, consider the emotional state of *feeling* 5.3
sad. In particular, consider the sadness of another person.

Illustrating the knowledge claim: How do you know that this person is sad?
The behavioristic answer is very close to the commonsense answer. You
know by what they do and what they say. They frown, they cry, they
mope. They say things like "I feel sad."
Illustrating the meaning claim: What does the word "sad" *mean*? What does
one understand when one understands claims like "Mary is very sad

---

This Is Philosophy of Mind: An Introduction, First Edition. Pete Mandik.
© 2014 John Wiley & Sons, Inc. Published 2014 by John Wiley & Sons, Inc.

today"? The behaviorist says that the meanings of such words can be spelled out in terms of behavior. If we describe someone as being in a mental state of "sadness," then *by definition* we are describing them as having, or being prone to have, behaviors such as frowning, weeping, and moping.

Illustrating the metaphysical claim: There are two versions to this claim, one that we can call *reductionist* and the other that we can call *eliminativist*. The reductionist version says that sadness *just is* a kind of behavior or behavioral disposition. The eliminativist version says that, there really is no such thing as a mental state of sadness, and that what exists instead are certain behaviors or dispositions. We will have more to say about eliminativism in chapter 10. Throughout this chapter we will mostly focus on the reductionist version of the metaphysical claim.

5.4   One thing that is especially noteworthy about behaviorism is how well it is suited to *other* minds. As we already noted, the basic behaviorist view of how we know about other minds is very close to the commonsense view—our knowledge of the minds and mental states of other people is mediated by observed behavior. Since there's very little scientific evidence for the existence of telepathy, there is no serious reason for thinking we can directly know the minds of others. We have to go on what they do or say and figure it out from there.

5.5   While behaviorism seems well suited to other minds, it may not be well suited as a view of one's own mind. At least, this has been a complaint of many philosophers against behaviorism. Consider how you know of your own sadness. Which seems the more plausible of the following two accounts?

Account 1: You observe your own behavior and notice that you are frowning and weeping. You conclude that you are probably sad.

Account 2: You simply *feel* sad and thereby know your sadness. You don't need to rely on any observations of your behavior. You just introspect and directly feel the sadness inside of you.

Many people will regard account 2 as much more plausible and for that reason resist behaviorism. Relatedly, one of the most prominent objections to behaviorism concerns certain subjective aspects of the mind—qualia—that we allegedly know directly via introspection. We will explore such objections later in this chapter. First, however, we turn to behaviorism's history.

The History of Behaviorism

"Behaviorism" is a label for two distinct historical movements, one in psy- 5.6
chology and one in philosophy. The psychological movement is called
"psychological behaviorism," "methodological behaviorism," or "empirical
behaviorism." The philosophical movement is called "philosophical behaviorism," "logical behaviorism," or "analytical behaviorism." These two
movements emerged due to different historical forces and have different
main topics of concern, although there is overlap.

The main topic of concern for psychological behaviorism is a question 5.7
of what methods are best suited for conducting scientific research in psychology. Psychological behaviorism rebelled against introspectionism,
which favored introspective methods for studying the mind.

The main topics of concern for philosophical behaviorism were semantic 5.8
and metaphysical. Historically, philosophical behaviorism emerged from
the philosophical movements of logical positivism and ordinary-language
philosophy. Ordinary-language philosophers were suspicious of philosophical theses such as Cartesian dualism that were not stated in the terms of
ordinary language. Logical positivists believed in a verificationist theory of
the meaning of terms. On this theory, the meaning of a term is given by
specifying the observable conditions that would verify its application. So,
the meaning of "oxygen" is given by specifying the experimental conditions
in which one can verify statements such as "there is oxygen present."

Behaviorism can be seen as a consequence of applying verificationism 5.9
to mentalistic terminology like "belief" and "desire." At least insofar as we
focus on other people, it is plausible that the only evidence we have for
verifying whether they believe or desire something is evidence concerning
their behavior. If we assume the verificationist theory of meaning, we wind
up with the behaviorist view that behaviors are part of the very meanings
of mentalistic terms like "belief" and "desire."

Despite the historical and topical differences between behaviorism in 5.10
psychology and behaviorism in philosophy, there is considerable overlap,
with commonalities in the answers given to the three core questions we
mentioned earlier (the questions we identified as epistemological, semantic, and metaphysical). Nonetheless, the discussion in the present chapter
will be primarily focused on philosophical behaviorism.

For any philosopher whom someone calls a behaviorist, controversy 5.11
arises about whether that philosopher really is a behaviorist. Nonetheless,

it is worth mentioning some of the key philosophers who are often associated with behaviorism, namely Gilbert Ryle, Ludwig Wittgenstein, W. V. O. Quine, and Daniel Dennett. In the present section, we will focus on two especially influential figures from the early days of philosophical behaviorism: Gilbert Ryle and Ludwig Wittgenstein.

Ludwig Wittgenstein and the private language argument

5.12   One of the central ideas that behaviorists rebel against, an idea with close associations with Descartes and his dualism, is the idea of the privacy of the mental. This idea of privacy is that you can only have knowledge of your own mind. You can make an educated guess about other minds, but you can only know, or only know with certainty, your own mind.

5.13   One early and influential attack on this idea of privacy originates with Ludwig Wittgenstein in his *Philosophical Investigations*. Wittgenstein expresses his antipathy towards privacy in his "beetle in a box" passage (from section 293 of the *Investigations*):

> Suppose everyone had a box with something in it: we call it a "beetle." No one can look into anyone else's box, and everyone says he knows what a beetle is only by looking at his beetle. Here it would be quite possible for everyone to have something different in his box. One might even imagine such a thing constantly changing.
>
> Suppose the word "beetle" had a use in these people's language? If so it would not be used as the name of a thing. The thing in the box has no place in the language-game at all; not even as a something: for the box might even be empty. No, one can "divide through" by the thing in the box; it cancels out, whatever it is. That is to say: if we construe the grammar of the expression of sensation on the model of "object and designation" the object drops out of consideration as irrelevant.

5.14   In Wittgenstein's discussion, the beetle in a box is a metaphor for sensations, especially as sensations are thought of from a Cartesian point of view. From a Cartesian point of view, sensations are known only privately. Others can observe your behaviors, but only you can experience your sensations. From the point of view of someone on "the outside" your sensations might be very different or altogether missing. Such an idea is reminiscent of the thought experiments about zombies and inverted qualia that we discussed in chapter 3. For someone on the outside, you might as well have no sensations at all. Wittgenstein's point here is even stronger: Even for you, you might as well have no sensations. You might as well have nothing in your "box."

How can we reach this even stronger conclusion? Isn't it just obvious 5.15 that there might be private sensations, that there might be a "beetle in the box"? Part of Wittgenstein's point is to focus on the words we would use to even try to frame such a question, words such as "sensation." "Sensation" is a word in English, a language shared by multiple people. As such, "sensation" has a public use. But also as such, whatever private things accompany our public uses of "sensation," they might as well not be there—"sensation" would still have its public use.

This line of thinking gets developed in Wittgenstein's famous *private* 5.16 *language argument*. The conclusion of this argument is that it is impossible for there to be a language that referred to private things, a language about sensations that could only be understood by a single person. Central to Wittgenstein's discussion is a thought experiment in which you try to imagine devising a language with which you could keep a diary of your own private sensations, a language that only you understand.

Suppose you devise a sign, "S," that you intend to stand for a particular 5.17 sensation that you just had. You write "S" down in your private diary. Wittgenstein invites us to wonder how you would know that "S" did indeed stand for that sensation and not some other (or stood for nothing at all). According to Wittgenstein, in keeping this private journal, you will not ever be in a position to distinguish whether, on some occasion, you used "S" to correctly refer to some sensation as opposed to merely *seeming* to yourself to have used it correctly. And since, by hypothesis, this is supposed to be private, no one else will be in a position to distinguish between a correct use of "S" and a mere *seemingly correct* use of "S." Since there is no one—not you, and not anyone else—who can distinguish between a correct usage and an incorrect usage of a sign in this language, there is no such distinction. But, according to Wittgenstein, where one cannot grasp a distinction between correct and incorrect uses, there just is no place for a notion of correctness at all. The sign "S," as well as the rest of the signs in this so-called language, is thus meaningless, and this is no language at all. The conclusion that Wittgenstein urges is that there cannot be a genuinely private language. Languages, then, are necessarily public, as are the things that we refer to using language. Whatever sensations are, then, they cannot be private. For the word "sensation" has a public use, and that's the only use that matters.

Gilbert Ryle versus the ghost in the machine

5.18 The philosopher Gilbert Ryle, in his book *The Concept of Mind* (1949), parodies Descartes' view of the mind as a view of "the ghost in the machine." Descartes' solution to the mind–body problem is to think of the mind as a ghost that inhabits our body (the machine). Part of what's wrong with this view, according to Ryle, is that it treats the mind and the body as each a kind of thing. Only on such an assumption would it make sense to say that the mind is literally *in* the body (like a ghost might be in a machine). But regarding the mind as itself a kind of thing is to make a mistake that Ryle calls a "category mistake."

5.19   A category mistake is the mistake of treating something that belongs in one logical or conceptual category as if it belongs in another. Here's an illustration of Ryle's: Imagine that one day you visit a university and join a tour of the buildings on campus. You are brought to the library, the science building, the sports building, and so on. Imagine further that you interrupt your tour guide and say, "Thank you so much for showing me the library, the science building, the sports building, etcetera, but when are you going to show me the *university*?" The mistake here is thinking that the university belongs in the same category as the various buildings, as if it were yet another building that you could be led to.

5.20   Ryle sees dualists as committing various category mistakes in the way they talk about the mind. The central category mistake is that of thinking of the mind itself as a thing that has its own properties and is made of its own substance. Instead we should think of talk concerning mind and mental states (like believing and thinking) as a way of tracking the behaviors and behavioral dispositions of people. The behaviors that a physical being can engage in do not themselves constitute a separate thing that the physical thing is related to. A dance is not a thing separate from the dancer. For Ryle, the mind is no *thing* at all!

5.21   Another important strand of Ryle's thinking is his *regress argument* against intellectualism and his closely related distinction between *knowing-how* and *knowing-that*. The *intellectualism* that Ryle targets can be represented as the view that any act that anyone does intelligently must be preceded by some episode of thinking. So, for example, if you intelligently glue a small component on to a model you are building, this action must be preceded by some thought of the form "the component should be glued in *this way* . . ." Ryle sees this as leading to an infinite regress since he sees thinking as itself a kind of action that can be done either intelligently or unintelligently. If an intelligent action must be preceded by some thinking, presumably the thinking must itself be *intelligent* thinking (since some stupid thinking can't be the cause of some nonstupid acting). And if the thinking itself is an intelligent action, then some other thought must precede it, and so on for infinity. Thus, an infinite regress arises.

The way Ryle's own view avoids leading to this intellectualist regress is 5.22 by drawing a distinction between two kinds of knowledge—knowing-how and knowing-that. In knowing-that (what others have called *propositional knowledge*) there is some thought or proposition that you know to be true. For instance, in knowing *that* the Earth is round, what you know is that the proposition *the Earth is round* is true. In contrast, in knowing-how (what others have called *procedural knowledge*), your knowledge is had by having an ability, a disposition to behave in a certain way. When you know how to ride a bike, you are, for example, disposed to move forward while pedaling the wheels and not falling off. According to Ryle, such ability cannot be summed up in the form of one or more propositions *that* one knows. The intellectualist regress is thus broken by having occasions of knowing-that, and intelligent action more generally, be grounded in know-how, a kind of knowledge that itself is not grounded in any other knowledge.

Objections to Behaviorism

We will examine three objections to behaviorism: (1) the qualia objection, 5.23 (2) Sellars's objection, and (3) the Geach–Chisholm objection.

The qualia objection

One sort of objection that philosophers have raised against behaviorism is 5.24 an objection that hinges on qualia. To really appreciate the force of this objection, it helps to focus on the aspect of philosophical behaviorism that has to do with the meanings of mentalistic terms, or, as we might put it, the structure of our mentalistic concepts. Behaviorism holds that the very concept of a mental state like desire or fear is connected to concepts having to do with behavior. So, for example, the very concept of someone being afraid of dogs is connected to concepts having to do with dog-related behaviors, such as moving away from any dogs that are nearby or speaking with a trembling voice whenever the topic of dogs comes up. If being afraid of dogs is conceptually linked to certain dog-related behaviors, then it ought to be *inconceivable* for someone to have a fear of dogs but not be in any way disposed toward dog-avoiding behaviors. Conversely, if it is so conceivable—if we can indeed conceive of someone being afraid of dogs independently of conceiving of them of having any dog-related behaviors— then that counts against this version of behaviorism.

5.25   Now, let us return to the question of qualia. Consider a red quale. Are there any behaviors such that they are conceptually linked to the concept of a red quale? Certain familiar thought experiments are relevant to answering this question. Consider, for example, the inverted spectrum thought experiment that we discussed in chapter 3. In this thought experiment, it is supposed to be conceivable that two people are alike in all their behaviors and behavioral dispositions, including their behaviors and dispositions regarding the sorting and naming of color samples, but have completely different qualia from each other. If such a situation is conceivable, then having a red quale cannot be conceptually linked to having such-and-such behaviors and dispositions.

Sellars's objection

5.26   Another sort of objection to behaviorism originates with the philosopher Wilfrid Sellars. The gist of Sellars's point is that (1) it is part of our very concept of a mental state like a belief that it is the cause or explanation of certain behaviors, and (2) genuine causal explanations cannot be circular, but (3) behaviorism would make the resulting causal explanations circular. Let us take a closer look at (1) and (3).

1. *It is part of our very concept of a mental state like a belief that it is the cause or explanation of certain behaviors.*

5.27   Consider verbal behavior. Consider, for example, someone who says sincerely, "Turnips taste best when harvested in August." Compare that case to a case where similar sounds are produced by a recording or a well-trained parrot. What makes the person's utterance count as a genuine piece of verbal behavior? What makes it a genuine speech act as opposed to merely the production of sound? Plausibly, only in the case of the person is the noise produced an expression of a belief or a thought. And what it means here for the speech to be an expression of a thought is for the thought to be a cause of the speech and that the thought and the speech have roughly the same content. What it means to say that they have roughly the same content in this example is that the person both thinks and says that *turnips taste best when harvested in August*. What's important here in the present context is not so much the content part of this story as is the causal part of the story, namely, that the thought is the cause of the speech that expresses it.

A similar line of thought can be extended to nonverbal behaviors. 5.28 Compare a person who kicks their leg out intentionally (perhaps they are kicking a ball in a game) and a person doing it unintentionally (perhaps in their sleep because an insect tickled their foot). What makes the first kicking a genuine intentional action and the other a mere bit of involuntary reflexive motion? Arguably what's important in the intentional case is that the kicking is the result of some prior plan or intention. The person has some goal or aim in mind and this mental state caused the movement of the foot. In the reflexive response to being tickled by the insect, there is no prior plan or intention.

3.   *Behaviorism would make the resulting causal explanations circular.*

To see this point, it will help to consider a very simplified version of 5.29 behaviorism. Suppose a behaviorist offered the following definition of sadness: Being sad *just is* having certain behaviors, such as crying and frowning. Now, according to Sellars, it is part of our commonsense grasp of terms like "sad" and "sadness" that we use them to explain certain behaviors. Why is Mary frowning and crying? Here's a commonsense explanation: She is crying and frowning because she is sad. But if the behaviorist is right, that explanation turns out to be circular. Since the behaviorist has defined sadness as having the behaviors of crying and frowning, the commonsense explanation winds up being equivalent to the following obviously circular explanation: Mary is frowning and crying because Mary is frowning and crying.

The Geach–Chisholm objection

One highly influential criticism of behaviorism is attributed to the philoso- 5.30 phers Peter Geach and Roderick Chisholm. The gist of this objection is that mental states cannot be individually connected with behaviors, but can only be connected to behaviors in concert with other mental states in a way that makes behaviorism an intractably complex theory.

To see why this presents a problem for behaviorism, let us begin by 5.31 taking a look at a particular mental state. Suppose that Jane fears tigers. Suppose also that Jane is on an expedition in the jungle and there is a tiger only five feet away from her. What behavior will her fear of tigers result in? What behavior she engages in depends to a large degree on what other mental states she has. First, it depends on whether she believes there is a tiger near by. Suppose she hasn't seen the tiger or has seen it but believes it is her friend in a tiger suit trying to play a trick on her. Without any belief that there is a tiger near by, the mere desire to avoid tigers is unlikely to trigger any particular behavior on this occasion.

5.32   The story of Jane and the tiger helps us to see that the desire to avoid tigers is not all by itself connected to tiger-avoiding behavior. It is only in concert with other mental states such as beliefs that a desire is connected to a particular kind of behavior.

5.33   This point does not just apply to desires. We can make the point about any mental state. Consider belief. Suppose there is a tiger five feet away from George and that George believes this—George believes that there is a tiger five feet away. What will his behavior be? Suppose George believes tigers are friendly and like to be petted. Suppose further that George desires to pet tigers. That might lead to one sort of behavior. But if George has a different desire, then he might behave differently.

5.34   Given that a mental state can only be connected to a behavior by also being connected to a bunch of other mental states, what's the problem for behaviorism? The problem is that the project of saying which behavior a mental state is connected to is so complicated as to be totally intractable. We are never in a position to give a definition of a particular mental state in terms of behavior, since we must bring in some other mental states in the definition. But how will we define each of those other mental states? Each of them can only be connected to behavior by reference to other mental states, including the mental state that we started with, and thus are we led in a circle.

5.35   Given that much of behaviorism is concerned with characterizations of the minds of others, it is natural at this point to delve deeper into the philosophical problem of other minds.

The Philosophical Problem of Other Minds

5.36   The problem of other minds is largely an epistemological problem—while most of us *believe* that there are minds other than our own, how can we each come to *know* that there are other minds? What *justifies* our belief in the existence of other minds? The problem can be felt as especially acute if we make certain Cartesian assumptions. One such assumption is that there is a stark difference between the way we know of our own minds and the way we know of the minds of others. On the Cartesian view, I know my own mind with certainty. However, my knowledge of things external to my own mind is mediated by my senses. And, since my senses may be deceived, nothing I know through them is known with certainty. Worse, the possibility arises that maybe I don't know anything at all about things external to my mind.

In the next two subsections we will examine two general strategies for 5.37 solving the problem of other minds. The first strategy accepts that there is an important asymmetry between the way one knows one's own mind and the way one knows the minds of others. The second strategy denies any deep asymmetry—the way each of us knows our own mind is not importantly different from the knowledge of the minds of others.

The rise and fall of the argument from analogy

The first solution that we will look at is known as the *argument from* 5.38 *analogy*, which can be spelled out in four steps.

The first step is to note the existence of one's own mind. You know that 5.39 you have a mind and various mental states. You know you have beliefs, desires, perceptions, memories, thoughts, feelings, and so on.

The second step is to note that on many occasions, certain kinds of your 5.40 mental states are correlated with certain kinds of behavior. You notice that when you are happy, you tend to walk with a bounce in your step and wear a smile on your face. You notice that when you are sad, you tend to frown and sulk. You notice that when you believe things, such as that $2 + 2 = 4$, you are disposed to say so.

The third step is to notice the other human bodies in the world and to 5.41 note the various behaviors they engage in. Sometimes those bodies walk with a bounce and smile. Other times those bodies frown and sulk. Sometimes those bodies engage in verbal behaviors. They say things like "$2 + 2 = 4$."

The fourth step is the step that gives the argument its name. The fourth 5.42 step involves reasoning by drawing an analogy and then making an *analogical inference*. Here the analogy is between your own body and the bodies of others. These bodies behave in analogous ways. Just as your body smiles and walks, so do the bodies of others. The *analogical inference* is to infer that the other people are similar to you in having mental states.

5.43   So, is this argument any good? We should note here that analogical infer- ence is a kind of reasoning that we employ often and such inferences are regarded as a respectable way to think about things. For instance, suppose that you've opened over a thousand peanut shells in your life, and that every peanut shell that you've ever opened so far has contained two seeds. It is reasonable, then, to expect that the next peanut shell that you open will also contain two seeds. What's the analogy here? The analogy concerns resemblances between the unopened peanut and the ones you've already opened. The unopened peanut resembles the other peanuts in having a similar shape and having come from a similar plant. You reason that, given these similarities, the new peanut will be similar in other ways as well.

5.44   Since analogical reasoning is a respectable form of reasoning, the mere fact that the argument from analogy deploys an analogical inference is not a problem. Nonetheless, the argument from analogy has a serious flaw. It is a *hasty generalization*. To see what's wrong with hasty generalizations, consider a variation of the story with the peanuts. Suppose George has only ever encountered or even heard about a single peanut. This single peanut contains two seeds. Suppose George concludes from observing this single peanut that on every future occasion of opening peanuts, they will be revealed as containing exactly two seeds. George is leaping to a conclusion. Having observed only one peanut, he doesn't have enough evidence to justify his claim about *all* peanuts. A claim about *all* peanuts is a generaliza- tion about peanuts, and in basing his generalization on only a small amount of evidence, George is making a hasty generalization.

5.45   What makes the argument from analogy a hasty generalization? Given the Cartesian assumption that you only have direct access to your own mental states, the only mind you "observe" is your own mind. But there are billions of human beings alive on the planet Earth. The crucial flaw of the argument from analogy is that it is making a generalization about what must be true of billions of people based on "observable" correlations between the behaviors and mental states of only one person.

Denying the asymmetry between self-knowledge and knowledge of other minds

5.46   Perhaps what makes the problem of other minds especially problematic is the Cartesian assumption that there's an asymmetry between the way you know your own mind and the way you know the minds of others. One strategy for solving the problem of other minds is to deny any deep asymmetry between knowledge of one's own mind and knowledge of the minds of others. Call this the "symmetry strategy."

One version of the symmetry strategy is behaviorism. According to behaviorism, since mental states can be defined in terms of bodily behavior, there is no *special* problem about knowing the minds of others. Knowing the minds of others is no more difficult than knowing the existence and motions of various physical bodies. This is a version of the symmetry solution because it claims that you know your own mind in the same way that you know the minds of others, namely, via knowledge of bodily behaviors. However, as discussed earlier, behaviorism is vulnerable to several powerful objections. 5.47

Another version of the symmetry strategy holds that knowledge of other minds, and knowledge of minds generally, is a kind of theoretical knowledge similar to the knowledge codified in the form of various scientific theories, theories such as the atomic theory of matter. 5.48

Crucial to this view of theories is the idea that theories posit the existence of unobservable entities (such as entities too small to be seen) as an *inference to the best explanation* of the observable data. In the case of the atomic theory of matter, microscopic particles invisible to the naked eye are posited in order to explain the observable interactions between various chemical samples. 5.49

Many philosophers follow Wilfrid Sellars and hold that our own knowledge of minds is codified in terms of a theory that we implicitly grasp, a theory referred to as *folk psychology*. The key entities in this theory are mental states such as beliefs and sensations. The existence of such mental states is posited to explain certain patterns of behavior. As we discussed earlier in connection with Sellars, such posits cannot simply be defined in terms of the behavior they are posited to explain, for the various explanations would then turn out to be circular. So, it is crucial on this view that the behaviorist program to define mental states by reference to behavior be rejected. In chapter 10 we will discuss further the idea that our grasp of minds is constituted by a grasp of a theory. 5.50

Conclusion

Some form of behaviorism seems especially plausible as an account of our knowledge of other minds. What else do we have to go on besides the behaviors of others when we try to understand what is going on in their 5.51

minds? We can ask them directly, but their answers are just a form of behavior—verbal behavior. Some of the biggest obstacles to behaviorism, however, concern the knowledge of aspects of our own minds. I seem to have an acquaintance with my own conscious experience that is unmediated by observations of my behavior.

Annotated Bibliography

Dennett, Daniel (1997) "True Believers: The Intentional Strategy and Why it Works," in John Haugeland (ed.), *Mind Design II: Philosophy, Psychology, and Artificial Intelligence* (Cambridge, MA: MIT Press). An exposition of Dennett's "behaviorism," especially as it applies to beliefs and other propositional attitudes.

Dennett, Daniel (2003) "Who's on First? Heterophenomenology Explained," *Journal of Consciousness Studies*, 10(9–10), 10–30, full text available from http://ase.tufts.edu/cogstud/papers/JCSarticle.pdf, accessed February 6, 2013. Dennett's "behaviorism" is applied to consciousness in the form of what he calls "heterophenomenology," a method for studying consciousness that is not restricted to so-called first person methods.

Hauser, Lary (2005) "Behaviorism," in *Internet Encyclopedia of Philosophy*, full text available from http://www.iep.utm.edu/behavior/, accessed February 6, 2013. A useful overview of both psychological behaviorism and philosophical behaviorism.

Hyslop, Alec (2010) "Other Minds," in Edward Zalta (ed.), *The Stanford Encyclopedia of Philosophy*, full text available from http://plato.stanford.edu/archives/fall2010/entries/other-minds/, accessed February 6, 2013. A wide-ranging overview of various versions and aspects of the problem of other minds.

Ryle, Gilbert (1949) *The Concept of Mind* (London: Hutchison). Ryle defends a kind of behaviorism while attacking Cartesian dualism as a kind of "category mistake" which casts the human mind as a "ghost in the machine."

Sellars, Wilfrid (1956) "Empiricism and the Philosophy of Mind," in Herbert Feigl and Michael Scriven (eds.), *Minnesota Studies in the Philosophy of Science, Volume I: The Foundations of Science and the Concepts of Psychology and Psychoanalysis* (Minneapolis: University of Minnesota Press), pp. 253–329, full text available from http://www.ditext.com/sellars/epm.html, accessed February 6, 2013. Sellars develops both a critique of philosophical behaviorism and a defense of what he calls "methodological behaviorism," the view that behavior is the best route we have to knowledge of one another in psychological terms.

Wittgenstein, Ludwig (1953) *Philosophical Investigations*, trans. G. E. M. Anscombe (Oxford: Basil Blackwell), full text available from http://gormendizer. co.za/wp-content/uploads/2010/06/Ludwig.Wittgenstein.-.Philosophical. Investigations.pdf, accessed February 6, 2013. One of the greatest philosophical works of the 20th century, the source of Witttgenstein's private language argument, and much else besides.

6

MIND AS BRAIN

Introducing Mind–Brain Identity Theory

The theory that we will examine in the present chapter—the mind–brain 6.1
identity theory (aka "type-identity theory," "psycho-neural reductionism,"
"central-state materialism," and often simply "the identity theory")—can
be stated simply. It is the view that the mind is the brain and that mental
states are brain states. Mind and brain are one and the same—they are
identical.

Since the brain is physical, mind–brain identity theory is a kind of physi- 6.2
calism. It denies both substance dualism and property dualism. It denies
substance dualism since it denies that the mind is a nonphysical thing. It
affirms that the mind is a thing, but it is a physical thing—it is the brain.
Mind–brain identity theory denies property dualism because it denies that
mental properties, such as qualia, are nonphysical properties. They are
indeed properties, according to this view, but they are one and the same as
certain brain properties.

It is worth here noting a key difference between mind–brain identity 6.3
theory and behaviorism, the other physicalist theory that we've examined
so far. The main difference might be put like this: Where the behaviorist
defines mental states directly in terms of *outward* behavior, the mind–brain
identity theorist defines mental states as something literally *inner*, since a
person's brain is something literally inside of their body.

This Is Philosophy of Mind: An Introduction, First Edition. Pete Mandik.
© 2014 John Wiley & Sons, Inc. Published 2014 by John Wiley & Sons, Inc.

Advantages of Mind–Brain Identity Theory

6.4 Let us briefly recount some of the problems that arose for the theories we've discussed so far, and reflect briefly on how mind–brain identity theory better solves them. We can summarize the main problems for the previous theories as follows:

- *Substance* and *property dualism* lead to epiphenomenalism and serious problems concerning mind–body interaction. Further, they make exceptions to the scientific worldview whereby everything is bound by the laws of physics.
- *Idealism* and the related theories of *solipsism* and *panpsychism* are deeply contrary to common sense.
- *Behaviorism* doesn't preserve the commonsense idea that many of our mental states are *causes* of behaviors.

The contrast between dualism and the identity theory is especially worth remarking on. Besides the general worry that dualism is not really consistent with a generally scientific worldview, a worldview that is overwhelmingly physicalistic, there is also the worry that arises having to do with *the problem of interaction*. The problem of interaction is especially acute for Cartesian substance dualism, which holds that minds are so radically different from physical bodies that they do not even have spatial locations. How, then, can a substance that is nowhere at all have causal effects on my body (as when I intentionally raise my hand)? A closely related problem is the problem of explaining why it is that my mind has a direct effect only on my own body. If your mind and my mind are equally nowhere, then why is it that my thoughts can have a direct influence on my body but not yours? And why does damage to your body cause suffering to arise in your mind but not mine?

6.5 The identity theory has a straightforward way of dealing with all of these questions and problems. Question: How can the mind affect the body and the body affect the mind? Answer: In the general way that physical objects affect each other, since the brain is as much a physical object as the rest of your body. Question: Why is it that damage to my body causes pain in me and not you? And why can I intentionally raise my own hand, but cannot directly raise your hand intentionally? Answer: Your brain is directly connected to the rest of your body, but not to my body, whereas my brain is connected to my body and not yours. Relatedly, identity theory does not lead to the troubling thesis of *epiphenomenalism* as property dualism does. Qualia are causally efficacious properties because they are brain properties, which are causally efficacious generally.

Let us now consider comparisons between identity theory and the mind-   6.6
centered views of idealism, solipsism, and panpsychism. Unlike idealism and solipsism, identity theory takes a more commonsensical approach to existence. There are many physical objects that exist independently of our minds because our minds are just our brains and there are many physical objects that exist besides brains. Unlike panpsychism, which draws no strict division between physical systems that have minds and physical systems that do not, identity theory is able to draw a strict division. Physical systems lacking brains thereby lack minds.

Aside from the virtues of identity theory already outlined—virtues such   6.7
as explaining mind–body interaction in a satisfying way and avoiding epiphenomenalism—an argument sometimes given in favor of identity theory is that it is simpler than its main competitor, dualism. As discussed in chapter 4, the idea that the simplest of competing theories is the preferable one is known as Occam's razor. Occam's razor arguably favors identity theory over dualism. Whereas dualism postulates entities in addition to brains and mental properties in addition to brain properties, mind–brain identity theory is simpler for dealing with just brains and brain properties. If dualism is identity theory's only competitor, then identity theory wins the competition for simplest theory.

However, we shouldn't be too quick in concluding that Occam's razor   6.8
settles all debates in favor of identity theory. As we know from chapter 4, there are other competitors besides dualism—there are the varieties of idealism, such as solipsism. Some of these are very simple indeed. If only your own mind exists, that would indeed be very simple! This is not to say that your mind is simple. The point here is that your mind plus an external world is more complex than your mind alone. And the larger point is that the question of which theory is simplest is itself not so simple!

Before moving deeper into the complexities of the philosophical debates   6.9
over mind–brain identity theory, it will be useful to briefly review some of the science relevant to the mind and brain.

A Very Brief Overview of Neuroscience

Neuroscience is the scientific study of the brain and other parts of the   6.10
nervous system of humans and other animals. The brain, especially the

brain of humans, is one of the most complex things in the universe. Accordingly, neuroscience is a complex field of study. Nonetheless, we can briefly say some things about the main features of our scientific understanding of nervous systems.

Major parts and functions of the nervous system

6.11 The nervous systems of animals (humans included) serve as the major means via which information is relayed, processed, and stored within their bodies. Vertebrate animals, including humans, have two main portions to their nervous systems—the central nervous system and the peripheral nervous system. The central nervous system includes the spinal cord and the brain and thus is the portion of the nervous system most directly involved in cognition and consciousness. The peripheral nervous system relays signals to and from the central nervous system. It relays signals from sensory organs and signals to muscular systems. In vertebrates, the brain is located in the skull and close to the major sensory organs, especially those for vision, hearing, taste, smell, and sense of balance.

Major parts and functions of the brain

6.12 Of the major portions of the brain, the portion that most distinguishes humans from other vertebrates is the cerebral cortex (often just called "the cortex"). The cortex is especially complex and large in humans compared to other animals, with the most significant differences having to do with the frontal cortex (the front part of the cortex). The cortex forms the wrinkled outer surface of the brain. It is highly wrinkled in humans compared to other animals because of how much more of it must be crammed into the comparatively small space of the skull. (Think of how very wrinkled clothes can get when a lot of them are crammed into a very small piece of luggage!) Various cognitive functions can be somewhat localized in distinct regions of the cortex. However, localization studies comprise an area of ongoing research and much remains to be discovered about which regions of the cortex perform which cognitive functions and how. Nonetheless, there is widespread agreement about the following rough assignment of functions: The posterior (back) half of the cortex is largely dedicated to sensory processing, with a very large portion of that (the backmost portion) dedicated to vision. The frontal half of the cortex is largely dedicated to motor processing (processing that eventuates in muscular movements) and executive functions such as the planning and control of voluntary behaviors.

Neurons, neural activations, and brain states

Nervous systems are composed primarily of two sorts of cells—neurons, 6.13 which relay electrochemical signals to one another, and glia (also called "glial cells"), which are largely dedicated to supporting the functioning of neurons. Protruding from the body of each neuron is a long *axon* and many, profusely branching, *dendrites*. A *synapse* is the site of connection between a neuron and another cell via which the neuron relays a signal to the target cell. Electrical and chemical signals move both within neurons and between them at the synapses. Short-lasting electrical events, known as "action potentials," "nerve impulses," or "spikes" play a central role in neural signaling. When a neuron emits an action potential, it is said to "fire." There are many kinds of specialized neurons. One kind is the photoreceptor neurons in the eye that transduce light into electrochemical neural signals. Another kind is the somatic neurons that connect directly to skeletal muscles and are crucial for bodily movement.

Lesions, imaging, and electrophysiology

Neuroscientists have developed many techniques for studying the function- 6.14 ing of living brains. One class of techniques involves observing spared and impaired functions associated with damage (lesions) to regions of the brain, including both accidentally caused and deliberately caused lesions. Other techniques involve machines that can create images of brain regions and the activity within them. One such technique, known as functional magnetic resonance imaging (fMRI) detects changes in blood flow associated with changes in neural activity. Yet another class of techniques measures electrical activity in various brain regions, either by recordings from electrodes on the scalp or by small sensors inserted directly into individual neurons.

Localism and holism

One general line of questioning in neuroscience concerns the degree to 6.15 which a cognitive function is performed by a specific part of the brain that is specialized for just that one function. The view known as *localism* is the view that cognitive functions are localizable in brain regions dedicated to performing those functions. So, for example, there would be a specific brain region for language, a different region for memory, and still a different one for vision. The view known as *holism* opposes localism. In its most extreme form, holism is the view that the entire brain subserves each cognitive function and that any particular part of the brain plays a role in every cognitive function. For any particular function, such as the visual perception of color, controversy surrounds the question of how localized (versus distributed) a function is in the brain. An early and extreme version of holism held that damage to a part of the brain may result in an overall degradation in cognitive functioning, but would not completely wipe out just a single function. More recent lines of evidence point away from this extreme holism. For instance, damage to a specific part of the brain can destroy a person's ability to consciously perceive the shapes of objects while leaving intact other aspects of vision as well as nonvisual cognition.

Learning and synaptic plasticity

6.16   Neuroscientists believe that one of the main ways in which the nervous system supports learning and memory is through changes in the synapses, changes that are related to the amount of use of the synapse. Synapses can change with respect to how "strong" they are, where the idea of synaptic strength here is the idea of how much the firing of one neuron (the "presynaptic" neuron) can influence the firing of another neuron that it is connected to via a synapse (the "postsynaptic" neuron). The stronger the synapse, the higher the degree of influence. The general process of such change in synapses is known as *synaptic plasticity*.

6.17   One highly influential hypothesis concerning learning and synaptic plasticity originates with Donald Hebb. Hebb's postulate can be summarized by the motto "cells that fire together wire together." The idea here is that if two connected neurons fire at the same time, their synaptic connections will be strengthened. After synapses have been strengthened, the firing in the presynaptic neuron is more likely than before to result in the firing of the postsynaptic neuron. Such a mechanism is thought to underlie the kinds of learning by conditioning studied by psychological behaviorists.

Computational neuroscience and connectionism

6.18   Computational neuroscientists create and study computer models of the functioning of single neurons and collections of neurons. Some computational neuroscientists are motivated by the belief that the brain itself is a kind of computer (see chapter 7). One school of thought concerning the creation of such computer models is known as *connectionism*. Connectionists study models, artificial neural networks or ANNs, in which large numbers of simplified neurons are connected to each other by connections with varied and modifiable connection "weights." Such weighted connections can be thought of as emulations of synapses of varying strengths. Learning is implemented in connectionist models via automated procedures that introduce changes in the connection weights.

Connectionist models of various kinds of cognitive tasks have been created. Examples include connectionist models of visual face recognition and reading aloud. One intriguing feature of such connectionist models is that, when they are "lesioned," there is an incremental degradation in performance that is markedly similar to the degradation associated with lesions of real brains. That is, a small amount of damage does not result in a total shutdown of functioning, but is instead associated with a relatively small decrease in functioning. 6.19

Neural correlates of consciousness

One sort of project pursued by neuroscientists interested in consciousness is the quest for the *neural correlate of consciousness* or NCC. The quest for the neural correlate of consciousness involves trying to figure out not just *where* in the nervous system conscious functioning can be localized, but also *what* sorts of neural activity are most closely correlated with conscious processes. Among researchers who believe that there is such a thing as the neural correlate of consciousness, there is a widespread agreement that consciousness can be localized somewhere in the cortex. Beyond that there is much disagreement. One point of disagreement concerns whether, for example, visual consciousness can be localized in the cortical areas in the very back of the brain (and thus be closely associated with the earliest stages of sensory processing in the cortex) or whether instead the location will involve more frontal areas (and thus be closely associated with areas associated with executive functioning or working memory, or both). 6.20

On pain and c-fibers

Often when philosophers discuss identity theory they use as an example the identification of pain and c-fiber firing. Pain is a kind of experience, an experience that is prototypically unpleasant and usually the result of 6.21

bodily damage and disturbance. A c-fiber is a fiber in the peripheral nervous system and the firing of a c-fiber is a state of activation involved in the transmission of pain signals. It should be noted that, given their location in the peripheral nervous system (as opposed to the central nervous system, which includes the brain) it is quite inaccurate for philosophers to call c-fiber firings a kind of *brain* state.

6.22   It should be further noted that associating pains only with c-fibers is quite simplistic and that the contemporary neuroscience of pain portrays a much more complex picture of how pain information is processed in the human nervous system. Nonetheless, there is a tradition in the philosophy of mind of talking in terms of "pain and c-fiber firings," and the present discussion will follow this tradition.

Some General Remarks about Identity

6.23   Before getting deeper into mind–brain identity theory, we are going to pause here to discuss the general notion of "identity." What does it mean to talk, in a general way, of things being *identical*?

6.24   The core notion of identity that is relevant here is the notion of "being one and the same as." Suppose that a family member gave you a book, say a copy of *Moby-Dick*. You unwrap the book at your birthday party. You keep this book with you for very many years, not just because you like the story, but because that very book, the one that you unwrapped as a gift, has become precious to you. Suppose one day you lose the book. If you go to the store and purchase a replacement, is the book that you bought *identical* to the one you lost? It has the same story and perhaps the same number of pages, but it is not *one and the same* book. In the strict senses of "identity" and "identical" that matter for the present chapter, the book you purchased is *not* identical to the book you received as a gift. They are not *one and the same* book but, instead, *two different books.*

6.25   The relation that the second book bears to the first one is not identity but instead mere similarity. One way of distinguishing this strict sense of "identity" from looser senses of the word is in terms of a distinction between *numerical identity* and *qualitative identity*. In the case of the two books, the first book may be qualitatively identical to the second book (meaning that they share qualities—they are similar) but the first book is not numerically identical to the second book (they are not one and the same). When we talk of twins being "identical twins" what we really mean is that the twins are qualitatively identical. They are not numerically identical. If they were, they wouldn't be twins (because there'd only be one of them).

In discussing the mind–brain identity theory, it is also important to keep 6.26 in mind a distinction between *a priori* identities and *a posteriori* identities. But before saying more about identity, let's give a rough indication of what *a priori* versus *a posteriori* amounts to. Putting this *very* roughly, we can say that the distinction concerns kinds of knowledge and that *a priori* knowledge is knowledge one can obtain *prior* to having a sensory experience whereas *a posteriori* knowledge is knowledge one can obtain only by having a sensory experience.

Let's consider an illustration. Consider the question of how many people 6.27 are in the White House right now. Unless you are there and have just recently counted the number of people in the White House (or have been in communication with someone who has), you will not know the answer to this question. Now, consider this question: Is it true of the number of people in the White House that it is either equal to or greater than zero? If you think about it for just a moment, you'll realize that the answer must be "yes." There can't be a *negative* number of people in the White House. In the case of the first question, the knowledge we are seeking is *a posteriori*. You can only know how many people are in the White House if you've counted them or been in communication with someone who has. Either way, you must have a sensory experience that ultimately connects you with the White House and the people in it. In the case of the second question, the knowledge sought is *a priori* knowledge, for we didn't need any particular sensory experience concerning the White House in order to figure out the right answer. As long as we know the meanings of the relevant words, words like "number" and "White House," the rest can be figured out just by reasoning.

Now that we have a rough grasp of the distinction between the *a priori* 6.28 and the *a posteriori*, let us turn to apply the distinction to identity statements, statements of the form "X is identical to Y" and "X is identical to X."

Here is an *a posteriori* identity statement: "The murderer of Jones is the 6.29 owner of the grocery store." This is *a posteriori* because we would have to conduct some sort of investigation, an investigation that ultimately involves our senses, in order to figure out whether it was true.

Here is an *a priori* identity statement: "The murderer of Jones is the 6.30 murderer of Jones." No investigation is needed to know that this is true. It is just *obvious* that it is true. As long as we know the meanings of the relevant words, we can figure out the truth value of the sentence by reason alone, with no additional assistance from the senses. Here is another *a priori* identity statement: "The oldest son of Sandra Mandik is identical to the oldest male offspring of Sandra Mandik." Again, no investigation is needed to figure this one out, just a knowledge of the meaning of the words in the sentence.

6.31   With these ideas in hand, we can now appreciate an important point about the mind–brain identity theory: All of the central identity statements relating mind and brain are *a posteriori* identity statements. Statements such as "pain is identical to c-fibers firing" is not supposed to be *a priori*. It is not supposed to be simply obvious or something you could just figure out as long as you knew the meanings of the relevant words. Instead, it is a statement that requires investigation to figure out whether it is true. More specifically, it is a statement that requires *scientific* investigation to figure out its truth. Mind–brain identity theorists see the relevant mind–brain identity statements as very similar to other sorts of identity statements found in the sciences. Such examples include "water is identical to H_2O," "lightning is identical to atmospheric electrical discharge," and "heat is identical to average molecular kinetic energy."

Arguments against Mind–Brain Identity Theory

6.32   We will examine three arguments against the identity theory. They are (1) the zombie argument, (2) the multiple realizability argument, and (3) Max Black's "distinct property" argument.

The zombie argument

6.33   Just about any argument that can be used as an argument *for* property dualism (chapter 3) can also be used as an argument *against* the mind–brain identity theory. One especially noteworthy example is what is known as the "modal argument," especially the version formulated in terms of zombies. Since we went over this in chapter 3, we will not go into as much detail in the present chapter. But briefly, here is a sketch of the argument adapted to be against identity theory:

Premise 1: If identity theory is true, then, since having a quale would be having a certain pattern of neural activation, it would be impossible to have that neural activation without having any qualia. (Another way of putting the same point is to say that if it is possible to have any given neural state without any qualia, then identity theory is false.)

Premise 2: If something is conceivable, it is possible.

Premise 3: Zombies are conceivable. Further, the sort of zombie that is conceivable and relevant to identity theory is a zombie that is just like you with regard to its brain and neural properties.

Premise 4: Zombies are possible, that is, something could have all the same neural properties as you but lack qualia.

Conclusion: It is possible to have any given neural state without qualia, so identity theory is false.

The multiple realizability argument

The gist of the multiple realizability argument can be stated simply, but the simple statement will require some supporting explanation. First, let's look at the simple statement. 6.34

If identity theory is true, then it must be true at the level of types, that is, each type of mental state is one and the same as a type of physical state. However, it is false that each mental state-type is identical to a single physical state-type, since mental state-types are multiply realizable by physical state-types. 6.35

That simple statement is unlikely to make much sense by itself. To help explain it, there are two ideas we need to grasp. The first is the idea of a *type*. The second is the idea of a *realization*. 6.36

Let's think about the general idea of types by considering the specific idea of types of words. Consider this question: How many words are in the sentence, "The dog bit the cat"? There are two ways of understanding the question. One way is to understand it as asking a question about how many *types* of words appear. The other is to understand it as asking how many word *tokens* appear. Understanding the question as being about *types* leads to this answer: There are four words in the sentence—"the," "dog," "bit," and "cat." Understanding the question as being about *tokens* leads to this answer: There are five words in the sentence—two tokens of "the" and one token each of "dog," "bit," and "cat." 6.37

Let us now turn to apply the type–token distinction to mental states. Suppose that two different people, Jones and Smith, have each stubbed their toe and are both in pain. They are each in a state of pain. Each is in the same *type* of mental state, namely a state of being in pain. So, Smith's 6.38

pain and Jones's pain are two mental state tokens of the same mental state-type.

6.39   The mind–brain identity theory is a thesis about types. The mental state-type pain is supposed to be identical to a physiological state-type. As philosophers of mind like to say, pain is identical to c-fibers firing. That is, pains in general are identical to c-fibers firing. The identity theory as we are here presenting it is *not* saying simply that Jones's pain is identical to Jones's c-fibers firing. That would leave open the possibility that Smith's pain is identical to something else—q-fibers firing maybe.

6.40   Let us turn now to consider the idea of a *realization*, a technical concept in philosophy.

6.41   To illustrate, let's begin by thinking about the relationship between water and the specific chemical elements of which it's made. I'm drinking a glass of water right now, and likely other people all over the world are also drinking water right at the moment that I write this. And here's something that we know about each of those samples of water—each of them is composed of two parts hydrogen and one part oxygen. This is why the chemical formula for water is "H_2O."

6.42   There's only one way of arranging subatomic particles to give rise to water. The arrangement has to involve a 2-to-1 ratio of hydrogen to oxygen. Contrast this feature of water with a feature of the various containers that people drink water from. Cups, mugs, glasses, bottles, etc., are all suitable for drinking water. However, there is no single way of arranging microphysical particles to give rise to a drinking vessel. Some such containers may be made of metal and others may be made of glass. There's no single chemical that is required to make something that can serve as a drinking vessel. Multiple chemically distinct arrangements of particles can give rise to a container suitable for drinking.

6.43   We can summarize these different facts about water and containers in the following way. Containers are *multiply realizable*. Water is not. Containers have multiple physical realizations. Water has only one. There are multiple physical ways in which to realize a container. There is only one physical way in which to realize a sample of water.

6.44   We can relate the idea of multiple realizability to the ideas of types and tokens in the following way: The type *sample of water* is identical to the type *sample of H_2O*. Every token of the type *sample of water* will also be a token of the type *sample of H_2O*. However, things are different when we turn our attention to multiply realizable types. The type *vessel for drinking* is *not* identical to any chemically specifiable type. For instance, the chemically specifiable type *container made from aluminum* is not one and the same as the type *vessel for drinking* since not every token of the type *vessel for drinking* will also be a token of the type *container made from aluminum*.

We are now in a position to understand the multiple realizability argu- 6.45 ment. Consider this question: Are minds and mental states more like water or more like drinking vessels? According to the multiple realizability argument, they are more like drinking vessels. They are multiply realizable. Consider an octopus and a person who are both in pain. These two different creatures have incredibly different nervous systems, so it's unlikely that the physical properties that give rise to pain in the octopus are of the same type as the physical properties that give rise to pain in the human. Despite these physical type differences, the human and the octopus are in the same type of mental state. They are both in pain.

The issues and ideas involved in the multiple realizability argument have 6.46 been hugely influential in the philosophy of mind. They intersect with questions such as "Can machines such as computers think?" Computers are made of very different stuff than are humans. So, the question of whether mentality is multiply realizable is closely connected to the question of artificial intelligence. We will explore these issues and ideas further in chapters 7 and 8.

Max Black's "distinct property" argument

One famous argument against the mind–brain identity theory originates 6.47 with the philosopher Max Black. Here's the gist: According to identity theory, the relevant statements of mind–brain identity are *a posteriori*. However, in order for an identity statement to be *a posteriori*, the two different referring expressions in the statement must be associated with distinct properties of the referent. This fact about *a posteriori* identity statements leads to property dualism, which is inconsistent with identity theory. That's the gist. Let's turn to explain this more carefully now.

Are you familiar with the star known as the morning star? How about 6.48 the evening star? The morning star is a bright heavenly object that rises in the morning. The evening star is a bright heavenly object that rises in the evening. It turns out that neither is actually a star and that each is actually one and the same as the planet Venus, the second planet from the sun in our solar system. Now, consider the *a posteriori* identity statement "The morning star is identical to the evening star."

6.49   How it is possible that this identity statement is *a posteriori*? What keeps it from being *a priori* like the identity statement "The morning is identical to the morning star"? Arguably, the key factor allowing an identity statement to be *a posteriori* is something about how the two different referring terms or referring expressions are each related to their referent. In this example the two different referring expressions are the phrases "the morning star" and "the evening star." These referring expressions both have the same referent. That is, there is just one thing to which they each refer, namely the second planet from the sun, the planet Venus. And here is a proposal about how the two different expressions are differently related to Venus: Venus has two different properties, each of which is associated with just one of the two different referring expressions. The first property is the property of being a bright heavenly object that rises in the morning, and this property is associated with the expression "the morning star." The second property is the property of being a bright heavenly object that rises in the evening, and this property is associated with the expression "the evening star."

6.50   If this line of thinking is correct, then there always have to be two distinct properties associated with every *a posteriori* identity statement. We indicated earlier that when we apply this generalization to the central relevant identity statements of mind–brain identity theory we are led to a kind of dualism, and, of course, dualism is totally incompatible with mind–brain identity theory.

6.51   To see how this line of thought is supposed to lead to dualism, consider the identity statement, "Pain is c-fiber firing." Here the two distinct referring expressions are "pain" and "c-fibers firing." What distinct properties could plausibly be associated with these distinct expressions? In the case of "c-fibers firing," the relevant property is some electrochemical property detectible via scientific methods. And plausibly, the crucial property associated with the term "pain" is the subjective painfulness of pain—a pain quale. But here's the problem: If a pain quale is distinct from neuroscientifically specifiable electrochemical properties, then that's property dualism.

Conclusion

6.52   One of the simplest and most straightforward versions of physicalism holds that minds are brains and that mental states just are brain states. However, despite its straightforward appeal, mind–brain identity theory has encountered forceful challenges from both property dualists, who think that the theory can't adequately account for qualia, and functionalists, who think that the theory is falsified by the multiple realizability of the mental. Property dualists were, of course, the central focus of chapter 3. Functionalists will figure prominently in chapters 7 and 8.

Annotated Bibliography

Bickle, John, Mandik, Pete, and Landreth, Anthony (2006) "The Philosophy of Neuroscience," in Edward Zalta (ed.), *The Stanford Encyclopedia of Philosophy*, full text available at http://plato.stanford.edu/archives/spr2006/entries/neuroscience/, accessed February 6, 2013. An overview of work at the intersection of philosophy and neuroscience, including *neurophilosophy*, the application of neuroscientific findings to address problems in philosophy, especially philosophy of mind.

Braitenberg, Valentino (2007) "Brain," *Scholarpedia*, 2(11), 2918, full text available at http://www.scholarpedia.org/article/Brain, accessed February 6, 2013. Concise overview of the brain by a famous neuroscientist.

Place, Ullin (1956) "Is Consciousness a Brain Process?," *British Journal of Psychology*, 47, 44–50. Considered, along with Smart (1959), to be one of the key initial defenses of the mind–brain identity theory.

Place, Ullin (2002) "Identity Theories," in Marco Nani and Massimo Marraffa (eds.), *A Field Guide to the Philosophy of Mind*, full text available at http://host.uniroma3.it/progetti/kant/field/mbit.htm, accessed February 6, 2013. An overview of versions of mind–brain identity theory by one of its founding defenders.

Smart, J. J. C. (1959) "Sensations and Brain Processes," *Philosophical Review*, 68, 141–156. Considered, along with Place (1956), to be one of the key initial defenses of the mind–brain identity theory.

Smart, J. J. C. (2008) "The Identity Theory of Mind," in Edward Zalta (ed.), *The Stanford Encyclopedia of Philosophy*, full text available at http://plato.stanford.edu/archives/fall2008/entries/mind-identity/, accessed February 6, 2013. An overview of the mind–brain identity theory by one of its founding defenders.

7

THINKING MACHINES

Can a Machine Think?

In many science fiction movies and books, highly advanced robots and 7.1
computers match, and even exceed, the intelligence of the average human
being. Is this only possible in fiction? Or is it instead possible that the real
world will one day contain genuine examples of artificial intelligence
(AI)—machines that, despite being manufactured, have the genuine ability
to think, and perhaps even the ability to feel?

There are two general positions on what the best answer to this question 7.2
is. These two positions are sometimes called "strong AI" and "weak AI."
According to proponents of weak AI, so-called artificially intelligent computers will never be anything more than mere *simulations* of intelligence.
They will no more count as really intelligent than a computer simulation
of a hurricane can really make you wet. Proponents of strong AI are much
more optimistic and hold that a suitably complex computer program will
be really intelligent, not just a mere imitation of intelligence. Just as a
computer really can store a phone number in its memory, so will it be able
(one day) to really understand what phones are and to really think about
who it might like to talk to on the phone.

Before we go further and examine what philosophers of mind have said 7.3
about the questions of artificial intelligence, it will be worth your while to
pause and ask *yourself* some of the relevant questions. Do you think a
computer or robot will ever (at least in theory) be able to . . .

This Is Philosophy of Mind: An Introduction, First Edition. Pete Mandik.
© 2014 John Wiley & Sons, Inc. Published 2014 by John Wiley & Sons, Inc.

1.   . . . *think* about things and *understand* what people mean when they talk and write?
2.   . . . *consciously experience* colors, pains, emotions?
3.   . . . have *free will* and be able to *make decisions* for itself?
4.   . . . *learn* on its own and modify its behaviors based on what it has learned instead of simply doing what it has been programmed to do?

Did you give the same answer to each of these questions, that is, answer them all "yes" or all "no"? Or did you instead answer "yes" to some and "no" to others?

7.4   Another sort of question to think about is this one: Of the various theories that you've learned about in the philosophy of mind—theories such as dualism, behaviorism, and mind–brain identity theory—what sorts of answers do you think that proponents of each of the theories would give to questions 1 through 4 about AI? For example, do you think that a behaviorist would be more likely than a dualist to answer "yes" to one or more of these questions?

7.5   One thing that we'll come to appreciate in this and the next chapter is that there's a special kind of philosophical position most closely associated with strong AI—it is the view known as *functionalism*. Many of the core ideas of AI and functionalism can be traced back to a single significant thinker—Alan Turing.

Alan Turing, Turing Machines, and the Turing Test

7.6 If there were such a thing as a thinking machine, what kind of machine would it be? There is widespread agreement amongst philosophers of mind that such a machine would be a computer—a computing machine. Another way of putting this point is to say that if one wanted to make a machine that had a mind, one should start off with a computer and then figure out an appropriate way to program that computer.

7.7   But now this question arises: *Why* do philosophers think that computers are a good starting point for making thinking machines? Here's a related question: *What* do computers and minds have in common such that computers seem like good candidates for potentially intelligent machines?

7.8   To get a handle on the answers to these questions, it will help to think a little bit about what computers are. And in order to do that, it will help us to think about one of the greatest early researchers on computers—Alan

Turing. We'll discuss his groundbreaking work on how to define computation and his invention of an idea that has come to be known as a Turing machine. Also, we'll discuss his proposal for how to tell if a machine is genuinely intelligent—the Turing test.

Alan Turing

Alan Turing (1912–1954) was a mathematician and one of the first and 7.9 most influential computer scientists. During World War II, he worked as a code breaker for the British. One of his most significant contributions to the fields of mathematics, computer science, and artificial intelligence is his development in the 1930s of a formal notion of computation.

Nowadays, we are used to the idea of computing machines. Computers 7.10 are a pervasive part of our lives. They exist not just as our desktop and laptop computers, but are also built into many of our phones and cars. It is important to keep in mind that back in Turing's day, there were no such machines. In fact, Turing's work on the notion of computation helped pave the way for the electronic computers that we are familiar with. Another thing to keep in mind is that the earliest uses of the word "computer" didn't refer to a kind of machine, but instead referred to a kind a person—a person who computes, that is, a person who figures out the answers to mathematical problems.

Turing developed his formal notion of computation and his related 7.11 special notion of a computing machine (a Turing machine) in order to tackle a theoretical problem in mathematics. This problem can be stated as this question: Is there a method (an effective procedure) for determining, for any particular mathematical proposition, whether that proposition can be proven? In tackling this problem, Turing developed a notion of what an "effective procedure" is that can equally be carried out by a person and by a machine. The basic idea here can be thought of in terms of reading and writing symbols according to certain rules. In developing his idea of how a machine can do this, Turing developed the idea of what has since come to be known as a *Turing machine.*

Turing machines

Turing did not himself build a Turing machine (although, since then, 7.12 actual Turing machines have been built). In Turing's mathematical work his machine was more of a thought experiment than an actual machine.

At the heart of a Turing machine is a *finite-state machine*, a machine that can only be in one of a finite number of states at a time. The transitions from state to state are controlled by a finite look-up table—a finite program that specifies what, for any given state the machine is in, its next state should be. The finite-state machine controls a read/write head that can move back and forth along an infinite tape and read, write, and erase symbols on that tape. Different Turing machines have different look-up tables. A *universal* Turing machine can emulate the behavior of any other Turing machine.

7.13   Using his notion of a computing machine, Turing was able to prove that there is no general method for deciding, for any selected mathematical proposition, whether it is provable. Along the way Turing was able to prove that anything that can be computed can be computed by a universal Turing machine.

7.14   One important aspect of the idea of a Turing machine is the way that it can do something that a person can do. It can follow rules to read and write symbols and thus arrive at the solution to a problem. It is perhaps unsurprising, then, that in his later work Turing thought explicitly about what it might take for a machine to exhibit human-level intelligence. One question that arises in considering the possibility of artificial intelligence is the question of how one would know whether a machine did indeed have human-level intelligence. (Such a question should remind you of the problem of other minds that we discussed in chapter 5.) In response to such a concern, Turing proposed what has now come to be known as the "Turing test."

The Turing test

7.15   Turing's test is designed to bypass irrelevant factors in deciding whether a being is intelligent. Such irrelevant factors include whether the being looks like a human. There is no good reason to think that something would need to look like a human in order to have human-level intelligence. In the Turing test, a human investigator conducts multiple conversations via a text-based interface (such as typing on a keyboard and reading text on a screen) with multiple participants, one of which is a machine and the rest of which are humans. If the investigator cannot determine, based on the ensuing conversation, which participants are humans and which is the machine, then the machine has passed the Turing test.

7.16   This leads to a question around which there is much controversy: If a machine passes the Turing test, does it really follow that the machine is genuinely intelligent? We turn now to examine a famous argument that the answer to this question must be "no."

Searle's Chinese Room Argument

One of the most famous and widely discussed philosophical arguments 7.17 concerning AI is John Searle's Chinese room argument. The point of Searle's argument is that no matter how much a computer's outward behavior might resemble a human's it will never have genuine intelligence or understanding. The point can be put in terms of a program that, perhaps in the far future, allows a computer to hold a conversation in Chinese with a human. We can imagine a suitably programmed computer that allows a human to type questions and responses on a keyboard and read the computer's printed questions and responses on a video screen. Or perhaps we can imagine an interface that is so sophisticated as to allow the human to speak into a microphone and listen to the computer's audio outputs via speakers or headphones. Either way, the program that the computer is running can be thought of as a set of instructions that, when followed by the computer, give the computer the outward appearance of understanding Chinese. And the way these instructions work is to allow the computer to match the right outputs to various inputs.

Thinking of a computer program as a set of instructions is important 7.18 for understanding a crucial step in Searle's argument. According to the way many people think about computers, it doesn't matter how the instructions are followed to match inputs and outputs. What matters is *that* the instructions are followed. This point is pretty much the idea behind *multiple realizability* discussed in the previous chapter. Searle exploits this point about the multiple realizability of computers to conduct the central thought experiment in his argument, the thought experiment of the Chinese room.

In Searle's thought experiment, he imagines the computer being replaced 7.19 with a large room in which Searle himself sits and follows a set of instructions that implement the Chinese-understanding computer program. Central to the thought experiment is the following supposition of Searle's: Searle, who himself understands no Chinese, can follow a program written in English that will allow for the *simulation* of a being that understands Chinese.

In Searle's Chinese room thought experiment, the computer is replaced 7.20 by Searle's room, and the input and output interfaces (keyboard and monitor) of the computer are replaced by slots in the wall of the room—one slot for incoming cards and one slot for outgoing cards. Printed on the cards are Chinese symbols that Searle does not understand. The instructions that Searle follows are printed in the form of several large books that contain various pictures of Chinese symbols and instructions, written in English, explaining what cards to send out of the room in response to cards sent into the room. A human on the outside of the room will form the impression that they are having a conversation with a being who understands Chinese. The room will thus pass a Turing test for Chinese comprehension. However, according to Searle, Searle can run the so-called Chinese-understanding program without himself actually understanding Chinese. So the room with Searle in it passes the Turing test without actually being intelligent. Or so says John Searle.

7.21   How exactly is Searle's argument supposed to work as an argument against strong AI? We can sum up the argument against strong AI like this:

Premise 1: If strong AI is true, then any system or entity that runs the so-called Chinese-understanding program thereby understands Chinese.
Premise 2: Searle can run the so-called Chinese-understanding program without understanding Chinese.
Premise 3: There is at least one system or entity that runs the Chinese-understanding program without thereby understanding Chinese (this follows from Premise 2).
Conclusion: Strong AI is false (this follows from Premises 1 and 3).

Responses to the Chinese Room Argument

7.22 Proponents of strong AI have not simply given up in the face of Searle's argument. Instead, many have produced counterarguments—arguments that Searle has made one or more errors in the formulation of his own argument. One response to Searle is to deny premise 2, the premise that says that Searle can run the so-called Chinese-understanding program without understanding Chinese.

7.23   One highly discussed reason for denying premise 2 is something that has come to be known as "the systems reply." According to the systems reply, the reason premise 2 is false is that Searle is not actually running the program all by himself. He is a mere part of a larger system, a system that also includes the cards and the rulebook and perhaps the whole rest of the Chinese room. It is this larger system that is running the program. It is irrelevant that Searle doesn't understand Chinese. The whole system of which he is part does understand Chinese.

Searle had anticipated the systems reply and has his own counter-reply. 7.24 Searle claims that he can internalize the whole system. He can, at least in theory, memorize all of the rules and, when presented with a sequence of Chinese symbols, consult the rules and produce an appropriate response. Further, he can do all this without understanding Chinese.

Another kind of reply to Searle's Chinese room argument grants that 7.25 there's something right about it, but only insofar as it targets a certain kind of approach to artificial intelligence, namely, a *disembodied* approach that tries to build a mind without putting it in a body that can interact with its environment. This "robot reply" claims that if the Chinese room were made to function as a "brain" in the body of a (giant) robot, then the running of the program *would* give rise to genuine understanding. Part of the thought behind the robot reply is the idea that in the disembodied version of the Chinese room, the symbols that are manipulated don't have any genuine meaning. Lacking genuine meaning, they do not give rise to genuine understanding. There needs to be a process of "symbol grounding" whereby, for example, one symbol can come to genuinely represent water, another can come to represent trees, and so on. The idea behind the robot reply is that symbols can only count as genuine mental representations if they are interacting in ways that connect them to the behaviors of a body and, through that, to items in the body's environment. This idea of symbol grounding is something we will explore further in chapter 13, which covers intentionality and mental representation. We turn now to another line of thought in favor of strong AI.

The Silicon Chip Replacement Thought Experiment

One line of thought in favor of the possibility of thinking machines is based 7.26 on a thought experiment that we'll call "the silicon chip replacement" thought experiment. The gist of the thought experiment involves imagining gradually having each of the neurons in your brain replaced by a silicon microchip that performs the same functions as the neuron it replaces, namely, receiving signals from and sending signals to its neighboring units.

Before conducting the thought experiment concerning replacing parts 7.27 of the brain, let us do a preliminary thought experiment concerning replacing other parts of the body. Imagine that you live in a future where there is a common disease that gradually destroys parts of the body. While this is an unfortunate fact about this imagined future, there is some good news. The technology exists to enable any human body part to be replaced with a mechanical analog that fully reproduces the information-relaying and information-processing functioning of the body part that it replaces. So, for example, human eyeballs can be replaced with digital cameras that have the same color sensitivity and resolution as human eyes. Human ears can be replaced with microphones that pick up exactly the same sounds that ears can. Human hands can be replaced with robotic hands that have pressure sensors and temperature sensors distributed across their surface. These robotic hands are able to make the same movements and pick up the same information about temperatures and textures as hands made of flesh.

7.28   When the eyes, ears, and hands are replaced by robotic components, wires in the components are connected to nerves in the body, allowing the same sorts of signals that were exchanged between the brain and the old organs to be exchanged between the brain and the new parts. For example, messages that would previously be sent to the brain by the eyes can now be sent to the brain by the cameras. And here is a crucial component of the thought experiment: As long as all the same information-related functions are in the camera as are in the eye, there would be no difference in the way things look through eyes and the way things look through the camera. Similar remarks apply to every part that gets replaced. So, for instance, things smell the same through a cybernetic nose and the original flesh version that it replaces.

7.29   Imagine, then, that at some future date, you catch this disease, and, as each body part fails, futuristic doctors replace it with a cybernetic replica. Part by part, flesh body parts that are made of fats and proteins get replaced by mechanical devices made of silicon, metals, and plastics.

7.30   Imagine that your central nervous system is the last place that the disease takes hold. Before any of your brain's neurons get replaced with microchips, all of your sensory organs (eyes, ears, etc.) and muscular systems (arms, legs, etc.) have been replaced. As stated already, you would be able to move through and perceive the world in all the same ways as before. You'd smell all the same odors, see all the same colors, etc.

7.31   Now we come to the crucial part of the thought experiment. Suppose that one of your neurons is replaced by a microchip that receives and sends signals in exactly the same way as the neuron it replaces. It is highly plausible to suppose that such a replacement would not result in any noticeable change in your mental life. You would still have all the same sorts of thoughts and experiences as before. Of course, this plausibility may be due to the fact that only one of your trillions of neurons has been replaced. But perhaps it doesn't matter how many of your neurons get replaced by microchips. Perhaps as long as the chips receive and send signals in the same pattern as the neurons, then no noticeable change in your mental life will occur.

Suppose the scientists and doctors replace the neurons in your nervous   7.32 system one by one until all of your neurons have been replaced. There are two competing hypotheses about how your mental life appears to you during this series of replacements.

Hypothesis 1: At some point—perhaps the first point at which more neurons have been replaced than remain—there is a change in your mental life. Perhaps the change is radical—your mentality disappears altogether. Perhaps the change is less radical than that—perhaps you undergo a qualia inversion.

Hypothesis 2: At no point does your mental life change. Even after all of your neurons have been replaced, you still have the same sorts of thoughts and experiences as you did before any of your neurons were replaced.

Which of these two hypotheses is more plausible? Will there be a mental difference between neural-you and microchip-you? Will you change mentally as you undergo the physical change from having a neural brain to having a microchip brain? In considering these questions, keep in mind some things that clearly *won't* change as you undergo the physical change from having no microchips in your nervous system to having only microchips in your nervous system. First, there will be no change in your behaviors. Since the chips will process and relay information in all the same ways as the neurons they replace, the chip version of you will, for example, respond to stimuli in all the same ways as the neural version of you. If we hold up a blue coffee mug under standard lighting conditions and ask, "What color is this?" chip-you and neural-you will give the same answers. Second, neural-you and chip-you will have all of the same memories. Since having a memory is storing a certain piece of information, and you will retain all your information-related capabilities even after all your neurons are replaced, you will retain all of your memories. Further, you will create new memories in all the same ways. That is, even after total neural replacement, you will have all the same capacities for *learning*.

A third similarity follows from the second one. Your capacity to *notice*   7.33 *changes* will be the same. To see this point, consider the way that noticing change is related to memory. If a light changes from green to red, in order to notice that the now red light has changed, you need to remember that it used to be something other than red. Further, you need to have some information-bearing state concerning the way the light is now that you can compare to the memory. If the information-bearing state about the present and the memory state say the same things (like, they both say that the light is red) then you will notice no change in the light.

7.34   Suppose, then, that hypothesis 1 is true. Suppose that you do undergo a change in your mental life—perhaps a qualia inversion—at some point during the series of neural replacements. Here's a problem with that supposition: You wouldn't notice any such change. As we've already seen, there will be no change in the overall pattern of information processing and storage. So, whatever changes are introduced, none of them are changes that you could notice. Your memories will all be the same as before, including your memories of what qualia you had. Further, you will gain no information about any new qualia, because you won't gain any information that you wouldn't have gained with just a neural brain. If you think a change in your qualia cannot be something that is in principle unnoticeable by you, then you are going to find hypothesis 2 superior to hypothesis 1.

7.35   What does this thought experiment show? It shows that, in principle if not in practice, there is at least one way to build a machine that thinks and feels in just the way that a human does. All you need to do is to make a machine out of microchips that exactly reproduces the information-processing features of the neurons in an actual human brain.

7.36   Another argument that moves from certain features of human brains to the conclusion that there can be thinking machines is attributable to Alan Turing himself. He argues that if a human brain can only be in a finite number of states, then there is a Turing machine that is equivalent to a human brain. However, is it true that the brain can only be in a finite number of states? Plausibly, the answer is "yes." This is because brains are made out of a finite number of particles that can interact in only a finite number of ways.

Symbolicism versus Connectionism

7.37 If there were such a thing as a thinking machine, indeed, if we ourselves are thinking machines, then the question naturally arises of how such machines would work. What general principles would an engineer need to follow to build a thinking machine? Perhaps any such machine will have to closely mimic the human brain. One approach to AI that seeks to mimic the brain is known as *connectionism*. We discussed connectionism briefly in chapter 6. An older approach is known as *good old fashioned artificial intelligence*, or GOFAI for short. This approach to understanding minds, especially thought of as an approach that applies equally to natural and artificial intelligence, is sometimes referred to as *symbolicism*.

Symbolicism attempts to understand minds by thinking of them as 7.38 computers in very much the same sense that Turing thought of computers— as mechanical systems that manipulate symbols in accordance with a set of rules. On this view, cognition is rule-governed symbol manipulation. Closely related to symbolicism is the language of thought hypothesis (aka LOT) developed by the philosopher of mind, Jerry Fodor.

According to the language of thought hypothesis, thinking is a process 7.39 whereby a finite number of mental symbols are combined in rule-governed ways to form thoughts. So, for instance, if you think the thought *Dogs bark*, this thought is a combination of two mental symbols or mental representations (or concepts)—one that represents dogs and one that represents barking. We can denote these symbols here by using all capital letters. To illustrate, suppose that someone has the following four mental representations in their language of thought: CATS, DOGS, BARK, and MEOW. They are now in a position, by combining those representations, to think the following thoughts: CATS MEOW, DOGS BARK, CATS BARK, and DOGS MEOW.

Just as the combination of words in a spoken language is governed by 7.40 certain rules (the rules of English grammar) so is the combination of mental representations in the language of thought governed by certain rules. Such rules might, for example, rule out combinations such as CATS DOGS and BARK DOGS MEOW CATS CATS. However, such rules would not rule out CATS BARK and DOGS MEOW. While it might be false to say that cats bark and dogs meow, the error here is getting the world wrong (for the world lacks barking cats and meowing dogs); it does not violate the rules of English grammar. Similarly, thinking the corresponding thoughts would not violate the "grammar" of the language of thought.

What reasons are there for believing in the language of thought hypoth- 7.41 esis? Jerry Fodor emphasizes certain features of human cognition that can be explained by hypothesizing the existence of a language of thought. Fodor calls these features "productivity" and "systematicity."

Productivity is the feature of human cognition whereby we are able to 7.42 think an indefinitely large number of thoughts. Given that we are finite beings, how is it that we are able to grasp a potentially infinite number of thoughts? Consider, for a moment, a sentence that you are unlikely to have ever been exposed to before, a sentence such as the "There are three tablespoons of peanut butter on a golden doorknob." How is it that you are able to understand this sentence? How are you able to grasp the thought that such a sentence expresses?

7.43   The explanation given by the language of thought hypothesis is this: Even though you have never been exposed to this sentence before, you do have a prior grasp of the parts of which it is composed (the words "tablespoons," "doorknob," etc.) as well as a grasp of the rules according to which such parts may be combined. By analogy, the way you are able to think thoughts that you have never thought before is by constructing them out of a finite store of mental representations (the concepts TABLESPOONS, DOORKNOB, etc.) according to rules governing their combination (rules that you grasp implicitly). According to Fodor, you are able to think an indefinitely large number of thoughts by combining a finite set of representations to form an indefinitely large number of combinations.

7.44   *Systematicity* is the feature of human cognition whereby thoughts bear certain systematic relations to one another. No human thinker capable of thinking the thought MARY KISSED JOHN is *incapable* of thinking JOHN KISSED MARY. Why is this so? Why don't we ever encounter a human who can think the one thought and not the other? The explanation offered by the language of thought hypothesis is that both thoughts are composed of the same mental representations combined in accordance with the same rules. Thus, once you have the raw materials and abilities to construct the first thought, you automatically have the raw materials and abilities required for the second thought.

7.45   One sort of controversy that surrounds the language of thought hypothesis concerns the question of whether it is consistent with certain assumptions about the way the brain functions. One such assumption, closely associated with connectionism, is that the representations utilized by the brain are widely distributed in their physical implementation. Often, representations in a connectionist network cannot be localized in any one part of it. Instead, each representation is holistically spread across the whole network. For example, a connectionist network trained to visually distinguish male faces from female faces doesn't have just one neuron that encodes the information about what a male face is, another for female faces, and so on. The knowledge of what distinguishes male faces from female faces is distributed across the network. Each piece of knowledge is encoded as a *distributed representation*.

In contrast to such a view of representations is the view that mental 7.46 representations have *discrete* physical implementations. The language of thought hypothesis seems committed to a thesis of discrete physical implementation. One metaphor for thinking of physically discrete representations is a set of refrigerator magnets, each of which has an English word printed on it and can be combined to create sentences. In the refrigerator magnet metaphor, what it means for the separate representations CATS and DOGS to be physically discrete is that each representation is a distinct magnet.

What does it mean to take the discreteness hypothesis literally as a 7.47 hypothesis about the physical implementation of mental representations in the brain? If it means that there are spatially distinct portions of the brain for distinct representations, then that is a hypothesis for which we have little direct evidence. There's little reason to suppose that for every concept that we grasp, we have a discrete chunk of brain tissue—a CATS brain chunk, a DOGS brain chunk, and so on. Further, even if there were such brain chunks, their combination into sentence-sized thoughts (like the thought that *Cats meow and dogs bark*) is not likely to closely resemble the way the refrigerator magnets are combined. Chunks of brain tissue are not moved around inside of your head.

Many adherents of connectionism view LOT as a highly improbable 7.48 hypothesis of how the brain works. Many adherents of LOT regard connectionism as not really offering a genuine alternative. They see connectionism as instead supplying a mere description at the level of implementation, a description that is consistent with LOT. One kind of consideration along these lines appeals to notions of computation and computing machines as developed by Turing. Anything that can be computed can be computed by a Turing machine, so any genuinely computational process can be described at some level as doing what a Turing machine does, which is to manipulate symbols in a rule-governed manner. Connectionist networks are one of many multiple realizations of such a functional characterization of cognition.

Conclusion

Skeptics about artificial intelligence doubt that computers and robots will 7.49 be able to do anything beyond merely giving the outward appearance of having thoughts and experiences. On the inside, they are mere machines and have no mentality whatsoever, artificial or natural. However, if such entities become sufficiently sophisticated to insist that they do indeed have minds, we may have no other choice but to take their word for it! We may be forced, then, to embrace the idea that the mind is a multiply realizable functional system that *cannot* be defined in terms of implementation-level facts about the brain. Such an idea is central to *functionalism*, the topic of the next chapter.

Annotated Bibliography

Anderson, David (2012) *The Mind Project*, full text available at http://www.mind.ilstu.edu/, accessed February 7, 2013. Lots of terrific stuff here pertinent to thinking machines and other areas of cognitive science and the philosophy of mind.

Bourget, David and Chalmers, David (2009) "Can Machines Think?," *PhilPapers*, full text available at http://philpapers.org/browse/can-machines-think, accessed February 7, 2013. A frequently updated online bibliography on the question of thinking machines, including in many cases abstracts and links to the full text of articles.

Fodor, Jerry (1975) *The Language of Thought* (Cambridge, MA: Harvard University Press). Classic defense by the most famous defender of the language of thought hypothesis. Additionally, the text contains an influential attack on mind-brain identity theory.

Fodor, Jerry and Pylyshyn, Zenon (1988) "Connectionism and Cognitive Architecture," *Cognition*, *28*, 3–71. A classic source for skepticism about the merits of connectionism. The authors argue that connectionism at best merely supplies an account of implementation details of cognitive systems that must nonetheless utilize a language of thought.

Garson, James (2008) "Connectionism," in Edward Zalta (ed.), *The Stanford Encyclopedia of Philosophy*, full text available at http://plato.stanford.edu/archives/win2008/entries/connectionism, accessed February 7, 2013. An overview of key issues, including the debate between connectionists as symbolicists.

Hofstadter, Douglas and Dennett, Daniel (eds.) (1981) *The Mind's I: Fantasies and Reflections on Self and Soul* (New York: Basic Books). A terrific collection of philosophical essays and science fiction stories on the nature of minds and thinking machines, not least of which is Arnold Zuboff's "The Story of a Brain" containing the silicon chip replacement thought experiment. This is the book that got me into the philosophy of mind way back when I was still in high school. I still love it.

Gauker, Chris (2002) "Language and Thought," in Marco Nani and Massimo Marraffa (eds.), *A Field Guide to the Philosophy of Mind*, full text available at http://host.uniroma3.it/progetti/kant/field/lat.htm, accessed February 7, 2013. Excellent overview of philosophical issues concerning the relations between language and thinking.

Searle, John (1980) "Minds, Brains, and Programs," *Behavioral and Brain Sciences*, 3, 417–457. A classic source of skepticism about AI, containing Searle's famous Chinese room argument.

Turing, Alan (1950) "Computing Machinery and Intelligence," *Mind*, 59(236), 433–460, full text available at http://mind.oxfordjournals.org/content/LIX/236/433, accessed February 7, 2013. Turing's classic discussion of the possibility of genuinely intelligent computers and his proposed test for machine intelligence (his "imitation game") that has since come to be known as the Turing test.

8

FUNCTIONALISM

The Gist of Functionalism

Functionalism has a positive part and a negative part. The positive part 8.1
concerns what mental states are defined in terms of. According to functionalism, a mental state is defined by certain causal relations it bears to input
states (sensory states), output states (verbal and nonverbal behaviors), and
other mental states.

The negative part of functionalism concerns what mental states are *not* 8.2
defined in terms of. The negative part is the *multiple realizability* thesis,
discussed previously in chapters 6 and 7—mental states are not defined in
terms of the material substances of which they are composed (in contrast
to the way that water is defined by its chemical composition). This negative
part serves to contrast functionalism and mind–brain identity theory. The
mind–brain identity theorist holds that, for example, pain is identical to
c-fiber firing. The functionalist instead holds that c-fiber firing is only one
of multiple ways that pain can be physically realized. (Further, some functionalists hold that it is possible for mental states to have nonphysical
realizations, and thus functionalism is consistent with nonphysicalist positions such as dualism. However, we will mostly focus on versions of functionalism that are physicalistic.)

There's another negative thesis that's important to functionalism, and 8.3
this one highlights a contrast between functionalism and behaviorism. The
negative point here is that the functionalist says, against the behaviorist,

---

This Is Philosophy of Mind: An Introduction, First Edition. Pete Mandik.
© 2014 John Wiley & Sons, Inc. Published 2014 by John Wiley & Sons, Inc.

that mental states cannot be defined solely by reference to behavior. Reference to behavior is only *part* of the defining features of mental states— reference must be made as well to sensory and other mental states.

8.4   Two key ideas that functionalists have appealed to in developing their position are the ideas of a *functional kind* and of a *multiply realizable kind*. A kind is a grouping of things or entities, usually grouped in terms of one or more features common to members of the group. Examples of kinds include cats, diamonds, planets, and mousetraps. To illustrate the idea of a multiply realizable kind, let us draw a contrast between diamonds, which are not multiply realizable, and mousetraps, which are. What makes something a diamond? First off, a diamond has to be made out of carbon. Anything superficially resembling a diamond that is not made out of carbon is not a genuine diamond. Crystals of zirconium dioxide superficially resemble diamonds, but are composed of the chemical elements zirconium and oxygen. Further, the carbon atoms that compose diamonds need to be arranged in a certain way (tetrahedral lattices). Carbon atoms not so arranged make up coal and graphite, not diamonds.

8.5   Diamonds may be physically realized in only one way—with tetrahedral lattices of carbon atoms. Thus they are *not* multiply realizable. Contrast this with mousetraps, which are multiply realizable. There are many ways to make a mousetrap. Some involve metal spring-loaded killing bars mounted on wooden platforms. Others involve a strong sticky glue applied to a flat surface on which the mouse gets stuck. There is no particular chemical element that is necessary for making a mousetrap.

8.6   Mousetraps help to illustrate not just the idea of multiply realizable kinds, but also the idea of functional kinds. Functional kinds are defined by what they *do*, and are so named because they are defined by the function they perform. Mousetraps perform the function of restraining or killing mice. Functional definition and multiple realizability often go hand-in-hand. As long as a system is able to achieve its defining function, it is largely irrelevant which physical stuff it happens to be realized by.

8.7   Much of the contemporary enthusiasm for functionalism stems from enthusiasm about analogies drawn between minds and computers, analogies that we discussed in chapter 7. Computers are clearly both functional kinds and multiply realizable kinds. What makes something a computer is what it does—it computes, that is, it reads and writes symbols in a rule-governed way. All sorts of materials can be deployed to construct computers. Computers have been built from transistors and other electronic components. Others have been built from mechanical components such as cams and gears. A computer that plays tic-tac-toe has even been constructed out of Tinkertoys!

One upshot of the analogy between minds and computers is that it 8.8
allows us to think of the relation of the mind to the brain in terms of the relation, in a computer, between software and hardware. One and the same piece of software, such as a video game or a word processor, can be run on physically distinct computers. Therefore, a program is not identical to the activity of a *particular* computer. If brains made out of brainy stuff can just as well give rise to a mind as an electronic computer made out of nonbrainy stuff, then perhaps the solution to the mind–body problem is to think of the mind as the software that is running on the hardware of the brain.

A Brief History of Functionalism

While functionalism has ancient roots and can be traced to the works of 8.9
Aristotle, the central defining works of functionalism emerged in the latter half of the 20th century. Functionalists draw much of their inspiration from advances in artificial intelligence and computer science more generally. But the core point of functionalism—that mental states are definable in terms of what they do—is not a point that needed the advent of electronic computers for someone to make it.

An important idea in the philosophy of Aristotle (384–322 BC) is the idea 8.10
of the *form* of a thing: that which contributes to the performance of the thing's defining function or purpose. The form of a sword enables it to cut, and the form of an eye enables it to see. One crucial aspect of Aristotle's thinking about forms is that they are not a thing separate from the thing that has them. The form of a sword is not one thing and the substance of the sword a second thing. These are two aspects united in a single thing—the sword itself. Aristotle resisted the view of Plato (427–347 BC) that the soul is an immaterial thing distinct from the body (a kind of substance dualism, as we discussed in chapter 2). Instead, according to Aristotle, the human soul is not separable and distinct from the body—it's the form of the body. Keep in mind that form encompasses more than mere shape, but also the functioning of the body and its parts. As Aristotle puts the point, "If the eye were an animal, then sight would be its soul."

Another key historical antecedent to the functionalism of the 20th and 8.11
21st centuries derives from the philosopher Thomas Hobbes (1588–1679). Anticipating the *multiple realizability* central to functionalism, Hobbes has

a mechanistic view of living systems including humans. In the introduction to his *Leviathan* he writes "why may we not say that all automata (engines that move themselves by springs and wheels . . .) have an artificial life? For what is the heart but a spring; and the nerves but so many strings, and the joints but so many wheels . . .?" Further, Hobbes holds one of the earliest versions of the *computational view of cognition* central to so many versions of functionalism as well as schools of thought in artificial intelligence and cognitive science. Hobbes writes in *Leviathan* (chapter 5) that reasoning is "nothing but reckoning, that is adding and subtracting, of the consequences of general names agreed upon for the marking and signifying of our thoughts."

8.12   More recent historical antecedents to 20th-century functionalism involve philosophical and scientific developments that we detailed in the previous three chapters. These developments involved the advent of and subsequent dissatisfaction with behaviorism (chapter 5) and the mind–brain identity theory (chapter 6) as well as the promising early successes in linking the notions of cognition and computation in the field of artificial intelligence (chapter 7). Functionalism inherits from behaviorism an emphasis on the important relations between mental states and behavior. Functionalism inherits from mind–brain identity theory an emphasis on mental states as being distinct from behaviors. Functionalists and identity theorists agree that mental states are inner states that are the causes of behavior. Functionalism inherits from artificial intelligence the view that mental states can equally be had by creatures with brains and entities controlled by nonbrainy machines (especially machines that compute).

Arguments for Functionalism

8.13   The main arguments for functionalism are also arguments against its main physicalistic competitors—behaviorism and mind–brain identity theory. We will examine two arguments for functionalism. The first, the causal argument, grows out of concerns raised against behaviorism. The second, the multiple realization argument, grows out of concerns raised against the mind–brain identity theory.

The causal argument

8.14   Recall a line of thought that we discussed as a critique of behaviorism in chapter 5. Since our very idea of mental states is that they can serve to causally explain certain kinds of behavior, the behaviorist mistakenly renders such causal explanations circular when he or she defines mental states as being either patterns of behavior or dispositions to behave. Part of the very idea of a mental state is that it can play certain kinds of causal roles. From here it is a short step to a certain kind of functionalism— *analytical functionalism*. According to this form of functionalism, mental states are, by definition, states that play certain causal roles and, further, different mental states can be defined in terms of the different causal roles that they play.

We can relate this to a line of thought pressed against both substance   8.15 dualism and property dualism. Recall the complaint that certain forms of dualism lead to epiphenomenalism and thus violate the commonsense idea that mental states have causal effects. Again we encounter the proposal that mental states have certain causal effects *by definition*. This proposal fits closely with analytical functionalism, according to which the definitions of commonsense concepts of mental states can be given in terms of the causal roles that they play.

So, what are the causal roles that are definitive of mental states? Such   8.16 causal roles will involve characteristic causal relations between, on the one hand, the mental state in question, and, on the other hand, sensory or input states, behaviors or output states, and other mental states. To illustrate, let us consider a rough sketch of how a functionalist might try to define a state of fear in terms of causal relations to inputs, outputs, and other states.

First, consider fear and its relations to inputs. What sorts of sensory   8.17 inputs can trigger a fear reaction? Often such inputs will be perceptions of potentially harmful things or situations. Examples include perceiving that a highly poisonous snake is nearby or that that one is standing too near to the edge of a cliff.

Second, consider fear and its relations to outputs. The are many behav-   8.18 iors that we recognize as expressive of fear. Those behaviors can figure in a functionalist definition of a fear state. These will include avoidance behaviors, such as avoiding spiders and snakes. They will also include verbal behaviors, such as saying "get those spiders and snakes away from me." Besides behaviors, the functionalist might also appeal to certain outwardly observable effects of fears that are better thought of as reflexes or physiological responses than outright behaviors. Such effects might include increasing heart rate, turning pale, and sweating.

Third, consider fear and its relations to other mental states. There are   8.19 certain mental states that are characteristic causes of fear states. And there are other mental states that are characteristic effects of fear states. One characteristic mental cause of a fear state is a belief that something harmful is happening or about to happen. For example, the belief that the noisy machine nearby could explode at any moment might cause you to go into a state of fear. One characteristic mental effect of fear is the formation of a plan or intention to do something to alleviate the fear. One such example is an intention to get away from the nearby poisonous snake at the first available opportunity.

8.20   Putting these three kinds of causal relations together would yield a definition of what it means to be in a fear state. The definition refers to characteristic inputs that lead to fear, characteristic outputs that fear brings about, and mental causes of and effects of fear.

The multiple realization argument

8.21 There are two general strategies that rely on the notion of multiple realizations in defending functionalism. The first appeals to alleged *actual* multiple realizations of mental states. The second appeals to the *mere possibility* of multiple realizations of mental states.

8.22   Perhaps one of the earliest and most famous multiple realizability-based arguments is a line of thought presented by Hilary Putnam, a line of thought designed to both promote functionalism and defeat mind–brain identity theory. According to Putnam, if mind–brain identity theory is true, a mental state of being in pain must be identical to a certain physical-chemical state and further . . .

> the physical-chemical state in question must be a possible state of a mammalian brain, a reptilian brain, a mollusc's brain (octopuses are mollusca, and certainly feel pain), etc. At the same time, it must not be a possible (physically possible) state of the brain of any physically possible creature that cannot feel pain. Even if such a state can be found, it must be . . . certain that it will also be a state of the brain of any extraterrestrial life that may be found that will be capable of feeling pain before we can even entertain the supposition that it may be pain. (Putnam, 1967, p. 436)

8.23   Contained in this quotation from Putnam we can find two suggestions, both of which count against identity theory and in favor of functionalism. The first suggestion hinges on what is actually the case. The second hinges on what might be the case. We can call the first suggestion "the argument from actual multiple realizations" and the second suggestion "the argument from possible multiple realizations."

Actual multiple realizations: Octopuses   The argument from actual multi- 8.24
ple realizations presumes that there actually are creatures who have some of the same mental states as humans—pain, for instance—and further, that such creatures differ physically from humans with respect to which physical properties give rise to those mental properties. We can put the point, as Putnam does, in terms of molluscs. Molluscs feel pain, but the portions of their nervous systems responsible for their pains differ chemically and physically from the portions of our nervous systems responsible for our pains.

One problem with this argument is that it presumes facts about crea- 8.25
tures, both mental facts and physical facts, that may not actually be facts. The argument presumes that molluscs have pain, and further that their pains are similar to our own. The argument also presumes that molluscs have nervous systems that are relevantly chemically–physically distinct from our own. Both presumptions may be questioned. First, we can question whether molluscs actually feel pain. This is, of course, to press a version of the other minds problem that we discussed in chapter 5. Molluscs may writhe or withdraw when presented with a stimulus that damages their tissues, but conceivably such behaviors occur in the absence of pain, perhaps in the absence of any mental state whatsoever. Another possibility is that molluscs do feel a form of pain, but it is quite different from the pains that we would feel when subjected to similar stimuli. Perhaps a stimulus that would cause a sharp searing pain in us would cause a dull throbbing pain in a mollusc and vice versa.

Even if it were true that molluscs feel the same sorts of pains as humans 8.26
do, another problem remains. It is an unsettled question whether mollusc nervous systems diverge from human nervous systems in a way that is relevant to the question of the multiple realizability of pain. Of course, there are *some* differences between mollusc nervous systems and human nervous systems. Mollusc nervous systems have fewer neurons than human nervous systems. Further, molluscs have more limbs than humans and thus differences in their nervous systems for the control of those extra limbs. But there are nonetheless similarities between their nervous systems and ours. Both are made of neurons. The basic functioning of our neurons and their neurons, and the chemicals responsible for that functioning, are highly similar. It remains an open question, then, whether the aspects of

neural functioning responsible for mollusc pain are the same as or different from the aspects of neural functioning responsible for human pain.

8.27   It is plain, then, that the actual multiple realizations argument is beholden to empirical evidence and that the empirical evidence is not all in yet. As is common amongst philosophers, many defenders of functionalism have been uncomfortable making their position beholden to actual empirical evidence. They prefer to see philosophical theories as distinct in this way from scientific theories. They thus formulate arguments that hinge not so much on what actually is the case but instead on what is possibly or conceivably the case. The next argument is one such argument.

8.28   *Possible multiple realizations: Artificial intelligence*   At the heart of the possible multiple realizations argument for functionalism is the idea that it is *possible* that mental states have multiple realizations. One such possibility is the possibility of strong artificial intelligence (as discussed in chapter 7). Another such possibility is that intelligent extraterrestrial life. Perhaps space aliens have human-level intelligence while having physical forms radically different from humans.

8.29   To get a feel for how these sorts of possibilities can be used to argue *for* functionalism, it will be useful to first take a look at how these sorts of possibilities can be used to argue *against* mind–brain identity theory. And, before proceeding, we need to answer the following question: Why would the *mere possibility* of something be of any consequence for a philosophical theory? The gist of the answer to this question is that the mere possibility of something can serve to defeat a claim that it is impossible. Suppose that mind–brain identity theory is committed to the claim that it is *necessary* that kinds of mental state are one and the same as kinds of physical state. On such a reading of mind–brain identity theory, it is necessary that mental states do not have multiple physical realizations. Another way of putting this point is to say that on such a reading of mind–brain identity theory, it is *impossible* for mental states to be physically realized in more than one way. Stating mind–brain identity theory in this way makes it look like a very strong claim, a claim that would be defeated if only it could be shown that it is possible for mental states to be multiply realized.

8.30   The next question to consider, then, is whether it *is* possible for mental states to be multiply realized. Here many philosophers of mind will appeal to the *conceivability* of multiply realized mental states. Of course, for conceivability to be relevant in the present context, there needs to be some sort of general principle that can connect conceivability to possibility, and, as we've discussed in chapters 2 and 3, that there is such a general principle is a matter of controversy.

The Varieties of Functionalism

We will discuss three varieties of functionalism—Turing machine func-   8.31
tionalism, analytic functionalism, and empirical functionalism. While Turing machine functionalism is historically significant, nowadays most functionalists are either analytic functionalists or empirical functionalists.

Turing machine functionalism

The earliest worked-out version of 20th-century functionalism is the view   8.32
originating with Hilary Putnam known alternately as *Turing machine func-*
tionalism and *machine state functionalism*. This version of functionalism views any creature with a mind as a Turing machine. As we discussed in chapter 7, one especially attractive aspect of Turing's idea is the way it helps to show how a purely physical and mechanistic system can engage in pro-cesses we regard as mental. This is especially true for the process of arriving at a solution to a problem. Such solutions are arrived at by Turing machines by manipulating symbols in a rule-governed way. The rules that govern a Turing machine's symbol manipulations are specified by the machine's *machine table* or *look-up table*. The rules are instructions that make up the machine's program. The instructions can be thought of as having a form such as "If the machine is in state S1 and receives input I1, then it goes into state S2 and produces output O1."

The set of such instructions helps define which kind of Turing machine   8.33
a machine is. The basic idea of Turing machine functionalism is that a creature's mental states can be defined by reference to instructions in a machine table. One of the main advantages that initially attracted philosophers to Turing machine functionalism was the way in which it overcame a problem that befell behaviorism, namely that behaviorists try to define mental states solely by reference to inputs (stimuli) and outputs (behavior) and make no provision for the way that mental states are related to inputs and outputs in virtue of also being related to other mental states. Turing machine functionalism, in contrast, allows for speci-fications of mental states in terms of inputs, outputs, *and* other mental states. However, the way in which other mental states figure in Turing

machine functionalism leads to one of Turing machine functionalism's greatest flaws. The flaw is that Turing machine functionalism makes no allowance for multiple simultaneous mental states. To see the "one at a time" nature of Turing machine functionalism, look again at the sample machine table instruction "If the machine is in state S1 and receives input I1, then it goes into state S2 and produces output O1."

8.34   Here the "then" can be read as indicating that we are dealing with a process that takes place over time. First the machine is in state S1, and then it leaves state S1 and goes into state S2. It doesn't allow for the machine to be in those two states simultaneously. Why is this a bad thing? The problem is that sometimes humans can be in more than one mental state at a time. For instance, you can have a sensory experience and a thought at the same time. Perhaps the sensory experience is that you smell some smoke and the thought is "Maybe something is burning in the kitchen." Since this is something that sometimes happens to humans, but can't happen to Turing machines, Turing machine functionalism is a flawed theory of human cognition.

8.35   Turing machine functionalism was important as an early alternative to behaviorism and mind–brain identity theory, but few functionalists nowadays adhere to this version of functionalism. Instead they are either analytic functionalists or empirical functionalists.

Analytic functionalism versus empirical functionalism

8.36   Each version of functionalism can be viewed as a theory of mental states wherein mental state definitions are descriptions of the *roles* those states play. Of course, there are many roles that mental states play and perhaps not all roles that a mental state plays will be essential for defining that mental state. For example, one role that my current thought plays is that it is the most recent thing that has happened to me today. However, that it is the most recent event in my biography is inessential to defining it as the mental state that it is. Much more important in defining it are descriptions of what it is a thought about and, if functionalists are right, descriptions that relate it to, for example, certain perceptual inputs, like my perceiving that I'm writing this paragraph right now.

8.37   Descriptions of mental state roles are crucial to all versions of functionalism. However, different versions of functionalism may be distinguished by the sorts of role descriptions they see as essential. Turing machine functionalists give pride of place to descriptions that can be stated in terms of machine-table instructions. The next two versions of functionalism differ over whether the role descriptions definitive of mental states are knowable *a priori* or are instead knowable only *a posteriori*. The view that the relevant descriptions are knowable *a priori* is known as *analytic functionalism*. The view that the relevant descriptions are knowable only *a posteriori* is known as *empirical functionalism* or sometimes *psycho-functionalism*. This view is called "psycho"-functionalism because of the central role given to the science of psychology in uncovering the relevant role descriptions.

The distinction between analytic and empirical functionalism is signifi- 8.38 cantly parallel to the distinction (discussed in chapter 5) between analytic and empirical behaviorism. Recall that analytic behaviorists were attempting to give a theory that would capture what is meant by commonsense uses of mental terms such as "belief" and "desire." The analytic functionalist has a similar goal, but will differ from the analytic behaviorist about what theory will best accomplish that goal. In contrast to these analytic theories (theories aiming to analyze commonsense term meanings), empirical behaviorism and empirical functionalism care less about common sense and are more inclined to defer to scientific psychological theories. What the empirical behaviorists and empirical functionalists disagree about are which psychological theories are the best ones. The empirical behaviorist will be suspicious of explanations that posit cognitive states intervening between stimulus and response and will prefer instead explanations of behavior given in terms of comparatively simple laws that directly relate stimulus and response. In contrast, the empirical functionalist will be more comfortable with theories that posit cognitive intermediaries between stimulus and response. Further, they will be more inclined to view the relations between stimulus and response as involving a complex relation that involves these intermediaries.

Arguments against Functionalism

Many arguments that we've discussed in connection with other issues can 8.39 be adapted for use as arguments against functionalism. One example is the zombie argument against physicalism (discussed in chapter 3). Another is the Chinese room argument against artificial intelligence (discussed in chapter 7). We'll just focus on these two, but there are others besides. For instance, one can adapt the inverted spectrum argument from chapter 3 to argue against functionalism.

Adapting the zombie argument to be against functionalism

8.40   Recall the zombie argument:

Premise 1: If physicalism is true then it is impossible for there to be two beings exactly alike physically but differing in that only one of them is a zombie.
Premise 2: It is conceivable that two beings are alike physically but only one of them is a zombie.
Premise 3: If something is conceivable, then it is possible.
Conclusion: Physicalism is false.

8.41   The main way to adapt this argument so that it targets functionalism is to replace words like "physically" and "physicalism" with words like "functionally" and "functionalism." Replacing words along such lines results in the following argument:

Premise 1: If functionalism is true then it is impossible for there to be two beings exactly alike functionally but differing in that only one of them is a zombie.
Premise 2: It is conceivable that two beings are alike functionally but only one of them is a zombie.
Premise 3: If something is conceivable, then it is possible.
Conclusion: Functionalism is false.

8.42   One of the parts of this new argument that may be called into question is a part that is also questionable in the old argument. And that part is premise 3—the part that links conceivability to possibility. The functionalist may want to respond to this argument by denying premise 3. However, whether this is an appealing move for the functionalist to make will depend on whether the functionalist in question is an *analytic* functionalist or instead an *empirical* functionalist. An analytic functionalist will not get very much mileage by resisting the "conceivability entails possibility" premise. This is because there is a version of zombie argument against analytic functionalism that doesn't depend on such a premise. Such an argument can be formulated in the following way:

Premise 1: If analytic functionalism is true, then it is inconceivable that two beings can be alike functionally but differ in that only one of them is a zombie.

Premise 2: It is conceivable for there to be two beings exactly alike functionally but differing in that only one is a zombie.
Conclusion: Analytic functionalism is false.

Since analytical functionalism is a theory about our *concepts* of mental   8.43
states (instead of a theory about the scientifically discoverable *nature* of
those states), it is especially vulnerable to conceivability-based considerations such as the zombie thought experiment. Empirical functionalism, in
contrast, is less vulnerable to such considerations.

Adapting the Chinese room argument to be against functionalism

The version of functionalism most directly threatened by adapting the   8.44
Chinese room argument is Turing machine functionalism. This is because
both the Chinese room argument and Turing machine functionalism can
be stated in terms of programs. Turing machine functionalism has programs at its heart because it is committed to the view that mental states
can be defined in terms of program instructions from a look-up table for
a Turing machine. At the heart of the Chinese room argument is Searle's
claim that a "Chinese understanding" program can be run by a person who
doesn't actually understand Chinese.

One interesting question is whether versions of functionalism besides   8.45
Turing machine functionalism can be targeted by the Chinese room argument. Arguably, analytic functionalism is vulnerable to the Chinese room
argument because Searle's central claim can be interpreted as a conceivability claim. While it is far fetched that anyone will *actually* do what Searle
invites us to imagine him doing, it is *conceivable*. It is conceivable that
Searle can run any program without himself thereby understanding
Chinese. Insofar as analytic functionalism is a claim about our *concepts* of
mental states, it is hostage to what we can and cannot *conceive* about them.
Empirical functionalism seems far less vulnerable to such a line of argu-
mentation, since empirical functionalism is geared toward defining mental
states in terms of the best scientific theory of the behavior of certain creatures. Further, it remains to be seen what, for example, the best theory is
of what it takes to understand Chinese. From the point of view of empirical
functionalism, what Searle can or cannot conceive of seems hardly relevant
to the question of what mental states really are.

Conclusion

8.46 Functionalism is the most popular current position on the mind–body problem, and its adherents see it as combining the best elements of antidualistic positions such as behaviorism, mind–brain identity theory, and strong AI. However, opponents of functionalism, especially qualia-based property dualists, see it as no better than other antidualistic views in its treatments of consciousness and qualia.

Annotated Bibliography

Aristotle, De Anima, trans. J. A. Smith, full text available at http://www9.georgetown.edu/faculty/jod/texts/aristotle.soul.html, accessed February 7, 2013. See especially Bk. II, Ch. 1 for an ancient Greek precursor to contemporary functionalism.

Block, Ned (1980) "Troubles with Functionalism," in Ned Block (ed.), Readings in the Philosophy of Psychology (Cambridge, MA: Harvard University Press). A classic line of criticism of the adequacy of functionalist approaches. Contains Block's famous "Chinese nation" argument against functionalism (it's like Searle's Chinese room, but with a billion people acting like individual neurons of a brain).

Block, Ned (1995) "The Mind as the Software of the Brain," in Daniel N. Osherson, Lila Gleitman, Stephen M. Kosslyn, S. Smith & Saadya Sternberg (eds.), An Invitation to Cognitive Science (Cambridge, MA: MIT Press). A nice overview of key ideas of functionalism.

Block, Ned and Fodor, Jerry (1972) "What Psychological States Are Not," Philosophical Review, 81, 159–181. An early classic source of criticisms of functionalism, especially criticisms based on considerations of absent and inverted qualia.

Fodor, Jerry (1974) "Special Sciences; or, The Disunity of Science as a Working Hypothesis," Synthese, 28, 97–115. An influential argument spelling out the autonomy of psychology from physics and physiology due to multiple realizability considerations.

Hobbes, Thomas (1651) Leviathan, full text available at http://www.gutenberg.org/files/3207/3207-h/3207-h.htm, accessed February 21, 2013. In chapter 5, Hobbes puts forward the view that thinking can be viewed as mechanistic.

Putnam, Hilary (1967) "Psychological Predicates," reprinted as "The Nature of Mental States" in Ned Block (ed.) (1980), Readings in Philosophy of Psychology (Cambridge, MA: Harvard University Press). A key early defense of contemporary functionalism.

9

MENTAL CAUSATION

The Problem of Mental Causation

According to common sense, mental events can (1) cause and (2) be caused 9.1
by nonmental events. Here is an illustration of (1): You form the intention
to go to the nearest pizzeria, buy a slice, and eat it. Nothing prevents you
from acting on this intention, so you wind up with a stomach full of pizza.
The mental event caused the nonmental event. The forming of the intention caused the occurrence of a bellyfull of pizza.

Here is an illustration of (2): When you take your first bite of the pizza, 9.2
it's too hot and it burns the roof of your mouth. The heat of the pizza is
high enough that it both damages the roof of your mouth and activates the
pain receptors that carry signals to your central nervous system. The heating
of your mouth and its nerve endings are physical events. These physical
events have various causal consequences, one of which is the mental event
of being in pain.

In the present chapter, we will be especially interested in examples of (1), 9.3
examples of mental causes of nonmental events. Such examples, if there
are any, are examples of *mental causation*. (Another sort of thing worth
calling "mental causation" is (3) when one mental event causes another
mental event.)

The idea of mental causation plays a very important role in many 9.4
parts of our culture. Consider, for example, the way that mental causation
figures in criminal law. If one person does something that causes the
death of another person, one very important question is whether this was

This Is Philosophy of Mind: An Introduction, First Edition. Pete Mandik.
© 2014 John Wiley & Sons, Inc. Published 2014 by John Wiley & Sons, Inc.

purposeful or instead an accident. Further, if it did happen on purpose, we want to know what the killer's *intentions* were. Did they cause the other person to die out of self-defense, or were they instead hoping to steal their money? Depending on what intentions led to the death, the criminal justice system will draw very different conclusions about what to do to the killer. Such conclusions may result in a life-long prison sentence or worse.

9.5   These remarks so far have focused on the importance for criminal law of nonmental effects of mental causes, causal relations of type (1). However, there are also connections between criminal law and causal relations of type (2). Consider, for instance, the importance that eyewitnesses have in a murder trial. Their very status as an eyewitness presupposes the possibility of perceptions (mental events) being caused by the events that they are perceptions of—as when, for instance, an eyewitness observed the suspect pushing the victim down a flight of stairs.

9.6   That mental events can cause and be caused by other events is so commonsensical and so important that it may seem totally outrageous that philosophers of mind have raised serious problems for the very idea. Nonetheless, they have, and the present chapter will examine some of the main problems as well as some of the main proposed solutions. The central problem that we will investigate in this chapter is something we can call *the problem of mental causation*. The problem of mental causation is the problem of explaining whether mental causation is even possible. While common sense may say that it clearly is possible, it seems to be a consequence of certain philosophical considerations—for instance, versions of dualism and functionalism—that mental causation is not possible after all.

9.7   In this chapter, we will examine four lines of thought against mental causation. The first comes from substance dualism. The second is qualia-based property-dualistic epiphenomenalism. The third is closely associated with the thesis of *anomalous monism* developed by Donald Davidson. The fourth is Jaegwon Kim's *explanatory exclusion* argument. Before delving deeper into the problem of mental causation and these four lines of thought, we need to examine one of the key ideas involved in debates about mental causation. This key idea is a thesis concerning *causal closure*.

The causal closure of the physical

9.8 One of the central sources of trouble for the idea that there is such a thing as mental causation is a thesis that is known as *the causal closure of the physical* or instead *the causal completeness of the physical*. This thesis can be put very simply: It is the thesis that every physical event that has a cause is caused by an event that is fully physical. In other words, there are no non-physical causes of physical events.

Adherents of the thesis of causal closure see it as highly confirmed by modern science. Physical events such as the formation of the continents or the accumulation of rust on the surface of a piece of iron have causes that are themselves fully physical. This is to say that such events are brought about by systems of physical objects operating under physical laws. Even physical events that we might describe as having mental causes, as when you purposefully raise your hand, are events that we have reason to believe are caused by brain events that are fully describable in physical terms. 9.9

One line of scientific support for the thesis of causal closure is based on (1) the widely confirmed principle of the conservation of energy plus (2) a highly plausible assumption about the relation of energy to causation. 9.10

According to (2), causation requires energy transfer. For example, if a rock dropped into a pond causes ripples, then there is a transfer of kinetic energy from the rock to the water. A flame causing a pot of water to boil transfers thermal energy to the pot and the water. 9.11

According to (1), the total amount of energy in the physical universe can neither increase nor decrease. There can be increases in subregions of the universe, but these increases require commensurate decreases in other regions. As the Earth warms by absorbing sunlight (a local increase), the sun slowly runs out of energy as it consumes the hydrogen that fuels fusion reactions (a local decrease). 9.12

We can derive a closure thesis from (1) and (2). If there were nonphysical causes of physical events, then, according to (2), that would involve a transfer of energy into the physical universe and thus an increase in the total energy of the physical universe. However, according to (1), there can be no such increase. Therefore, there can be no nonphysical causes of physical effects. Physical events that have causes must have physical causes. 9.13

Let us turn now to consider this question: How does causal closure lead to problems for mental causation? Well, if mental events are simply identical to certain kinds of physical events, as the mind–brain identity theorists discussed in chapter 6 believe, then there's no obvious problem here. Problems start to arise on views wherein the mental is, in some sense, not identical to the physical. One of the clearest examples of such a view is the view of substance dualism that we discussed in chapter 2. 9.14

The problem for substance dualists

9.15 There are two sorts of ways in which the problem of mental causation arises for substance dualists. The first is that it is almost entirely unintelligible how there can be any causal interaction between such radically distinct substances as extended bodies and unextended Cartesian souls. As we discussed in chapter 2, this is a point that Princess Elisabeth of Bohemia raised against Descartes.

9.16 The second way in which the problem of mental causation arises for substance dualism depends on the idea of the causal closure of the physical. If, as the thesis of causal closure says, everything that has a cause has a physical cause, and, as the substance dualist says, nothing mental is also physical, then it follows that nothing that has a cause has a mental cause.

The problem for property dualists

9.17 The problem of mental causation doesn't just arise for substance dualism. For example, it also arises for property dualism. However, before we get deeper into the connection between property dualism and the problem of mental causation, we need to first take a brief detour and take a look at the idea of *property efficacy*.

9.18 Consider a baseball hitting a glass window pane and causing the pane to shatter. The baseball has a bunch of properties—it has a shape, a color, a mass. Among its properties are relational properties—it is traveling at a certain velocity when it hits the pane, and it is a baseball that once belonged to my uncle. Not all of the properties of the baseball are relevant to the shattering of the pane. Given its mass and velocity, the baseball hits the pane with a certain amount of force and that is directly relevant to why the pane ends up shattering. The color of the baseball or who it once belonged to is irrelevant. A ball with that mass hitting the glass at that velocity would have made it shatter even if the ball had been a different color or had a different owner. The ball's properties differ in their causal relevance to the breaking of the glass. We can sum up these differences in terms of a notion of *efficacy*. With respect to the pane's shattering, *causally efficacious* properties of the ball include its mass and velocity, but not its color or its history of owners.

9.19 Now that we have the idea of property efficacy in hand, we can turn to look at property dualism's trouble with mental causation. In order to do so, we need to consider a version of the causal closure thesis stated in terms of properties. According to this version, everything that is caused to happen happens solely because of physical properties. In other words, the only efficacious properties are physical properties. If mental properties are nonphysical, it would seem to follow, then, that mental properties are never efficacious. Nothing ever happens because of mental properties.

For an example of a mental property, consider a pain quale—the very 9.20 painfulness of pain. Common sense tells us that certain things happen because of painfulness. After stubbing your toe, you cry or swear *because* of the painfulness of the ensuing experience. However, if the property version of the causal closure thesis is true, and property dualism is also true, then common sense is wrong in this respect. You are not crying or swearing because of the painfulness of the pain, and it is a mere illusion that things seem otherwise. This resulting view is of course the epiphenomenalism associated with property dualism that we encountered in chapter 3.

Basic Views of Interaction

Traditionally there have been four main views on the topic of mental– 9.21 physical causal interaction. These four views are interactionism, parallelism, epiphenomenalism, and reductionism. The first three of these are versions of dualism. The fourth is a version of physicalism.

Interactionism and reductionism both agree that there are causal inter- 9.22 actions between the mental and the physical. They disagree about other relations between the mental and the physical. Interactionism is a form of dualism and so holds that the mental is nonphysical. Reductionism denies dualism and holds the mental to be a special case of the physical, that is, according to reductionism, the mental comprises a special subset of the physical. Mind–brain identity theory, discussed in chapter 6, is a form of reductionism.

Parallelism and epiphenomenalism both agree that there are no causal 9.23 interactions leading from the mental to the physical. However, they disagree over the question of whether there can be causal interactions in the other direction, that is, from the physical to the mental. Parallelism says "no" and epiphenomenalism says "yes."

Interactionism

One of the most prominent historical instances of interactionism is the 9.24 substance dualism of Descartes. It has the advantage of embracing the commonsense view that there are causal interactions running in both directions between the mental and the physical. However, at the heart of Descartes' substance dualism is the thesis that minds and physical bodies are radically distinct—physical bodies have spatial properties like size and location and minds or souls don't. Given this radical difference between minds and bodies, it becomes very difficult to understand how interaction between them is possible. Nonetheless, interactionists assert that such interaction does indeed take place. They lack, however, a credible account of *how* it takes place.

Parallelism

9.25 Parallelism embraces dualism while denying mind–body interaction. According to parallelism, mental and physical events form two distinct noninteracting streams—a stream of mental events and a separate but correlated stream of physical events. One of the main problems that arises for parallelism is the problem of explaining why there are any systematic correlations between the mental and the physical.

9.26   While it may be possible to deny that there are causal relations between mental and physical events, it is far harder to deny that there are certain systematic *correlations* between mental and physical events. One such correlation is the correlation between certain stimulations of your nervous system, such as red light going into your eyes, and certain kinds of experiences, such as seeing something as being red. Another correlation is that when you decide to do certain things, very often those things happen. For instance, you decide to brush your teeth and just a little while later, there you are, brushing your teeth. *Why* are there these correlations? It is not at all satisfactory to regard these as simply *brute* correlations, that is, correlations for which there is no explanation. We demand an account.

9.27   As discussed in chapter 2, there are two traditionally prominent accounts that parallelists have given. One is Malebranche's *occasionalism*. The other is Leibniz's doctrine of pre-established harmony. Both accounts bring God into the picture to explain the correlations. On both views, the correlations exist because God willed the events to be correlated. Even for philosophers who believe in the existence of God, this is far from satisfactory, and we already reviewed the problems in chapter 2. Let us turn, then, to the next two theories—epiphenomenalism and reductionism. They each seem to have better answers to the question of correlation than do the traditional versions of parallelism.

Epiphenomenalism

To get a picture of how the epiphenomenalist envisions the relation between   9.28
mental and physical phenomena, imagine some sea foam bobbing up and
down on the crest of a wave in the ocean. The foam moves up and down
because the wave moves up and down, and not the other way around. The
sea foam's movement doesn't affect the wave's movement. The foam is,
quite literally, merely along for the ride. According to the epiphenomenalist,
your mental properties and states are similarly merely along for the ride.
The real causes of your bodily movements are certain purely physical properties and states, such as the purely physical properties of states of your
brain. You limp and cry not because of the painfulness of the pain that you
experience after stubbing your toe. The limping and crying are caused by
a certain brain state—c-fibers firing. The occasion of c-fibers firing in your
brain causes certain things to happen in the rest of your body, things such
as movements of your musculoskeletal system. The occasion of c-fibers
firing also gives rise to a distinct state, a nonphysical mental state of pain.
But the event of pain itself, while caused by physical events, does not itself
cause any physical events. Like the sea foam on the wave, the pain is just
along for the ride.

Like parallelism, epiphenomenalism has the disadvantage of conflicting   9.29
with common sense about mental causation. However, unlike parallelism,
epiphenomenalism has an answer to the question of correlation that doesn't
invoke God. According to epiphenomenalism, the reason that the mental
is correlated with the physical is that the mental is an effect of the
physical.

It should be noted that if by "effect" here we mean "causal effect," then   9.30
epiphenomenalism is in danger of violating the principle of the conservation of energy. It's open, however, for epiphenomenalism to embrace a
noncausal reading of "effect," and thus avoid violating the conservation
principle. This will all require a bit of explaining.

First, let's address this question: Does epiphenomenalism violate conser-   9.31
vation? Recall the idea that causation requires energy transfer. If the effect
that the physical has on the mental is causal, and the mental is nonphysical,
then that would seem to imply a flow of energy out of the physical universe,
and thus an overall decrease of energy in the universe. However, according
to the principle of the conservation of energy, energy can only be moved
around in the universe—there can neither be an increase nor a decrease in
the sum total of the energy in the physical universe.

9.32   Perhaps, then, the effect that the physical has on the mental is a kind of effect that is *noncausal*. If this were true, then epiphenomenalism would have a way of answering the question of correlation without violating the principle of conservation. However, this strategy is not without its problems. One problem is that it remains unclear whether there really are such things as effects that are noncausal.

Reductionism

9.33   According to reductionism, the mental is just a special case of the physical. There are certain physical events—for example, certain physical events in the brain—that are identical to mental events. For example, the event of being in pain is just one and the same as having c-fibers fire. There's no problem in understanding how c-fibers can be caused by and cause other physical events, so reductionism has the advantage of being consistent with the commonsense view that there are causal interactions between the mental and the physical. Another advantage of reductionism is that it gives a clear answer to the question of correlation. The reason, for example, that pains occur whenever c-fibers fire is that pains just *are* c-fiber firings.

9.34   Despite these advantages, reductionism is not entirely unobjectionable. The main objections to reductionism are the ones we discussed in connection with mind-brain identity theory in chapter 6. Such objections hinge on qualia—arguments such as the knowledge argument, the explanatory gap argument, and the modal arguments featuring zombies and inverted spectra.

Qualia and Epiphenomenalism

9.35   As we've already discussed, if we assume a property-based thesis of causal closure, it would seem that property dualism leads to a form of epiphenomenalism. In the present section we will take a brief look at issues connected to epiphenomenalism about qualia.

9.36   Epiphenomenalism about qualia may strike many as one of the worst possible kinds of epiphenomenalism. This is because, arguably, there's a very tight connection in our commonsense thinking between qualia and causation. Consider two key examples of qualia—the qualia associated with pain and the qualia associated with pleasure. These qualia are the very painfulness of pain and the very pleasantness of pleasure. Arguably, its part of the very idea of pleasure and pain that it can be caused by certain physical stimuli and cause certain downstream effects on behavior. One of the main ways in which, for instance, you learn to not touch a hot stove is when you receive a *painful* burn upon touching it. It seems like the painfulness—the pain quale—causally matters in producing your subsequent stove-avoiding behaviors. And when you learn a new behavior that you've been rewarded for, the pleasantness of the reward—the pleasure quale—seems to matter as well. The causally efficacy of the painfulness of pain and the pleasantness of pleasure is deeply entrenched in common sense.

Whether qualia-based epiphenomenalism conflicts with phenomenal self-knowledge

One of the most perplexing issues that arises in connection with qualia-based epiphenomenalism is the question of how, on the assumption that qualia don't have any effects, anyone can come to *know* whether anyone, including themselves, have any qualia. To see how qualia-based epiphenomenalism may threaten to undermine the possibility of knowledge of qualia, it helps to first spell out some widely held assumptions. One assumption is that in order to have knowledge of a property, that property must be causally efficacious. Another assumption is that thoughts are distinct from qualia both in the sense that thoughts aren't themselves qualia and in the sense that thoughts themselves don't have any qualia. 9.37

When we combine these widely held assumptions with property-dualistic qualia-based epiphenomenalism, we are able to generate a very puzzling thought experiment—Daniel Dennett's thought experiment about a kind of zombie he calls a "zimbo." (Dennett's argument is from his book, *Consciousness Explained* (1991). It's an argument that we briefly touched on in chapter 3.) 9.38

Dennett's zimboes

Recall that a philosopher's zombie is a being that is similar to a normal human in some significant respect (e.g., physically or functionally) but lacks qualia. Dennett's zimboes are a kind of zombie—they lack qualia—and the significant similarities they bear to normal humans are that, in addition to being behaviorally identical to a normal human being, they have all of the same *thoughts* as some normal human being. 9.39

We are ready now to run the thought experiment. Imagine that some-where out there is your *zimbo duplicate*—a being that behaves just as you do and has all of the same thoughts as you do but lacks qualia. For the purposes of this thought experiment, the most important thoughts that 9.40

you have are thoughts about your own consciousness and the qualia that accompany your conscious states. If you were to bite your tongue a little bit and concentrate on the feeling you experience, you might think the thought "I am now experiencing a painful quale." At the same time that you are doing that, your zimbo counterpart is biting his or her tongue and thinking to himself or herself "I am now experiencing a painful quale." But here's the puzzling part of the thought experiment: Whereas you are thinking something true (you *really are* experiencing a painful quale), your zimbo duplicate is thinking something false (it really *isn't* experiencing a painful quale). Remember, we are here temporarily assuming (for the purpose of the argument) the truth of epiphenomenalism about qualia. Therefore, whatever it is that causes your thoughts, it's not qualia doing the causing. Thus, there's nothing to prevent your zimbo duplicate from having the very same thoughts that you have.

9.41   Now the crucial question arises: Given that everything you think about yourself is something that your zimbo duplicate also thinks about himself or herself, how can you *know* that you really do have qualia? Another way of asking what is essentially the same question is this: How do you know that you yourself are not a zimbo?

9.42   Many philosophers follow Dennett in thinking that the point of this thought experiment is to show that qualia epiphenomenalism is absurd because it leads to the absurd consequence that we cannot know whether we ourselves possess qualia. Other philosophers, however, have sought to maintain their allegiance to qualia epiphenomenalism in the face of this thought experiment. One way in which they do this is by rejecting the assumption that properties have to be causally efficacious to be knowable. Of course, the question arises as to how it is that inefficacious qualia can be knowable if they aren't causally responsible for our thoughts about them. Certain epiphenomenalists have offered that there is a special non-causal relation between qualia and certain thoughts about them—a noncausal relation of "acquaintance"—by which we know of our own qualia.

Anomalous Monism

9.43   One highly influential line of thought concerning mental causation grows out of Donald Davidson's view known as *anomalous monism*. The "monism" here is a physicalist monism, though it is distinct from the kind of physicalist monism we studied in chapter 6 on mind-brain identity theory. To grasp the distinction between these two kinds of physicalist monism, it helps to recall the distinction between types and tokens spelled out in chapter 6. This distinction helps us understand a distinction between type-physicalism and token-physicalism. Mind–brain identity theory is a kind of type-physicalism whereas anomalous monism is a kind of token-physicalism. Type-physicalists affirm that mental types are identical to physical types. Token-physicalism is consistent with the denial of type-physicalism. The core assertion of token-physicalism is that every mental token is identical to a physical token.

The reasons that Davidson gives for preferring token-physicalism to type-physicalism are tightly connected with the reasons why his monism is "anomalous." Let us now turn to say more about Davidson's argument. 9.44

The line of reasoning that Davidson develops in favor of anomalous monism grows from an attempt to resolve what seems to be a conflict between three independently plausible propositions. We can label these propositions (1) "mental causation," (2) "nomic subsumption," and (3) "the anomalism of the mental." 9.45

Proposition (1), mental causation, is simply the proposition that has been central to the present chapter—it is the commonsense proposition that mental events enter into causal relationships, especially relationships wherein mental events cause physical events, as in cases of intentional action. 9.46

Proposition (2) is nomic subsumption. The "nomic" in "nomic subsumption" has to do with laws, especially natural and scientific laws like the laws of physics. The proposition of nomic subsumption is the proposition that for each instance of one event causing another, there is some description of those events under which there is a law that events of the one type cause events of the other type. So, if my baseball breaks your window, there must be a description of the baseball and the window under which it is a law that events of one type cause another. Some descriptions will be better suited to this than others. Describing the baseball as an object that once belonged to my uncle is inadequate, since there is no law of nature connecting things owned by my uncle to things breaking. Better would be to describe the baseball with such-and-such mass, velocity, and momentum, for there is a law of nature concerning how physical magnitudes of mass, velocity, and momentum relate. 9.47

It is important for Davidson's larger argument that the laws in question are strict laws or exceptionless laws. Consider a case in which a white 9.48

billiard ball bumps into and moves a red billiard ball. There is a strict (exceptionless) physical law having to do with mass, velocity, and momentum that subsumes the events in question. It is a law of physical mechanics that objects colliding with such-and-such masses and velocities will move in so-and-so ways. There is not, however, a strict law relating ball movements to their colors. It is not a law of physical mechanics or any other branch of the sciences that white things make red things move.

9.49   Of course, waving a red flag at a bull can sometimes attract its attention and make it move. But this is not a strict law—it has exceptions. Sometimes the bull doesn't see the flag. Other times the bull does see the flag, but he is busy eating, so doesn't bother to charge at it. The sorts of laws that Davidson is focusing on do not have such exceptions.

9.50   Let us turn now to consider proposition (3), the anomalism of the mental. Davidson holds that the only strict laws are found in physics. It is only under descriptions in physical terms that events are subsumed under strict laws. Descriptions in other kinds of terminologies—terminologies other than the terminology of physics—do not subsume events under strict laws. One important kind of description that fails to subsume events under strict laws is mentalistic or psychological description, such as descriptions of an event as being an episode of believing or desiring.

9.51   Davidson holds that there are no strict laws that relate events in terms of their being beliefs or desires. What motivates Davidson to say this is a point that we are familiar with from the discussion of the Geach–Chisholm objection to behaviorism in chapter 5. Recall that the point raised there was that a belief cannot be related to a kind of action except in virtue of being related to a whole host of other states. These other states put conditions on whether the belief will be connected to action. Situations in which these conditions do not hold are situations in which there is an exception to a law relating the belief to a particular action. Thus, there is no exceptionless law relating belief to action. Whatever law relates belief to action will not be a strict law.

9.52   On the face of it, the set of propositions (1), (2), and (3) seems to be an inconsistent set. If, for example, it is true that (2), causation must be subsumed under strict laws, and (3), there are no strict laws that subsume mental events, then it would seem that it must be false that (1) mental events cause anything.

9.53   Davidson's token-physicalism helps to resolve this apparent conflict between (1), (2), and (3). The key idea here can be conveyed in terms of how we interpret proposition (1). Mental event tokens are identical to physical event tokens, and since physical event tokens are subsumed under strict laws, there is a sense in which (1) is true, mental events do enter into causal relations. They just don't enter into causal relations under their mental descriptions, but only under their physical descriptions.

Some philosophers have worried that anomalous monism leads to epi- 9.54 phenomenalism. However, it seems that in order to derive epiphenomenalism from anomalous monism, we have to import remarks about *properties* into the account of anomalous monism. Further, it's likely that Davidson would find such remarks disagreeable in that he may very well deny the existence of properties.

The way to bring properties into anomalous monism and generate a 9.55 version of epiphenomenalism goes like this: First, we start with the Davidsonian point that an event only enters into causal relations under physical descriptions. Second, we translate that Davidsonian point into property-talk. For example, we make the point that only an event's physical properties are causally efficacious. Its nonphysical properties, such as its mental properties are not efficacious. They are, instead, epiphenomenal.

Recall the example of causation concerning the white and red billiard 9.56 balls. There's a law that subsumes the balls with respect to their mass and velocity, but not a law that subsumes them with respect to their colors. We can put this point in terms of properties. The balls have color properties as well as properties of having such-and-such mass and so-and-so velocity. The mass and velocity properties are causally efficacious properties—those are the properties that allow the balls to be subsumed under a strict law.

We can use this property-based view of nomic subsumption to describe 9.57 anomalous monism in the following way: Mental events are identical to physical events, but are subsumed under laws only in virtue of their physical properties and not in virtue of their mental properties. Given these claims about subsumption on the property-based interpretation of anomalous monism, mental events don't cause anything in virtue of their mental properties, but only in virtue of their physical properties. Stated this way, it is clear that property-based anomalous monism is a version of property-based epiphenomenalism.

One possible response to this argument for epiphenomenalism is to deny 9.58 the existence of properties. To deny that there are such entities as properties is not an unheard of position in philosophy, and there is reason to believe that Davidson was attracted to it. However, the debate concerning property realism versus property antirealism is too far from issues central to the philosophy of mind. We will not discuss it in further detail.

The Explanatory Exclusion Argument

9.59 Jaegwon Kim's explanatory exclusion argument attempts to show that a certain kind of physicalism leads to epiphenomenalism. This kind of physicalism is what we'll here call "multiple-realizability based non-reductive physicalism," or just "nonreductive physicalism" for short. Recall from chapters 7 and 8 that multiple realizability is a core idea of functionalism, one of the most widely held views amongst philosophers of mind. Kim's argument thus serves to point out a serious problem with functionalism, and nonreductive physicalism more generally, namely that it perhaps leads to a kind of epiphenomenalism.

9.60   Nonreductive physicalism shares with property dualism the view that there are mental properties and that no mental property is identical to any physical property. Despite this commonality, what serves to make nonreductive physicalism nonetheless count as *physicalistic* is its commitment to the view that each instance of a mental property has a physical property as its *realization*. In short, nonreductive physicalism holds that the mental is *realized* by the physical. According to these nonreductive physicalists, the reason the mental is not *reducible* to the physical, that is, the reason that no mental property is identical to any physical property is that each mental property is *multiply realizable*. Given that there are two (or more) distinct physical properties that can realize a given mental property, the mental property cannot be identical to either one of the physical properties.

9.61   Suppose that there is some occasion of causation that we are tempted to describe as an instance of mental-to-physical mental causation. Suppose, for example, that person has just moved their body based on an intention to move their body. Call the physical property of having a bodily motion "P1." The intention to move the body is mental, so let us call the relevant associated mental property "M." Since M is physically realized, and is realized by a physical property other than P1, say some property of the brain, call the property that realizes M, "P2." Which properties are the efficacious ones, the ones in virtue of which P1 is caused? If we assume the thesis of causal closure, then that would exclude M from being the property that is efficacious with respect to P1. In short, we can say that it seems that P2 causes P1 and M is causally irrelevant. But if M is causally irrelevant, then this looks to be a version of epiphenomenalism about M.

9.62   The explanatory exclusion argument gets its name from the idea that since P2 explains why P1 occurred, it excludes M from being the explanation of why P1 occurred. If having such-and-such a brain state explains your hand going up, then that excludes your intention to raise your hand from being the explanation of your hand raising.

Conclusion

The idea that mental events can cause physical events and vice versa is 9.63 deeply rooted in common sense. However, there are various views in philosophy of mind, views such as substance dualism, property dualism, and even versions of functionalism, that make it seem especially difficult to explain how mental causation can even be plausible. However, rejecting mental causation and embracing epiphenomenalism strikes many philosophers of mind as an unacceptable option.

Annotated Bibliography

Davidson, Donald (1970) "Mental Events," in L. Foster and J. W. Swanson (eds.), *Experience and Theory* (Amherst, MA: University of Massachusetts Press, pp. 79–101). Reprinted in Donald Davidson (1980) *Essays on Actions and Events* (Oxford: Clarendon Press, pp. 207–225). Classic discussion of Davidson's anomalous monism.

Dennett, Daniel (1991) *Consciousness Explained* (Boston: Little, Brown). As rich and fascinating as it is controversial, it's a source of many excellent insights and arguments, including Dennett's "zimbo" argument.

Glymour, Clark (1999) "A Mind Is a Terrible Thing to Waste," *Philosophy of Science*, 66(3), 455–471. Ostensibly a review of Kim (1998), this turns out to be an irreverent and fun critique of key discussions in philosophy of mind, especially problems revolving around the issues set up by Davidson (1970).

Kim, Jaegwon (1998) *Mind in a Physical World: An Essay on the Mind–Body Problem and Mental Causation* (Cambridge, MA: MIT Press). Kim critiques nonreductive versions of physicalism on the basis of the exclusion problem.

Robinson, William (2011) "Epiphenomenalism," in Edward Zalta (ed.), *The Stanford Encyclopedia of Philosophy*, full text available at http://plato.stanford.edu/entries/epiphenomenalism, accessed February 7, 2013. Excellent overview of the main issues, written by a philosopher highly sympathetic to epiphenomenalism. See especially sections 2.3 and 2.4 dealing with problems of epiphenomenalism in connection with knowledge of other minds as well as knowledge of our own minds.

Yoo, Julie (2007) "Mental Causation," in *The Internet Encyclopedia of Philosophy*, full text available at http://www.iep.utm.edu/mental-c/, accessed February 7, 2013. Excellent and accessible overview of key issues. See especially section 1.c. for a nice framework for visualizing the main approaches to mind–body interaction.

10

ELIMINATIVE MATERIALISM

Introduction and Overview

Eliminative materialism (or "eliminativism") is an extreme form of physi- 10.1
calist monism that denies the existence of either (1) anything mental or,
more typically, (2) some limited range of mental phenomena. The "eliminative" in the name "eliminative materialism" reflects the recommendation
that we eliminate talk of mental entities (minds, mental states, mental properties, etc.) in attempting to truly describe what exists in the universe.

In its most extreme form, eliminative materialism is a startling view. It 10.2
contains a host of counterintuitive claims. Such claims include claims that
no one has ever had a belief, a hope, or a dream, that no one has ever
planned for the future or remembered the past, and that no one has
ever felt any pleasure or any pain. Part of the interest in examining such a
radical view is that it highlights questions of whether we really do have
good reasons for believing in any of these mental phenomena.

Historical precursors to contemporary eliminative materialism, espe- 10.3
cially the eliminative part, include the view that there is no such thing as free
will (a view to be discussed further in chapter 12) and the view that there is
no such thing as the self (a view to be discussed further in chapter 15).

In contemporary discussions of eliminative materialism, the super- 10.4
strong form that denies the existence of all mental phenomena is not as
widely discussed and as widely taken seriously as the weaker and more
limited forms that simply deny the existence of only one kind of mental
phenomenon. Nonetheless, these limited forms are still pretty shocking.

This Is Philosophy of Mind: An Introduction, First Edition. Pete Mandik.
© 2014 John Wiley & Sons, Inc. Published 2014 by John Wiley & Sons, Inc.

Consider, for example, the claim that no one has ever believed anything. Is this a claim that is at all plausible? Some philosophers have suggested that such a claim is self-undermining. One way of seeing this point is by reading the eliminative materialist as recommending that we *believe* the claim that there are no beliefs. However, if we believed that claim, then at least one belief exists and the claim that is believed turns out to be false.

10.5   As we'll discuss further a little later, eliminative materialism is *not* the same as mind–brain identity theory. Despite a superficial similarity, there is a deep difference. To see both the similarity and the difference, let us think about a simple form of mind–brain identity theory and a simple form of eliminative materialism. The simple form of mind–brain identity theory says that pains are nothing but a certain kind of brain state—c-fibers firing. The simple form of eliminative materialism says that there are no pains— there are only c-fibers firing. Both theories agree that c-fiber firings exist. But do both agree that there are no pains, that pains do not exist? No, they do not, and this is the key difference between them. The mind–brain identity theorist's statement in terms of "nothing but" may make it seem like the existence of pains is being denied, but this is not so. The "nothing but" claim—the claim that pains are *nothing but* c-fibers firing—is not telling us that pains are nothing at all. Instead, it is simply saying that pains are nothing *additional*, they are nothing *beyond* c-fibers. But, since pains are identical to c-fiber firings, and c-fiber firings exist, then pains exist. In contrast, the eliminative materialist is outright denying that pains are identical to c-fibers firing. Pains aren't identical to anything at all—they don't even exist according to the eliminative materialist.

10.6   In contemporary discussions of eliminative materialism, the central focus has been the denial of the existence of *propositional attitudes*, such as beliefs and desires. Though not as central in discussions of eliminative materialism, there has nonetheless also been significant discussion of the denial of the existence of qualia. In keeping with the contemporary trends, the discussion of eliminative materialism in the present chapter will focus mostly on propositional attitudes. There will, however, be a section toward the end of the chapter that covers eliminative materialism about qualia.

Basic Ingredients of Contemporary Eliminative Materialism

10.7   There are two ideas that form the main ingredients of contemporary versions of eliminative materialism. The first is the idea that folk psychology is a theory. The second is the idea of a contrast between elimination and reduction.

Folk psychology as a theory

Contemporary discussions of eliminative materialism take place against a   10.8
background of assumptions concerning how theories change in the history of science. Often in the history of science, one theory is abandoned in favor of a new theory. Further, when the new theory is adopted, the entities posited by the old theory—the theory's *theoretical posits*—are regarded as not existing. The posits are thus *eliminated*. Examples from the history of science include the elimination of, that is, rejection of:

- *caloric*, the alleged substance that flows into objects when they heat up;
- *élan vital*, the alleged substance that makes all living things alive;
- *phlogiston*, the alleged substance contained in flammable objects that flows out of them when they combust; and
- *the luminiferous ether*, the alleged medium through which waves of light and other forms of electromagnetic radiation propagate.

Contemporary eliminative materialists regard propositional attitudes as   10.9
importantly analogous to phlogiston, caloric, *élan vital*, etc. That is, they regard propositional attitudes as theoretical posits. But, in what theory are they posited? The relevant theory is a kind of "folk theory" about the mind—*folk psychology*.

What is a *folk* theory? It's a theory, implicitly held, concerning a domain   10.10
for which there is often a nonfolk, fully scientific, and explicit theory. Besides folk psychology, other examples include folk physics and folk biology. Often there is a disagreement between a folk theory and its scientific counterpart. Take, for example, folk physics. Folk physics contains implicit and commonsensical views about how objects move. An example is the view that an object moving in a curved path tends to remain moving in a curved path. According to folk physics then, if a rock tied to the end of a string is swung around in a circle over your head, when released from the string it will tend to follow a curved path instead of going in a straight line. However, this contradicts scientific physics, which states that the released rock will move in a straight line.

The central elements of folk psychology are propositional attitudes, such   10.11
as beliefs and desires. Folk psychological explanations account for the behaviors of humans and (some) nonhuman animals by reference to their

beliefs, desires, and other propositional attitudes. According to folk psychology, such mental states constitute the causes or reasons for behaviors. Take, for example, George, who is opening the refrigerator. An example of a folk psychological explanation of why George is opening the refrigerator would be to say that George desires to drink some beer and believes that there is beer in the refrigerator.

10.12   One important feature of folk theories that distinguishes them from scientific theories is that folk theories are *tacit* or *implicit* (as opposed to explicit). In the case of an explicit theory, there may be some distinct moment in which a person learns a relevant piece of the theory, as when one learns in a physics class that $E = mc^2$. In contrast to this piece of scientific physics, there is no clearly marked time in which one comes to learn a piece of folk physics. It is instead the sort of thing that one just picks up "by osmosis." Being a folk theory, we can expect that folk psychology similarly is not acquired due to explicitly learning it. Maybe it is instead implicitly acquired or even something inborn.

The contrast between reduction and elimination

10.13   At the beginning of this chapter we briefly discussed the important distinction between elimination and reduction in terms of the difference between eliminative materialism, on the one hand, and a reductive materialism, such as the mind–brain identity theory, on the other hand. The general contrast between reduction and elimination can be understood by reference to two kinds of relations between scientific theories over the history of the development of a scientific field. In science, old theories are discarded in favor of new theories. There are two general relations that can hold between the posits of the old theory and the posits of the new theory. One sort of relation is *reduction*—the posits of the old theory are reduced to the posits of the new theory. Another sort of relation is *elimination*—the posits of the old theory are eliminated in favor of the posits of the new theory.

10.14   For examples of reduction and elimination, we can turn to the history of chemistry. For an example of reduction, consider an old theory that posits the existence of chemicals such as oxygen and hydrogen and a newer theory that says that chemicals are composed of atoms that are in turn composed of electrons, neutrons, and protons. The posits of the old theory, chemicals, are reduced to the posits of the new theory, entities composed of nuclear particles (protons and neutrons) orbited by electrons. For an example of elimination, consider an old theory that explains combustion as the rapid release of *phlogiston* from a combustible material such as a piece of wood, and a new theory that explains combustion as a highly energetic oxidation reaction, a combination of oxygen with a fuel to form a chemical compound. Here, the posit of the old theory, phlogiston, is eliminated in favor of the posits of the new theory. Chemists no longer believe in the existence of phlogiston. When theoretical posits of an old theory are eliminated, the new theory posits neither the old entities nor anything that the old entities can be reduced to. There is nothing in contemporary chemistry that can plausibly be taken as something that phlogiston can be reduced to.

Putting the ingredients together

What does it mean, then, to combine the idea that beliefs are posits of a 10.15
folk theory—*folk psychology*—with the idea of the *elimination* of theoretical posits over the course of the history of theory change? The resultant idea is that folk psychology will be surpassed by a superior theory, one that neither posits mental states nor posits anything that mental states can be reduced to. What scientific approach is likely to be superior to folk psychology? One famous answer to such a question—championed by the husband and wife philosophical team of Paul Churchland and Patricia Churchland and other eliminative materialists—is that folk psychology will be surpassed by the neurosciences.

We will get an even clearer view of eliminative materialism when we 10.16
turn to examine some of the main arguments that have been advanced in favor of it.

Arguments for Propositional Attitude Eliminative Materialism

We will look at three arguments for eliminative materialism concerning the 10.17
propositional attitudes. They are:

1. Folk psychology is a stagnant research program.
2. Folk psychology is committed to propositional attitudes having a sentential structure that is unsupported by neuroscientific research.

3. Folk psychology makes commitments to features of mental states that lead to an unacceptable epiphenomenalism.

Folk psychology is a stagnant research program

10.18 Folk psychology has been around, arguably, for thousands of years. And there are many aspects of mind and human behavior that folk psychology is no closer to having satisfactory explanations of than it was thousands of years ago. Folk psychology has yet to provide any satisfactory answer to such questions as the following:

- Why do humans and other animals need to sleep, and why do they often have dreams while asleep?
- Why do certain head traumas result in amnesia—massive memory loss and inability to learn new information—without any impairment in an ability to speak language or loss of knowledge of what words mean?
- Why do some people suffer from debilitating forms of mental illness such as schizophrenia?
- Why can't you tickle yourself?
- Why does the full moon look larger when it's closer to the horizon than when it's closer to the zenith, even though there's no change in the size of the optical image that reaches the eye or a similarly positioned camera?

10.19 A scientific research program is considered stagnant when a considerable time elapses without making significant progress in answering key questions in its domain. Often, scientific research programs are abandoned if their progress in answering questions stalls for a few years. By comparison, folk psychology is even more stagnant, since it has stalled for several thousands of years.

Folk psychology is committed to propositional attitudes having a sentential structure that is unsupported by neuroscientific research

10.20 This argument is very much along lines that we discussed in chapter 7, especially the part where we discussed objections from supporters of *connectionism* against the *language of thought hypothesis*. According to this line of thought, folk psychology is committed to the existence of a language of thought, a commitment contradicted by neuroscience, especially neuroscientific research inspired by connectionism.

To illustrate, consider the propositional attitude of thinking that the 10.21 moon is round. Here, there is an attitude of *thinking* and the propositional content *the moon is round*. According to the language of thought hypothesis, thinking that the moon is round involves utilizing two distinct *mental representations* or *concepts*, one of which is a mental representation of the moon and the other of which is a mental representation of roundness. According to certain proponents of connectionism and connectionist-inspired neuroscience, there is no good reason to think that there are separate representations in the brain for the moon and for roundness. Instead, the moon and roundness are represented in a distributed or holistic way. The representations of the moon and roundness are spread out across a large number of neurons, no subset of which constitutes or gives rise to *distinct* representations.

Folk psychology makes commitments to features of mental states
that lead to an unacceptable epiphenomenalism

The general line of thought here is based on the supposition that science 10.22 has little room for posits that don't really do anything. Combine this general principle with one of the arguments for epiphenomenalism that we discussed in chapter 9, and you have another argument for eliminative materialism. Take, for example, the explanatory exclusion argument. If every bodily motion is caused by a brain state that no mental state is identical to, then whatever mental states are posited by folk psychology are states that don't really do anything to produce behavior. Instead, the brain states are doing all the work. In light of such considerations, the eliminative materialist recommends that we just eliminate any reference to the so-called mental state in explaining behavior.

Arguments against Propositional Attitude Eliminative Materialism

We will examine four lines of thought against eliminative materialism 10.23 about the propositional attitudes. They are:

1. Eliminative materialism is self-refuting.
2. The "theory" theory is false.

3. Folk psychology is indispensable.
4. Introspection reveals the existence of propositional attitudes.

Eliminative materialism is self-refuting

10.24 Eliminative materialists say that beliefs do not exist. In so saying, they *assert* "Beliefs do not exist." However, consider what distinguishes assertions from other kinds of utterances. Consider what distinguishes asserting "the cat is on the mat" from imitating or quoting someone who uttered "The cat is on the mat." Plausibly, one of the distinguishing features of assertion is that the speaker *believes* the proposition that their utterance expresses. Contrast this with imitation or quotation. I can doubt that there are any cats on any mats yet nonetheless imitate or quote someone by uttering "The cat is on the mat." For my utterance of "The cat is on the mat" to count as an *assertion*, it is necessary that I *believe* that the cat is on the mat.

10.25 Let us now return to the assertion made by the eliminative materialist. In asserting "Beliefs do not exist," it is necessary that they believe what they assert. However, this requires the existence of at least one belief, which contradicts the very thing that they are asserting. Thus, according to this line of thought, eliminative materialism about the propositional attitudes, especially the propositional attitude of belief, is self-undermining.

10.26 Of course, eliminative materialists need not surrender their position in the face of this argument. Instead, they can give an account of assertion that does not require the existence of beliefs. One sort of way the eliminative materialist can do this is by appeal to special neural states, states understood perhaps in connectionist terms as holistic patterns of neural activation, that are requirements for a speaker's utterance to count as an assertion, but are not themselves beliefs or any other kind of propositional attitude.

The "theory" theory is false

10.27 Let us call the proposal that folk psychology is a theory the *"theory" theory*. The "theory" theory, or TT for short, is an important component of many, if not all, arguments for eliminative materialism. One approach that has appealed to many critics of eliminative materialism has been to try to argue against TT.

10.28 If our folk psychological grasp of the minds of others is not due to a tacit *grasp of a theory*, then what is it due to? One proposal offered as an alternative to the "theory" theory is the *simulation* theory. According to the simulation theory, we do not understand one another's mental states by reference to a theory about such states, but instead, by *simulating* such states inside ourselves. So, for instance, if I see George opening the refrigerator, I don't *consult a theory* in order to come to the conclusion that he desires beer and believes that there is beer in the fridge. Instead, I imaginatively simulate myself opening the fridge, that is, I "put myself in George's shoes" and discover what mental states I would have if I were in George's position.

Regardless of whether TT is better or worse than the simulation theory, opposing TT does not seem to be a very strong way of defending the reality of propositional attitudes against eliminative materialism. Consider an analogy. Suppose it could be shown that no one ever subscribed to a theory that posited the existence of unicorns. Showing that wouldn't be a very powerful consideration against the existence of unicorns. In spite of the lack of a unicorn theory, it's possible that there could nonetheless be unicorns. Consider a different analogy. Several hundred years ago, no one had ever conceived of electrons, and thus, no one had ever subscribed to any theory positing the existence of electrons. Nonetheless, electrons existed all along. Indeed, electrons predate—by many billions of years—anyone holding the theory of electrons. Given these two analogies—the analogy concerning unicorns and the analogy concerning electrons—it seems reasonable to generalize in the following way: The failure to hold a theory of X is irrelevant to whether X exists, since the failure to hold a theory of X is consistent both with the existence of X (as in the case of electrons hundreds of years ago) and with the nonexistence of X (as in the case of unicorns). 10.29

Folk psychology is indispensable

Unlike the previous objection, which denies that folk psychology is a theory, this objection grants that it is a theory, but argues that it is a theory that we cannot do without: It is, instead, indispensable. But what is it indispensable for? What's so great about folk psychology? Arguably, folk psychology allows us to predict, explain, and otherwise understand one another's behavior in a way that we simply could not do without. 10.30

In order for this objection to work, it is not enough that we get pretty good predictions and explanations from folk psychology. It needs to be shown that the virtues of folk psychology are such that we simply could 10.31

not do without it. It needs to be shown that, for instance, there will not be a future neuroscientific theory that more simply, elegantly, and powerfully accounts for behavior than does folk psychology. But a prediction about what will never happen in the future is hard to invest a high degree of certainty in. Who knows what the future will bring?

Introspection reveals the existence of propositional attitudes

10.32 What is the best evidence that there is a piece of furniture near you? Arguably, the best evidence is that you can *perceive* it—you can either see or feel that there is a chair, or desk, or table near you. It doesn't seem to depend on any fancy *theorizing* to know that you are sitting in a chair right now. You can simply look and see that you are. Many philosophers regard introspection as importantly analogous to perception. (We'll have a lot more to say about perception in chapter 11.) Just as perception is a highly reliable indicator of the existence of its objects—objects such as the visible and tangible material objects in our immediate environment—so is introspection a highly reliable indicator of the existence of its objects. But what are the "objects" of introspection? Plausibly, they are the very mental states that eliminative materialists want to eliminate—beliefs, desires, etc.

10.33 Some critics of eliminative materialism regard introspection as giving much stronger grounds in *favor* of the propositional attitudes than does any neuroscience-inspired argument *against* propositional attitudes. One way of thinking of this alleged opposition between introspection and neuroscientific theory is that it is analogous to an alleged opposition between modern physics and common sense about whether such objects as rocks, trees, tables, and chairs are *solid*. Common sense says that they are solid and our best evidence of their solidity is perceptual—we push on them and *feel* that, unlike a gas or a liquid, they resist the pressure we apply to them. Our hand does not simply pass right through. However, modern physics tells us that a so-called solid object is actually mostly empty space. Most of the mass of a rock is restricted to the nuclei of the atoms that make up the rock—and compared to the volume taken up by the atomic nuclei, the volume of the rest of the rock is vast. So, does this mean that modern science contradicts common sense and the deliverance of perception? Does this mean that so-called solid objects aren't actually solid? Not necessarily. This is so because, arguably, the right way to interpret the relation between perception and science when it comes to rocks etc. is not that perception is incorrect when we perceive them as solid, or that science is incorrect when it says that rocks are mostly empty space, but instead that one and the same thing can be both solid and mostly empty space.

But how can this be? How can a rock be at the same time solid and mostly   10.34 empty space? The trick is to interpret the "solidity" of an object in a way that does not entail that the object is non-empty in the entirety of its volume. Perhaps, then, a similar reconciliation can be made between intro-spection and neuroscience. However, it goes beyond the space allotted here to supply an account of how such a reconciliation might go.

Qualia Eliminative Materialism: "Quining" Qualia

In this section we will turn from eliminative materialism about the propo-   10.35 sitional attitudes to eliminative materialism about phenomenal conscious-ness. Phenomenal consciousness is that aspect of our mental lives in virtue of which there is "something it's like" to be us. The clearest cases of phenomenal consciousness are most closely associated with sensory per-ception. Much contemporary philosophical discussion of phenomenal consciousness is conducted in terms of *qualia*, the subjective qualities of our conscious states, especially conscious states of sensory perception.

In this section, we will look at a case of eliminative materialism about   10.36 qualia, especially as that case has been developed by the philosopher Daniel Dennett in his (1988) article, "Quining Qualia." The verb "quine" is a word Dennett jokingly made up in dedication to the philosopher Willard van Orman Quine. Dennett's definition is "quine, v. To deny resolutely the existence or importance of something real or significant."

The general form of Dennett's argument against the existence of qualia   10.37 can be sketched as follows:

Premise 1: If qualia exist, then they are things that have properties W, X, Y, and Z.
Premise 2: Nothing has properties W, X, Y, and Z.
Conclusion: Qualia do not exist.

To fill this argument out, we need answers to two questions. First, what are the properties traditionally attributed to qualia? Second, what are Dennett's reasons for thinking that nothing has such properties?

What are the properties traditionally attributed to qualia? According to   10.38 Dennett, the traditional account of qualia holds that they have a fourfold essence. Qualia are supposed to be (1) ineffable, (2) intrinsic, (3) private, and (4) directly known.

10.39   Being ineffable means being indescribable or inexpressible in language. If your qualia are ineffable, then you cannot tell anyone else what your qualia are like.

10.40   Being intrinsic is best understood in contrast to being extrinsic. An extrinsic property is a relational property—a property defined in terms of relations. For example, the property of being a parent is an extrinsic property. In order to be a parent, you must be related to someone else in such a way that they count as your child. In contrast, then, intrinsic properties (if there are any) are supposedly had by an object independently of any relations it bears to any other object.

10.41   The alleged ineffability and intrinsicality of qualia play an important role in the classic inverted spectrum thought experiment. If Jones and Smith can be exactly alike in their verbal and nonverbal behaviors while differing in their qualia, then it seems that qualia must be both ineffable and intrinsic. They would be *ineffable* because everything Smith says about his red qualia is exactly what Jones would say about his green qualia, and thus their words cannot convey what it's like to have the one kind of qualia instead of the other. And the qualia would be *intrinsic* because the relations that, for instance, Smith's behaviors enter into with his environment and his own bodily states are exactly the same as the relations concerning Jones. Since Smith and Jones are exactly the same in terms of relations, qualia must be some nonrelational, and thus intrinsic, aspect of their mental lives.

10.42   The inverted spectrum thought experiment concerning Smith and Jones also allows us to illustrate the *privacy* and *direct knowability* of qualia. Both of these aspects of qualia have to do with *knowledge* of qualia. The claim that qualia are private is the claim that only you can have knowledge of your qualia. If other people as well as you could know about your qualia, then they would be *public* instead of private. The alleged privacy of qualia is sometimes discussed in terms of what is accessible only from the *first person point of view*, in contrast with such items as physical objects that are accessible from the *third person point of view*. Another closely related contrast used to differentiate qualia from the rest of the universe is that qualia are *subjective* whereas, planets, atoms, rocks, and trees are *objective*.

10.43   The claim that qualia are directly knowable is the claim that your knowledge of your qualia is not in any way mediated. Contrast this with the way in which we know about scientific theoretical posits such as electrons. That knowledge is mediated by certain instruments as well as a scientific theory that helps us understand what the readings of the instruments have to do with electrons. In contrast, allegedly, you do not need to grasp any theory in order to have knowledge of your own qualia. Such a contrast should remind you of our discussion from chapter 3 of the contrast between what can be known by description versus what can only be known by acquaintance.

Let us turn now to convey a bit of the flavor of Dennett's arguments 10.44 against anything answering to the description that the tradition assigns to qualia. One important part of the traditional claim about the *intrinsicality* of qualia is that they have their properties independently of any relations they bear to propositional attitudes such as the *thoughts* we might have about our sensory experiences. Dennett introduces a thought experiment to cast doubt on this. It is his thought experiment of the experienced beer drinker. Many people who enjoy drinking beer will claim that they did not like it when they first tasted it. It was only later, after several tries, that it became an acquired taste.

Consider, now, the flavor quale associated with the way beer tasted when 10.45 they first tried it. Is *that* the taste that they grew to enjoy? It is quite tempting to answer "no, if beer still tasted like *that* they would still dislike it." But this seems to show that propositional attitudes, such desiring or liking *that* such-and-such is the case, are relevant to the subjective aspect of a beer-tasting sensory state. But that seems to cast doubt on qualia being *intrinsic* properties. A quale can't be an intrinsic property of an experience if whether an experience has that property depends on relations that the experience bears to one or more propositional attitudes.

Another of Dennett's thought experiments targets the claim that qualia 10.46 are directly knowable. This is the thought experiment of Chase and Sanborn—two coffee tasters who have worked at Maxwell House for many years. One day, Chase announces that he has come to no longer enjoy the taste of Maxwell House coffee. Further, Chase claims that the coffee tastes the same to him, but that he just doesn't enjoy *that taste* any more. Sanborn claims to have undergone a similar change in that he no longer enjoys drinking Maxwell House coffee. However, he makes an additional claim that seems to conflict with Chase's. Whereas Chase claims that the taste is the same and he just doesn't enjoy that taste anymore, Sanborn claims that the taste has changed. Sanborn says that if the taste had remained the same, he would still enjoy the coffee, because what he liked was the way the coffee originally tasted when he was first hired.

10.47   We can put the key claims of Chase and Sanborn in terms of *qualia*. Chase is claiming that his coffee-associated qualia have remained the same. What has changed are Chase's judgments about his qualia. He used to judge those qualia to be enjoyable. Now he judges them to be unenjoyable. In contrast, Sanborn claims that his *qualia* have changed. Sanborn judges his old qualia to be enjoyable and the new ones to be unenjoyable.

10.48   Dennett invites us to contemplate how anyone—Chase, Sanborn, or anybody—could figure out which of the two tasters, if either, is correct about how things stand with respect to their qualia and their judgments about them. Suppose that there is some fact of the matter about which taster is correct and further, some empirical test to ascertain this. Perhaps such an empirical test would involve scanning different parts of the tasters' brains at different times to see if there are changes in the pre-judgment brain responses to coffee or only changes in the brain areas for the judgments themselves. Note, however, that if we rely on such tests to settle which of the two tasters have made the correct claims, we would be abandoning the claim that qualia are directly knowable. It would seem, instead, that knowledge of what is going on is achieved via the *indirect* route of brain scanning.

10.49   Dennett's arguments involve many more thought experiments than the ones we've reviewed here. However, we've seen some of Dennett's considerations for the view that nothing can have all of the properties that are traditionally attributed to qualia. Dennett urges an eliminative materialism about qualia—qualia don't exist.

Conclusion

10.50   The ideas that there are no propositional attitudes and no qualia are so odd as to seem perverse or like some kind of bad joke. At least, that's how some philosophers have reacted to various kinds of eliminative materialism. Nonetheless, eliminative materialism is a position that must be dealt with in one way or another in philosophy of mind, especially by those philosophers who hold that the basis for asserting the existence of psychological phenomena must ultimately be grounded in scientific facts. We must take seriously the possibility that—perhaps—science will overturn our commonsense and philosophical ideas about minds.

Annotated Bibliography

Churchland, Paul (1981) "Eliminative Materialism and the Propositional Attitudes," *Journal of Philosophy*, *78*, 67–90. Churchland's classic statement and defense of eliminativism about the propositional attitudes.

Churchland, Patricia (2008) "The Impact of Neuroscience on Philosophy," *Neuron*, *60*(39758), 409–411, full text available at http://philosophyfaculty.ucsd.edu/faculty/pschurchland/papers/neuron08impactofneuroonphil.pdf, accessed February 9, 2013. A concise overview by one of the most forceful advocates for the importance of neuroscience for philosophy.

Dennett, Daniel (1988) "Quining Qualia," in A. Marcel and E. Bisiach (eds.), *Consciousness in Modern Science* (Oxford: Oxford University Press), full text available at http://ase.tufts.edu/cogstud/papers/quinqual.htm, accessed February 9, 2013. Dennett's highly intriguing and entertaining defense of a thesis that outrages many philosophers of mind—qualia don't exist!

Gordon, Robert (2009) "Folk Psychology as Mental Simulation," in Edward Zalta (ed.), *The Stanford Encyclopedia of Philosophy*, full text available at http://plato.stanford.edu/archives/fall2009/entries/folkpsych-simulation/, accessed February 9, 2013. Overview by one of the many defenders of the simulation theory, an alternative to the "theory" theory of folk psychology.

Lycan, William (2005) "A Particularly Compelling Refutation of Eliminative Materialism," in D. M. Johnson and C. E. Erneling (eds.), *Mind as a Scientific Object: Between Brain and Culture* (Oxford: Oxford University Press, pp. 197–205), full text available at http://www.unc.edu/~ujanel/ElimWeb.htm, accessed February 9, 2013. Lycan critiques arguments for attitude eliminativism by complaining that their premises are far less plausible than the falsity of their conclusions.

Stich, Stephen (1996) *Deconstructing the Mind* (New York: Oxford University Press). In the title essay of this collection of articles by Stich, he expresses skepticism about ever resolving the debates over eliminativism. He casts the debates as turning on whether there exists anything that words like "belief" refer to, an issue that itself rests on intuitive judgments that may very well be hostage to biases that vary across populations.

11

PERCEPTION, MENTAL IMAGERY, AND EMOTION

Two kinds of mental state dominate discussion in philosophy of mind— 11.1
thoughts and sensations. These aren't the only kinds of mental state,
however. Perceptions, mental images, and emotions are three examples.
There are interesting philosophical problems associated with these other
kinds of state.

Perception

The philosophical problem of perception is the problem of explaining what 11.2
the *objects* of perception are. The objects of perception are those things that
we perceive when we perceive. Interesting questions about objects surround
perception-like phenomena—mental phenomena that aren't perceptions
despite certain similarities. Examples of such phenomena include illusions,
dreams, and hallucinations. But what are the *objects* of illusions, dreams,
and hallucinations? This question is addressed in the various versions of
the classical *argument from illusion*. In this section, we will take a look at
the commonsense view of perception and its objects, the difficulties raised
by the argument from illusion, and some of the main philosophical
responses to these difficulties.

Direct realism and the argument from illusion

Consider a typical case of perceiving something. Suppose you see a pencil 11.3
resting on a desk in front of you. What are the *objects* of perception in this

This Is Philosophy of Mind: An Introduction, First Edition. Pete Mandik.
© 2014 John Wiley & Sons, Inc. Published 2014 by John Wiley & Sons, Inc.

case? That is, what are the things that are perceived? On one view about how to answer to such a question, a view that philosophers often refer to as *direct realism*, the objects are the *mind-independent* objects that we ordinarily take ourselves to perceive. In this case the objects of perception are the pencil and the desk. What makes direct realism a version of *realism* is the claim that the objects of perception are *mind independent*. Direct realism thus opposes views, such as idealism, that deny that we ever perceive any mind-independent thing.

11.4   What's *direct* about direct realism is that it denies that mind-independent objects are perceived *indirectly*. It denies that mind-*independent* objects are perceived by first perceiving some mind-*dependent* entity. It thus opposes views, such as versions of the sense datum theory (versions known as *indirect realism* or *representative* realism), that hold that what we directly perceive are mind-dependent entities—sense data.

11.5   Many philosophers have thought that direct realism has a problem dealing with perception-like illusions, such as dreams, hallucinations, and illusions properly so called. The idea that direct realism cannot explain illusions motivates a famous line of thought against direct realism—*the argument from illusion.*

11.6   (To simplify discussion, we will use "illusion" to refer to a far broader class of cases than those that would be properly regarded as illusions. Strictly speaking, neither a dream nor a hallucination is an illusion. There are important differences between dreams, hallucinations, and illusions properly so called. Hallucinations are an abnormal occurrence, often associated with mental illness and intoxication. In contrast, neither dreams nor illusions are abnormal. Most people dream every night as a healthy part of their sleep cycle. And illusions are typical results of normally functioning perceptual systems. There's nothing abnormal or malfunctioning in your visual system when you look at an optical illusion and two figures that are really of equal size appear of different sizes. A further difference among these phenomena marks a contrast between perceptual illusions on the one hand and hallucinations and dreams on the other. In the case of hallucinations and dreams, one may hallucinate or dream a thing that doesn't exist at all, such as a winged pig or a pink elephant. In contrast, illusions do not involve the apparent perception of a nonexisting thing, but instead, the perception of an existing thing as having some features that it doesn't really have, as when one perceives a straight stick as being bent.)

11.7   Despite key differences, dreams, hallucinations, and illusions properly so called are interestingly similar to one another. And these states are interestingly similar to perceptions, especially in their subjective or phenomenal aspect. Further, there is an interesting *difference* between perceptions and illusions. Whereas perceptions are "factive"—you can perceive that there is a cat on a mat only if, as a matter of fact, there really is a cat on the mat— illusions are not factive. You can dream, hallucinate, or be under the illusion that there is a cat on a mat even when there is no cat, no mat, or no cat on a mat.

There are two key claims that are made about illusions that serve as key premises in the argument from illusion. The first is that illusions are subjectively or phenomenally similar to perceptions. This first claim can be put in terms of *the way things seem* to the subject of an illusion. When undergoing an illusion of a cat on a mat, the way things seem to you can be just like the way things seem when there *really is* a cat on the mat and you are perceiving it. 11.8

The second key claim is that in illusions you are nonetheless aware of *something*. This is so even in the case of a full-blown hallucination of a nonexistent animal, such as a unicorn. Even though no unicorn exists, there nonetheless is *something* that you are aware of. It is not as though you are aware of nothing at all. A case of being aware of nothing at all would be better regarded as a case of unconsciousness, as when one is in a coma or a deep and dreamless sleep. 11.9

With these two key points in hand, the proponent of the argument from illusion goes on to make a third point, a point that can be viewed as an *explanation* of why the first two points would be true. If, as the second point says, in even full-blown hallucinations you must be aware of *something*, and, as the first point says, the accurate perception and the inaccurate illusory case are *subjectively* the same, then (third point) what is the same in both cases is something subjective, that is, something mental or mind-dependent. In a dream or a hallucination of an eight-headed billy goat, you are not aware of an eight-headed billy goat, since no such thing exists for you to be aware of. But you are nonetheless aware of something. What is this something? It is a mind-dependent entity—it is the idea or mental image of an eight-headed billy goat. 11.10

The argument from illusion can be used alternately as an argument *against* direct realism or as an argument *for* one of the alternatives to direct realism, such as indirect realism and idealism. In the next section, we will examine several philosophical theories of perception, theories that differ in the way that they deal with the problems raised by the argument from illusion. Some of these theories are versions of direct realism. Proponents of 11.11

such theories see the argument from illusion as being flawed. Other theories see the main thrust of the argument as essentially correct.

Philosophical theories of perception

11.12   The central claim that distinguishes philosophical theories of perception concerns what perception's objects are. When you perceive, *what* do you perceive? Do you only perceive ideas in your mind? Do you instead perceive physical objects external to your mind? Or do you perceive some combination of ideas and external objects? There is also philosophical interest in the nature of the *relation* between the perceiver and the object perceived. Is the relation you bear to perceptual objects *direct*? Or is it instead *indirect*? Before turning to the distinct theories that differ regarding the objects of perception, we will consider some general remarks about the nature of the perceptual relation.

11.13   One thing that is especially interesting about the perceptual relation—the relation between a perceiver and a thing perceived—is the way it seems to distinguish perceptual states from other mental states, such as states of thought. What serves to distinguish *thinking* that there is a pencil on a desk from *perceiving* that there is a pencil on a desk? Consider, first, cases in which both the pencil and desk in question actually exist. Arguably, there are many more constraints on perceiving than on thinking. In the perceiving case, the desk and the pencil have to be sufficiently close to the perceiver so as to exert some causal influence on the perceiver. Further, the causal influence has to be of a sort that involves the perceiver's perceptual organs. For example, the pencil on the desk has to be sufficiently close so as to cause the perceiver to see it with her eyes, feel it with her skin, or hear it with her ears, and so on. In contrast, there seems not to be a similar causal constraint on thinking. Suppose, while traveling, I accidentally leave my favorite pencil on a friend's desk and do not remember its location until several days later and thousands of miles away. Even though I may be too remote for the pencil to have any effect on my eyes, ears, etc., that is no bar to my thinking about the pencil and thinking that it is on a desk.

11.14   We will now turn to examine four philosophical theories of perception that grapple with the concerns raised by the argument from illusion. The four theories are indirect realism, idealism, and two versions of direct realism: *intentionalism* and *disjunctivism*. There are several key issues that serve to define these theories. We can represent these issues in terms of three questions.

First question: In having an accurate perception that commonsense 11.15
describes as a perception of a mind-independent thing, is one indeed aware
of a mind-independent thing? Idealism answers "no" but the other three
theories answer "yes."

Second question: Is the claim at the heart of the argument from illusion— 11.16
the claim that there is a substantial commonality between perceptual states
and illusory states—correct? Disjunctivism answers "no" but the other
three theories answer "yes."

Third question: Regardless of whether one is, in perceiving, aware of 11.17
something mind independent, is one aware of something that is mind
dependent? Both indirect realism and idealism say "yes" and both intentionalism and disjunctivism say "no."

Indirect realism   Indirect realism affirms that we do indeed perceive mind- 11.18
independent objects, such as rocks and trees. However, it insists that we do
so only *indirectly*. To get a further feel for this claim about perceptual indi-
rectness, it helps to consider an analogy. Consider what happens when you
see someone on television or in a mirror. You perceive that person, but only
as a consequence of perceiving the image on the television screen or in the
mirror. Your perception of the person is *mediated*—it is mediated by the
perception of the image. By analogy, on the indirect realist view of perception, when you perceive a mind-independent object such as a tree, your
perception is mediated by a perception or awareness of a mind-dependent
entity, an entity variously referred to as a "sense datum" (plural: "sense
data"), "idea," or "mental representation."

Given that what we are *directly* aware of on this view is a mind-dependent 11.19
object, the question arises of how we ever manage to be aware of a mind-
independent object. Perhaps one way to think of the process of becoming
aware of a mind-independent object is by analogy to a certain kind of
scientific inference about the existence of such unobserved entities as
microscopic particles or the core of the earth. Scientists gather evidence by
observing the behavior of their measuring devices and other scientific
instruments. Then, based on the evidence that they gather, they infer the
existence of unobserved entities. Such unobserved entities are posited as
the causes of the observable behaviors of the scientists' instruments. By
analogy, on the indirect realist view of perception, our evidence about the
world external to our minds comes in the form of ideas or sense data that
we are directly aware of, and we infer the existence of mind-independent
objects that are the causes of those sense data.

11.20   If the indirect realist is proposing that we are ultimately aware of mind-independent objects only by performing some kind of inference or educated guess, then the indirect realist becomes vulnerable to a kind of skeptical worry. The skeptic about the external world denies that we can have knowledge of the external world. The skeptical worry that arises for indirect realism is that if our access to the external world is mediated by an awareness of sense data, then the possibility arises that the external world is not actually the way we infer it to be. The sense data that represent the external world may represent it incorrectly and thus we would not *know* what's really going on in virtue of our perceptions. If you are inclined to reject skepticism about the external world, then you might be similarly inclined to reject indirect realism, since it arguably leads to such a skepticism.

11.21   *Idealism*   Since much of chapter 4 concerned idealism, we will not spend a lot of time discussing it in the present chapter. The main thing to note here about idealism as a theory of perception is its main similarities and differences with the other theories, especially with indirect realism. Idealism is similar to indirect realism in that both deny the direct perception of mind-independent objects. Idealism is different from indirect realism (and the other theories discussed here) in denying that there are any mind-independent objects.

11.22   *Intentionalism (a version of direct realism)*   Intentionalism is so called because it views perceptual states as akin to other intentional states, that is, states that exhibit *intentionality* or *aboutness* (a central topic to be taken up in chapter 13). A core example of an intentional state is a belief. Beliefs can be either true or false. Intentionalism holds that both illusory states and accurate perceptions are the same sort of state, a certain kind of intentional state (though not necessarily a kind of belief). According to intentionalism, the main difference between an illusory state and an accurate perception is that one is false and the other is true.

11.23   One commonality between intentionalism and indirect realism is that both explain perception partially in terms of mental representations that represent a mind-independent object. The key difference between intentionalism and indirect realism is that it is not a requirement on intentionalism that this mental representation itself be something that you are aware of while perceiving.

Recall that one of the complaints raised against indirect realism was that 11.24
it seemed to lead to external world skepticism. A similar complaint arises
against intentionalism.

Disjunctivism (another version of direct realism)   At the heart of disjunctiv- 11.25
ism is its denial that there is any deep commonality between accurate
perceptions and illusory states. This denial serves to block one of the
key premises in the argument from illusion, a premise concerning an
alleged similarity between perceptual and illusory states. The indirect realist
affirms such a similarity and posits that what is similar between the two
cases is that both involve a direct awareness of a mind-dependent entity.
Disjunctivism denies such a similarity. Disjunctivism is named after a
disjunction—an either–or statement. The central disjunction that defines
disjunctivism is an either–or statement concerning the sorts of mental state
that may be regarded as subjectively indistinguishable and perception-like.
Such a state is *either* an accurate perception *or* an illusory state. The dis-
junctivist denies that there must be any deeper similarity between these
subjectively indistinguishable and disjunctively characterized states.

Mental Imagery

The previous section dealt with comparisons between accurate perceptions 11.26
and perception-like illusory states such as hallucinations, dreams, and illusions properly so called. In this section we will discuss philosophical problems that have arisen around a distinct class of perception-like states—mental
images.

Mental imagery encompasses a range of various phenomena. Let's focus 11.27
first on *visual* mental imagery. One such example is an eyes-closed imagining of a fanciful scene. For example, close your eyes and imagine a giraffe
jumping on a trampoline. Another kind of visual mental imagery is an
eyes-opened seeing of faces in the clouds or in patterns of wood grain. This
latter type of phenomenon is known as *pareidolia*.

Examples of visual mental imagery include the sorts of mental phenom- 11.28
ena we might describe as "picturing something in the head" or "examining
something with the mind's eye." The term "mental imagery" thus seems
especially apt for states that are visual in nature. However, there are also
cases of mental imagery associated with sensory modalities besides vision.
Examples include cases in which one imagines a sound or an odor. Nonvisual

cases of imagery, then, include cases such as olfactory imagery, auditory imagery, and so on.

11.29   There are several philosophical problems that arise in connection with mental imagery. One philosophical issue concerns the relations between mental images and such mental states as precepts and thoughts. One set of relations discussed are relations of similarity and difference. How similar, for instance, are imagery and perception? How similar are mental images and thoughts? Another set of relations include relations of origination. Do thoughts *originate* from the senses via a process of imagery formation? Another question that has intrigued philosophers is the question of how image-like or picture-like mental images really are. Actual pictures, such as photographs, resemble what they picture. Are mental images picture-like in this way? Does your mental image of a dog resemble a dog? Let's take a closer look at some of these philosophical questions concerning mental imagery.

How similar are mental images to other mental states?

11.30   There are two kinds of mental state that philosophers have been especially interested in comparing to mental images—percepts and thoughts. Let us first examine the comparisons between images and percepts. On one view percepts and mental images are highly similar and differ in only a few respects. One of the main differences cited is that whereas a perception of a cat needs to be caused by an actual nearby cat, a mental image of a cat does not need to be similarly caused. Even if it is true that I may have to have some *past* causal contact with cats to be able to form a mental image of one *now*, I can still imagine a cat *now* even if no actual cat is currently in view.

11.31   Another contrast between images and percepts is that, for instance, images of cats and not percepts of cats can be called to mind at will. If there's no cat nearby, I cannot simply decide to *see* one, but I can decide to *imagine* one.

11.32   Yet another contrast that some philosophers have cited in differentiating mental images and percepts is that percepts are more clear or vivid than mental images. A mental image of a pain seems nowhere near as intense, vivid, or clear as an actual pain. When one imagines seeing a red rose, or biting a wedge of lemon, the image seems not as lively as the percept you have when actually seeing the redness of a real rose, or tasting the zippy tang of actual lemon juice in your mouth.

It should be noted that these claims about the distinction between per- 11.33
cepts and mental images are not entirely uncontroversial. Plausibly, there
are counterexamples to the generalizations made above. For example, some
mental images seem to be both highly vivid and not under the direct
control of the will. One such example occurs when a person has a very
strong image that they just can't get out of their head.

Is mental imagery the basis for mental states such as thoughts?

One especially central and important class of mental states is thoughts, 11.34
examples of which include states of thinking, judging, and believing. One
view about the relation between imagery and thought, especially prevalent
among empiricists such as Berkeley and Hume, is that sensory imagery is
the basis for thought. This imagery theory of thought fits nicely with the
empiricist view that there is nothing in the mind that isn't first in the senses.
According to the empiricist view of the origination of thoughts, the primary
kind of mental state is the sensory impression—the sort of state you are in
when you see a red rose or feel a cold bucket of water. After you undergo
such a sensory episode, you can still call to mind faint, less vivid copies of
the sensory impressions. These faint copies are ideas or images.

These ideas can be combined to form new and complex ideas. So, for 11.35
example, after having seen horses and horns, one is in a position to combine
the relevant simple ideas to form the complex idea of a horned horse—a
unicorn. On this empiricist view of the operation of the mind, sensory
impressions are the original basis for other mental states, and when copies
of impressions—images—are reignited in the mind, these images serve as
the basis for thought. So, when you think that there is a triangular object
in front of you or believe that you left the stove on at home, such mental
states are really a form of mental imagery, images of triangles, stoves, etc.

To what degree, if any, is mental imagery genuinely imagistic or picture-like?

A key component of many philosophers' views on mental imagery— 11.36
including the views that we just attributed to certain empiricists—is the
view that mental images are literally a kind of image or picture. The crucial
part of claiming that something is literally a picture is that it resembles the
things that it pictures. To illustrate, consider a drawing or a photograph of
a blue triangle. In a typical instance, a picture of a blue triangle will itself

have a blue triangle in it. Thus, the picture resembles the thing pictured. A picture that contained only a red circle would be a poor picture of a blue triangle.

11.37   Contrast this way that pictures represent with the way linguistic items such as written and spoken words and sentences represent. The word "green" doesn't have to be printed in green ink in order to represent the color that it does. And even though the word "microscopic" is larger than the word "big," that doesn't stop it from representing very small things.

11.38   We can summarize these remarks by saying that pictures represent things in large part by resembling them. In contrast, other representations, especially linguistic symbols, need not resemble that which they represent.

11.39   The empiricists that we mentioned earlier held that ideas—mental images—were literally image-like in that they resembled what they represented. On this view, an idea resembles what it is an idea of. According to Berkeley, an idea of a triangle had to itself be triangular. Being itself triangular, and representing by way of resemblance, it could only represent the triangles that it resembled. So, an equilateral triangular idea was ill suited to represent triangles such as right-angled triangles that are not equilateral.

11.40   Many philosophers have come to be quite skeptical of the idea that mental images represent by resemblance, especially if imagery is supposed to serve as the basis for thoughts. It seems clear that we can have negative thoughts, such as the thought that there aren't any cats in the room. It also seems clear that we can have abstract thoughts, such as a thought about triangles in general that isn't about any specific or particular triangle. However, pictorial representations seem ill suited for representing negative and abstract subject matter. It is totally obscure, for instance, what would serve as a picture of there being no cats in the room as opposed to a picture of there being no dogs in the room. A picture of an empty room does not seem to determinately represent that there are no *cats* in the room. In contrast, it seems quite clear that such a thing can be determinately represented by a linguistic representation, such as the sentence "there are no cats in the room."

11.41   Yet another problem for the proposal that images serve as the basis of thought is a problem raised by Descartes. While we can grasp in thought the difference between a polygon with a million sides and a polygon with a million-plus-one sides, we can no more imagine the difference than perceive the difference. If we were to be perceptually presented with the two polygons, there wouldn't be a perceptible difference. In fact, they may not be perceptibly distinguishable from circles. Similarly, mental images of the two polygons would not be distinguishable either.

Besides being skeptical about whether resemblance-based representa- 11.42 tions can serve as the basis for thought, philosophers have also been skeptical about whether mental images themselves, regardless of whether they are the basis for thought, are genuinely pictorial. In fact, there is quite a bit of controversy between groups of philosophers and also between groups of scientists about whether mental images resemble their objects.

One powerful consideration in favor of the resemblance view comes 11.43 from experiments concerning "mental rotation." One kind of "mental rotation" experiment would be one in which a subject is shown a pair of images and asked to indicate whether the one on the left is the same as the one on the right. Sometimes the two images are the same except that one is rotated some amount, perhaps 90 degrees or 180 degrees. In measurements of the reaction times of the subjects, experimenters discovered that the further the one image must be "mentally rotated" to match the other, the longer the reaction time in giving an answer. Some philosophers and scientists have argued that such experimental results help show that mental images really do resemble the things that they are images of.

One kind of consideration *against* the resemblance view and in favor of 11.44 a more linguistic *description theory* of mental images concerns the *cognitive penetrability* of mental images. What it means for a mental state or process to be "cognitively penetrable" is that it is influenced by *cognitive* states such as beliefs or thoughts (as opposed to more sensory states such as sensations). In some mental manipulation experiments, the reaction times can vary depending on what *verbal* information subjects are given. An example of such verbal information is telling the subjects to imagine that the figures are 50 *inches* apart versus 50 *feet*. Since the verbal information and subsequent beliefs or thoughts seem to "cognitively penetrate" the mental imagery, this has been taken by some to suggest that mental images are more language-like than picture-like.

Emotion

Emotions are perhaps the most familiar of our mental states. They include 11.45 states of fear, joy, anger, and disgust. Emotions are also perhaps the most personally important of our mental states. They constitute our main motivators and the main sources of value and worthiness in our lives. We seek out certain activities, things, and people because of the joy that they bring us. And we avoid others because of the anxiety or anger that they would lead to. Emotions play a central role in the ways that we rank our preferences and life choices. They also play central roles in social cohesiveness and our sense of morality.

11.46   Despite the central and important roles that emotions play in our lives, emotions are sometimes seen as obstacles, especially obstacles to rationality. It is often said that we should avoid letting our minds be clouded by fear or anger and that we shouldn't let our passions or emotions "take control" of us. However, it is difficult to see how a life devoid of emotion would be a life worth living.

11.47   Issues of special interest to philosophers of mind concerning emotions are questions concerning (1) what it is that distinguishes emotions from other mental states and (2) what it is that distinguishes different emotions from one another. Supplying a satisfactory account of emotions, an account that answers these two questions, has turned out to be quite difficult. Some philosophers even doubt that there will ever be a satisfactory unifying account of emotions. However, we will here mention a few basic ideas that philosophers have proposed about these topics.

What distinguishes emotions from other mental states?

11.48   One proposal is that emotions are distinctive in the way they are so closely associated with certain bodily states. Whereas merely having a belief is not closely associated with any particular kind of bodily state, emotions such as fear and anger are associated with increases in heart rate and perspiration. Also, many emotions have characteristic kinds of facial expression, as with happiness and smiling, or with sadness and frowning. One early and particularly strong version of this bodily account of emotional states is the James-Lange theory (after William James and Carl Lange), which states that emotion is simply the awareness of certain bodily changes. On such a theory, anger is simply the perception of one's increased heart rate, clenched fists, etc. One finding that helped to undermine this theory is that experimental subjects injected with the stimulant epinephrine would report feeling either euphoric or angry depending on what sorts of actions an actor in the room was performing. This suggests that the cognitive content of the different beliefs gained in the different scenarios contributed to what emotion was felt. Thus, the suggestion seems to be that an emotion such as anger can't simply be the awareness of stimulation or arousal in bodily systems.

What distinguishes different emotions from each other?

There are many dimensions along which emotions may be differentiated 11.49
from one another. Three of the main dimensions that have been of interest
to philosophers are (1) intentionality, (2) intensity, and (3) valence.

The intentionality of emotion has to do with what the emotion is about 11.50
or directed at. Many, if not all, emotions have *intentional content*. So, for
example, in being afraid of dogs or angry that your wallet was stolen, the
content in question concerns dogs or your wallet being stolen. The proposal
that all emotions have intentional content is somewhat controversial. Free-
floating anxiety or a general depressed feeling may not be about anything
at all. Alternately, maybe they are about everything! Anyway, perhaps
one way in which intentionality may serve to differentiate emotions
from one another is that some emotions need to be about certain sorts of
things while other emotions need not be about anything at all. A state of
anger, or more specifically, a feeling of outrage or indignation is usually, if
not always, about people. While one may be disappointed that it is raining,
it is barely intelligible that one would be morally outraged or resentful that
it is raining.

The intensity of emotion serves to contrast emotions such as rage and 11.51
irritation from one another. Intensity also serves to help distinguish amusement and ecstasy.

The valence of emotion serves to contrast emotions in terms of whether 11.52
they are positive or negative. There is a very clear and intuitive sense in
which fear, anger, and disgust have a negative emotional valence in opposition to joy and amusement, which have a positive emotional valence.

The difficulties in giving a unified account of the emotions

One hypothesis about emotions is that they comprise a *natural kind* and, 11.53
as such, there is some, perhaps complex, characterization of what makes
them all hang together as one sort of thing. A contrary hypothesis is that
emotions do not hang together as a natural kind and it is instead a somewhat artificial way of classifying mental states to label some as emotions
and others as not.

One issue that is germane to the question of the naturalness of classifying 11.54
certain mental states as emotions hinges on whether emotions are culturally universal. Some researchers have proposed that at least some emotions
are present in all cultures and are associated with expressions that are
recognizable across cultures. Examples of such emotions include fear,

happiness, sadness, disgust, surprise, and anger. Other emotions may perhaps not be culturally universal. The German word "Schadenfreude" is not directly translatable into English, at least, there's no single word in English that seems synonymous. (A rough translation, however, would be something like "the joy taken in the misfortune of others.") Perhaps this is an example of a culturally specific emotion. If there are certain emotions that are culturally specific, then this might cast doubt on whether "emotion" is a natural (as opposed to artificial or culturally relative) way of classifying mental states.

11.55   Another obstacle to a unified account of emotions concerns the variations in the intentional contents across emotional states, variations even in whether a given state *has* intentional content. Given that some emotions may lack intentional content—free-floating anxiety may be one such example—perhaps having intentional content is not part of what unifies the emotions as a kind. Also, the lack of content of some emotions suggests that perhaps the ones we think of as having content are really cases in which the content is the content of another mental state, perhaps a judgment. So, for instance, in being angry that someone stole your wallet, perhaps the intentional content "someone stole my wallet" is not a content of the anger itself, but the content of a judgment that accompanies the anger.

Conclusion

11.56   Much discussion in philosophy of mind centers on the mental phenomena of thoughts and sensations. However, our mental lives seem to contain much more than these states. Foremost among these other sorts of states are emotions—the mental states that make life worth living. However, like perception and imagination, emotion is especially difficult to understand, and many philosophers would agree what we are still in the very early days of our voyage toward an adequate theoretical understanding of such phenomena.

Annotated Bibliography

Adelson, Edward (2012) *Edward Adelson's Illusion Pages*, full text available at http://web.mit.edu/persci/people/adelson/illusions_demos.html, accessed February 22, 2013. A fun collection of visual illusions.

Crane, Tim (2011) "The Problem of Perception," in Edward Zalta (ed.), *The Stanford Encyclopedia of Philosophy*, full text available at http://plato.stanford.edu/archives/spr2011/entries/perception-problem/, accessed February 22, 2013. Excellent overview of the philosophical problem of what the objects of perception are and what the nature of the perceiving relation is.

Descartes, René (1641) *Meditations on First Philosophy*, full text available at http://www.earlymoderntexts.com/de.html, accessed February 22, 2013. Descartes is careful to distinguish imagining from conceiving. See especially his discussion in the second meditation.

de Sousa, Ronald (2010) "Emotion," in Edward Zalta (ed.), *The Stanford Encyclopedia of Philosophy*, full text available at http://plato.stanford.edu/archives/spr2010/entries/emotion/, accessed February 22, 2013. Thorough overview of a difficult topic.

Hume, David (1748) *An Enquiry Concerning Human Understanding*, full text available at http://www.earlymoderntexts.com/he.html, accessed February 22, 2013. For Hume's account of how ideas are faint copies of sensory impressions, see sections 2 and 3.

Thomas, Nigel (2009) "Mental Imagery," in Edward Zalta (ed.), *The Stanford Encyclopedia of Philosophy*, full text available at http://plato.stanford.edu/archives/win2009/entries/mental-imagery/, accessed February 22, 2013. The imagery debates exist at an interesting intersection of philosophy and cognitive science and are well covered in this article.

12

THE WILL
WILLPOWER AND FREEDOM

The Problem of Free Will and Determinism

Debates over free will are among the most vexing debates in philosophy. 12.1
Here's the central question: Is the existence of free will compatible with
determinism—the thesis that every event, including every human action, is
determined, in the sense of being *pre*determined?

Think of some choice that strikes you as chosen *freely*. Suppose, for 12.2
example, that a person is presented with a choice of two different flavors
of ice cream for dessert—chocolate and vanilla. Suppose that this person
has enjoyed each flavor in the past, but tonight they decide to order two
scoops of vanilla. Now, with this ice cream scenario in mind, let's do a
couple of thought experiments.

Thought experiment #1: Let us suppose that this person's brain is under the
   control of a mind-influencing ray operated by some evil scientist. The
   scientist causes the person to utter the following words to a waiter at a
   restaurant: "Please give me two scoops of vanilla ice cream." Suppose
   further that the way the scientist causes the person to utter these words
   is by causing the person to *prefer* vanilla over chocolate at that moment.
   Now, here's the crucial question of the thought experiment: Is the person
   who is under the control of the evil scientist choosing vanilla of their
   own free will?
Thought experiment #2: This second thought experiment is a variation of
   the first. Let us remove the evil scientist and instead have all of the mental

---

This Is Philosophy of Mind: An Introduction, First Edition. Pete Mandik.
© 2014 John Wiley & Sons, Inc. Published 2014 by John Wiley & Sons, Inc.

and physical states of the person ordering ice cream fully predetermined by the decisions of actual ancient Greek gods. Suppose that Zeus and his fellow gods are really real and have made it so that our ice cream ordering subject was fated (since the beginning of time!) to order vanilla ice cream on this particular day. Again, ask yourself the crucial question: Is the person choosing vanilla of their own free will?

12.3   Many people who contemplate such thought experiments are inclined to answer "no" to the crucial questions posed. Perhaps you are one such person. But let us now consider a third thought experiment.

Thought experiment #3: This third thought experiment is a variation of the second, but with one major difference. Instead of the person's mental states and actions being fated by the gods, their mental states and actions are predetermined because of the laws of physics. Suppose that physicalism is true and that everything is physical. Suppose further, as we discussed in chapter 9, that that every caused event has a physical cause. Again, ask yourself the crucial question: Is the person choosing vanilla of their own free will?

12.4   Some people who contemplate this third thought experiment will answer "no" to the key question. They hold that the kind of *determinism* described is incompatible with free will. They hold a position known, for obvious reasons, as *incompatibilism*. Other people who contemplate this third thought experiment will answer "yes." Such people see no problem in supposing both that determinism is true and that free will exists. They hold a position known as *compatibilism*.

12.5   The philosophical debate between compatibilists and incompatibilists is especially pressing because of the way it connects with the notion of *moral responsibility*. The idea that people can be morally responsible for their actions plays a central role in our practical, ethical, and legal deliberations. And, arguably, whether someone is morally responsible for something seems to depend on whether they chose that thing of their free will.

12.6   Consider a case in which someone causes the death of a human being. Judgments about whether the killer deserves a punishment, and how severe the punishment should be, depend largely on judgments about whether they *freely chose* to kill. The killer may receive a less severe punishment or no punishment at all if it's discovered that their actions were compelled. Perhaps the killing was compelled either by circumstances, such as a gun to their head, or by internal factors, such as a brain tumor or chemical imbalance. According to many thinkers, free will is necessary for moral responsibility. However, as we've already glimpsed in the three thought experiments above, the question of whether any one has free will is arguably threatened by the proposition that their actions are determined in the sense of being *predetermined*. Further, there are powerful arguments in favor of the view that every event is determined in such a way.

Sources of Determinism

General remarks

There are two key components of the idea of determinism. The first is the 12.7 notion of one thing making another thing happen. A typical example involves two events related as cause and effect. The idea of causes coming before effects is closely related to conceptions of determination as *predetermination*. The second key component of determinism is the idea that, for any event that happens, it had to happen and could not have been otherwise.

   The two components of determinism are not wholly independent of 12.8 each other. If it is indeed the case that one event *made* another happen, then it would seem to follow that given the first event, the second event *had* to happen and could not have been otherwise. Consider, for argument's sake, the following contrary supposition: Suppose event $e1$ happens, and even though $e2^a$ happens next, it was still entirely possible that some other event, $e2^b$ had happened instead. It seems clear, then, that in such a case, $e1$ didn't *make* $e2^a$ happen. Perhaps $e2^a$ happened after $e1$ as a matter of random chance. Or perhaps what really made $e2^a$ happen was not $e1$ by itself but instead $e1$ in conjunction with some other event. To sum up, then, if an early event makes a later event happen, then, given the first event, the second event had to happen and could not have been otherwise. Thus, arguably, the two key ideas of determinism are not wholly independent of each other.

   Despite this dependence between the two components of determinism, 12.9 the two components figure in separate conflicts between compatibilists and incompatibilists. The component that has to do with earlier events determining later events arguably conflicts with conceptions of free will in which the agent is the ultimate source of their actions. The component that has to do with happenings that "could not have been otherwise" arguably con-flicts with conceptions of free will that require free agents to able to do or choose otherwise.

12.10 In the rest of this section we will examine five lines of thought in favor of determinism. These five lines of thought mostly agree on their conclusions. They mainly differ on the kinds of reasoning that lead to their deterministic conclusions. The five lines of thought can be sorted into two groups, groups that differ about how many events are determined. The first group concerns *global* determinism, the view that *all* events are determined. The second group concerns *local* determinism, the view that some restricted class of events is determined. In particular, the local determinisms we will examine focus on those events that can be classified as human actions. Global deter-minisms include physical determinism, theological determinism, and logical determinism. Local determinisms include ethical determinism and psychological determinism. Let's look at these five lines of deterministic thought in a bit more detail.

Physical determinism

12.11 The thesis of physical (or *causal* or *nomological*) determinism fits very closely with the kinds of physicalism that we studied in previous chapters, especially the physicalism of chapter 6. If we think of physicalism as the view that everything is either identical to or determined by arrangements of physical particles, and add to it the idea that every event is caused in a way that is fully governed by the laws of physics, then we are very close to the thesis of physical determinism.

12.12   To get a further grasp on the thesis of physical determinism, consider the following way of looking at the unfolding of events in the universe since its very beginning during the Big Bang. Consider the total state of the universe at the present moment. Everything that is happening at the present moment is the causal consequence of what was happening at a previous moment. We can sum this up by saying that the global state of the universe at time t is fully caused or fully causally determined by the global state of the universe at time t-minus-1. One way of summing up the key idea of physical determinism is by saying that any given state of the universe is determined by the previous state of the universe plus the natural laws. Another way of summing up this key idea is to say that every event is determined by a previous event plus the laws of nature.

Most of the empirical support for physical determinism comes from the 12.13 physical sciences and thus makes it a good fit with physicalism. However, strictly speaking physicalism neither entails nor is entailed by physical determinism. It is possible to embrace physicalism (the view that everything is physical) while also embracing indeterminism (the view that some events are not determined by prior events and the natural laws). It is also possible to embrace dualism while also holding that mental events are fully determined by previous events and special laws governing the mental.

Physical determinism is the variety of determinism that we will mostly 12.14 be concerned with in the present chapter. However, before leaving this section, let's take a brief look at the other kinds of determinism.

Theological determinism

According to many who believe in the existence of God, God is both the 12.15 creator of everything and omniscient (all knowing). An omniscient creator knows every fact. One assumption about what it means to be the creator is that God was present at the beginning of the universe. One assumption about what it means to know every fact is that even facts pertaining to the future are known. If God didn't know every fact about the future, then there would be at least one fact that he didn't know—he would not be omniscient. For any future event, then, it seems that there is only one way for it to turn out. This includes events concerning human action. If you turn left instead of right while walking in the park, God knew at the beginning of time that you were going to turn left instead of right. If you had turned right instead of left, this would have contradicted God's prior belief about what you were going to do. Given, then, that God knew billions of years ago what you are going to do at any given moment, then at each moment, there's only one thing you *can* do. For each thing that you do, you could not have done otherwise, for to do so would contradict God's perfect knowledge of the future.

Logical determinism

Logical determinism arises out of a puzzle discussed by Aristotle in chapter 12.16 9 of his *De Interpretatione*. Consider the sentence "There will be a sea battle tomorrow." According to many logicians and philosophers, it is a law of logic that every sentence is either true or false, and not both (and not neither). This would seem to entail, then, that the sentence "There will be a sea battle tomorrow" is either true right now or false right now. If it is true right now, then there must be a sea battle tomorrow. If it is false right now, then there must not be a sea battle tomorrow. But whatever happens tomorrow, it cannot contradict whatever the truth value of the sentence is today. If there is a sea battle tomorrow, then, when it happens, it will be true that it can't have been otherwise. Similarly, if there *isn't* a sea battle tomorrow, then it will be true that there couldn't have been a sea battle then.

Ethical determinism

12.17   The ancient Greek philosophers Socrates and Plato held that a person always chooses what they *think of* as good. This doesn't mean that people always choose what *actually is* good, since there is room for a difference between thinking that something is good and its actually being good. Perhaps the thing they think of as good really isn't good. Nonetheless, according to Socrates and Plato, whatever a person chooses is something that the person thinks of as good. If they didn't think it was good, then why did they choose it? Doesn't the mere fact that they choose it mean that they want it? And is there really any difference between wanting a thing and thinking of that thing that it is good? On this view, then, a person's choices are determined by what they think. And they are thus determined. Given what they think, there's only one thing that they'll choose—they won't choose otherwise. A person's choices are thus determined by their prior psychological states—their thoughts about what is good.

Psychological determinism

12.18   Psychological determinism is similar in an important respect to ethical determinism. Psychological determinism is the view that a person always chooses what they most desire. Like ethical determinism, a person's choice is determined by their prior mental state. Psychological determinism differs from ethical determinism if it turns out that there is a difference between desiring something and thinking that it is good.

12.19   We've reviewed these five kinds of deterministic thought to convey the idea that there are many ways to arrive at deterministic conclusions. Of course, each of these arguments have been criticized in various ways by various philosophers. However, coming up with a coherent argument against *all* forms of determinism is a highly difficult task. Determinism will not go away quietly!

We will now shift our attention to the question of the nature of free will, and whether it is the sort of thing that is compatible with determinism. 12.20

Compatibilism

Compatibilists hold that the existence of free will is compatible with determinism. (For simplicity's sake, we will primarily have physical determinism in mind for the ensuing discussion.) Recall the two key aspects of determinism that incompatibilists allege to be threats to the existence of free will. (1) According to determinism, your preferences and actions are determined by events that occur prior to them, including events that occurred prior to your birth. (2) Given the current state of the universe and the natural laws, there is only one possible future state of the universe, and thus, for whatever you actually do, it is false that you could have done otherwise. Compatibilists disagree with incompatibilists about whether (1) and (2) are threats to free will. 12.21

One line of thought in favor of compatibilism originates with the philosopher Harry Frankfurt. Frankfurt's argument can be seen as aiming to show the compatibility of free will and (2). According to Frankfurt's line of thought, it is not a requirement of having free will that one could have done otherwise. 12.22

Central to Frankfurt's argument are certain hypothetical scenarios or thought experiments, hypothetical scenarios that have come to be called "Frankfurt cases." Frankfurt cases are designed to show that having free will does not require that one be able to do otherwise. 12.23

To get a feel for Frankfurt cases, let us imagine a future in which brain-control technology has been perfected. In this future, certain people have access to microchips that can be implanted in other people's brains. These brain implants allow one person to remotely control another. Now imagine that there are two roommates, Alicia and Beyoncé, who have agreed to take turns vacuuming their carpets on alternate Mondays. The upcoming Monday, it will be Beyoncé's turn to vacuum, but Alicia is worried that Beyoncé won't do it. Alicia is expecting some very special guests and she wants the apartment to be very clean when they arrive. Alicia expects to be very busy doing other things in preparation for the guests, and will not be able (or willing) to do the vacuuming herself. 12.24

12.25   While Beyoncé is sleeping, Alicia implants a brain-controlling microchip into Beyoncé's brain. The way that this chip is designed to work is to monitor Beyoncé's brain, checking to see whether Beyoncé decides to vacuum on the upcoming Monday. If Beyoncé does not decide to vacuum, then the chip will switch from its monitoring mode to its controlling mode and *make* Beyoncé decide to vacuum. If, however, Beyoncé does decide to do the vacuuming, then the chip will remain in its monitoring mode and not do anything that effects Beyoncé's decisions or actions.

12.26   Suppose that Monday rolls around and Beyoncé does decide to do the vacuuming. She decides on her own, without any intervention from the chip. It seems intuitively plausible both that Beyoncé *could not have done otherwise* and that she is nonetheless *morally responsible* for the completed vacuuming. She could not have done otherwise because the microchip would have prevented her from doing otherwise. And she's morally responsible for doing the vacuuming, since her decision to do it and thus uphold her end of the agreement both resulted in a clean carpet and is morally praiseworthy.

12.27   On the assumption that free will is a requirement of moral responsibility, the following seems to be true of Beyoncé: Since Beyoncé was morally responsible for the resulting vacuuming, Beyoncé decided of her own free will to do the vacuuming. Her free will is thus compatible with her not having been able to do otherwise. The moral that many compatibilists draw from Frankfurt cases is this: Free will, at least the kind that is required for moral responsibility, is compatible with determinism.

Incompatibilism

12.28   Suppose, at least for a moment, that we define compatibilism as the view that affirms both (1) the existence of free will and (2) the truth of determinism. Given such a definition, there are thus three ways of denying compatibilism and affirming incompatibilism. The first way is to embrace a form of incompatibilism known as *hard determinism*, the view that denies the existence of free will and affirms the truth of determinism. The second way is to embrace a form of incompatibilism known as *libertarianism*, the view free will exists and that determinism is false. The third way denies both that free will exists and that determinism is true. This third way is not usually what people have in mind when they discuss incompatibilism, and there is not a widely agreed upon name for it.

In this chapter we will examine two arguments for incompatibilism. The 12.29
first is the *origination argument*. The second is the *consequence argument*.
The arguments don't take a stand on whether free will exists. Neither do
they take a stand on whether determinism is true. The point of these arguments is to support a conditional, an "if–then," statement. The aim of these
arguments is to show that *if* determinism is true, *then* free will does not
exist. A logically equivalent aim is to show that *if* free will does exist, *then*
determinism is false.

These two arguments can be distinguished in terms of two different 12.30
aspects of what incompatibilists think free will consists in. The first aspect
of incompatibilist free will is the idea of the ultimate source of free choice
residing in a person. On this conception, a person or some mental act of a
person is the true and ultimate source of his or her free actions. This aspect
of incompatibilist free will plays a key role in the origination argument.

The second aspect of incompatibilist free will is the idea that in having 12.31
free will one has genuine alternate possibilities to choose from. This is
the idea that there are genuine ways things *could* have been. These are possible events that would have been actual if only the person had chosen
them. In considering some future course of action there are genuine multiple alternate futures that one has some power to bring into actuality. This
aspect of incompatibilist free will plays a key role in the consequence
argument.

The origination or causal chain argument

The origination argument (or causal chain argument) hinges on the aspect 12.32
of determinism that involves past events determining later events. This
aspect of determinism conflicts with a certain conception of what free will
involves, namely that if one were to have free will then one would be the
ultimate source of the decisions that one makes.

How does the idea of past events determining later events conflict with 12.33
one's being the ultimate source of one's decisions? The key here is best seen
by contemplating events that happened before you make your decisions. If
it is true that each event that happens is determined by some prior event,
then this applies as well to each of your decisions, since each of them is an
event, a thing that happens. If determinism is true, then a decision of yours
is a link in a causal chain. Prior links make the decisions happen and the
decisions themselves make your actions happen. But if this causal chain
picture of determinism is correct, then neither you nor things happening

inside of you are the *ultimate* sources of your decisions, choices, and actions. Whatever the ultimate source is, it is something that happened prior to your decisions. Perhaps the ultimate source is something happening an incredibly long time ago, like the formation of the physical universe during the Big Bang.

12.34   Assume that having free will requires being the ultimate source of your choices and actions. If determinism is true, then neither you nor any aspect of you is the ultimate source. Therefore, if determinism is true, then you don't have free will.

The consequence argument

12.35   At the heart of the consequence argument is a conflict over the nature of time. The conflict concerns, on the one hand, what time needs to be in order for free will to exist and, on the other hand, what it needs to be in order for determinism be true. One way to put these conflicting positions is to say that they conflict over whether the future is open in a way that the past is not.

12.36   Many people hold that there's a big difference between the past and the future. The past is set. It is something that we no longer have any control over. We no longer have any say in how it turned out. What's past is over and done and there's nothing that can be done about it now. In contrast, the future is open.

12.37   Suppose that you are deciding what clothes to wear for your big job interview tomorrow. The choices are open—you can wear your blue outfit or your red outfit. We can put this point in terms of possible futures. One future has you going to your job interview in blue, another future has you going to your interview in red. It is up to you to choose one or the other. At least, that's what you would think if you thought you had a certain kind of free will.

12.38   But now let us consider what the nature of the future would be if determinism is true. On the hypothesis of determinism, it looks like there are not multiple branches ahead of you for you to choose from. If, as determinism says, any given moment is made to happen by some previous moment in conjunction with the laws of nature, then the present moment (plus the laws) determines only a *single* future. On this view of determinism, it looks like the future is just as set or fixed as the past. Free will requires that the future be open. But determinism entails that the future is closed. Determinism looks to be incompatible with the existence of free will.

What Might Free Will Be, If There Were Any Such Thing?

Let us turn now to the question, "What might free will be, if there were any 12.39
such a thing?" One way we can approach this question is by first addressing
the question, "Freedom aside for the moment, what is the will?"

Freedom aside for the moment, what is the will?

While it is not wholly uncontroversial in philosophy whether there is such 12.40
a thing or aspect of mind that is worth calling "the will," we will not spend
much time examining the controversy over whether the will exists. Instead,
we will sketch a brief account that says some general things about what the
will might be if there is such a thing. That is, we'll give a quick sketch of
an answer to the question of what sort of thing or things the phrase "the
will" might refer to.

The will as willings: Mental events that are common to both intentional action 12.41
and trying to perform actions   On one view, the term "the will" serves to
pick out a certain kind of mental state or mental event. These are states or
events that we can call "willings" or "acts of will."

One way of understanding willings is by comparing and contrasting 12.42
them to sensations. If we think of sensory perception as the interface at
which the external world influences the mind, then sensations are the first
mental link in a causal chain leading from the external object to the mental
event of perceiving it. In contrast to perception, which is closely linked to
the inputs to the mind, action is closely linked to the outputs of the mind.
Intentional action can be thought of as the interface at which the mind
influences the external world. Willings, then, can be thought of as the last
mental link in a causal chain leading from a plan or desire to a bodily
movement or action.

Recall our discussion of perception in chapter 11. There we faced the 12.43
problem of illusion. Recall that one motive for postulating things such as
sense data or sensations was to account for an apparent commonality
between accurately perceiving an object and hallucinating it. On one
account of perception, what both situations have in common is the presence of a sense datum or sensation. An analogous kind of line of thought
can be used in favor of *willings*. Here, the apparent commonality arises

between, on the one hand, intentionally and successfully performing some action and, on the other hand, trying but failing due to no fault of one's own. To illustrate, compare (1) successfully and intentionally throwing a paper ball into a wastebasket and (2) trying to do so but failing because, at the last moment, your muscles gave out or a breeze through an opened window blew the ball off course. In comparing these two situations, we notice a mental or psychological commonality between the successful doing and the mere trying. These are willings or acts of will. In both the successful and the failed trying there is the willing. There is an act of will to toss the paper ball, an act of will that results in the ball actually getting into the basket in (1) but not in (2).

12.44   *The will as a source of power and weakness: Willpower, akrasia, and weakness of will*   Another way of thinking about the will (and this is consistent with the previous way of thinking about it) is that it is something that varies along a spectrum of power versus weakness. Such variation has to do with *willpower*. Low degrees of willpower are associated with weakness of will—what philosophers sometimes call *akrasia*.

12.45   The idea of weakness of will is a commonsense idea. Many of us have experienced difficulty in doing something that we thought of as the right or preferable thing to do. We want to do a thing, but fail due to some failure inside of us. One such example might be trying to resist highly tempting junk food while trying to stick to a new and healthier diet.

12.46   Despite seeming to be rooted in common sense, the idea that there is such a thing as weakness of will has raised various philosophical problems. There is no clear consensus on how to solve the problems. We will here give a quick sketch of the heart of the problem.

12.47   Imagine that George resolves to quit drinking alcohol. George has certain mental states pertaining to alcohol. George *believes* that alcohol is damaging to his liver and he *desires* to no longer drink things that are damaging to his liver. In short, George both believes that alcohol is to be avoided and desires to avoid it.

12.48   George's beliefs and desires constitute his *reasons* for action. On any given occasion in which George performs an intentional action, we cite such mental states as his beliefs and desires to *explain* his actions. We cite his reasons for acting in answering questions of the form "*Why* did George do that?"

12.49   Acting for reasons distinguishes intentional action from involuntary behavior. When George does something on purpose, it is something brought about by his beliefs and desires. When George behaves in an involuntary way, as when his leg reflexively jerks upon being hit on his knee, the explanation of the leg's jerk involves something other than beliefs and desires.

Suppose George is at a party and he refuses a beer offered to him. Why did he refuse the beer? He refused it because he believes that it would be bad for his liver, and he desires to avoid damaging his liver. Those are his reasons for the refusal. 12.50

Now consider a case that looks like George exhibiting weakness of will. Suppose that there is an occasion in which, despite believing that alcohol is to be avoided and desiring to avoid it, George "caves in" and has an alcoholic drink. Later at the party, he is again offered a beer. He says, "Well, I really shouldn't," but then goes and drinks it anyway. 12.51

Why did George do that? It looks like this is an occasion in which he acted despite what he believed and desired. George acted in a way that went against his "better reason" or "better judgment." Nonetheless, in taking the drink, he acts intentionally. It is not like the drinking of the beer was involuntary, as in reflexive movements or sleepwalking. 12.52

So, what's going on here? One sort of answer would be to say that we must have been mistaken about what George *really* desired. Maybe in that moment he actually did desire alcohol more than he desired to avoid it. A different sort of answer appeals to a diminishment of willpower, a temporary weakness of the will. On this view, George's desires (and beliefs) about alcohol remained constant, but there was a fluctuation in his resolve, his strength of will. 12.53

What might the freedom of the will consist in?

Let us return now to the question of the *freedom* of will. What would it mean for the will to have the sort of freedom that matters for moral responsibility, the sort of freedom at the heart of debates between compatibilists and incompatibilists? 12.54

It should come as no surprise by now that there is a lot of controversy about how to answer such a question. This is what much of the controversy between compatibilists and incompatibilists boils down to. Here we will present just two of the many models of what freedom of will consists in. The first is one that fits more closely with compatibilism, and the second fits more closely with incompatibilism. 12.55

12.56 *The hierarchy of desires model of freedom of will: A compatibilist account of free will* This model of free will originates with philosopher Harry Frankfurt. There are two key notions in the model. The first is a distinction between first order and higher order (second order, third order, etc.) mental states, especially mental states such as desires. The second key notion is that of a desire becoming a volition.

12.57   First, let us consider the relevant notion of *order*. A second order desire is a desire about a first order desire. So, what's a first order desire? It's a desire about something that itself isn't a desire. Suppose George desires a beer. This is a first order desire. Suppose, despite having a desire for beer, George desires to be the sort of person who doesn't desire beer. George has a second order desire, then—a desire to not desire beer.

12.58   Next, let us consider what it means for a desire to become a volition, or, in other words, for a desire to become one's will or a willing. One might have a desire, but for some reason or other, fail to act on it. One desires to own a blue coat, but all of the blue coats for sale are too expensive, and so one buys a red one. In this case, the desire did not become what one willed, it did not become a volition. But, if on the following day one lucked into some prize money, or the prices of blue coats came down, then the desire for a blue coat could become a volition.

12.59   Combining the idea of second order desires with the idea of volitions gives rise to the idea of second order volitions. On this model, having free will consists in having second order volitions. On some particular occasion in which a person acts, they acted freely if the action is in accordance with their second order volition. All of this is compatible with all of the states of the person being determined by some prior state of the universe plus the physical laws. Therefore, the resultant view is a compatibilist view.

12.60 *The ultimate origination model of freedom of will: An incompatibilist account of free will* On this model of free will, a person or their will must be the ultimate originator of their choices or actions—if the will is itself caused or determined, then it is not free. One version of the origination model of free will is the agent causation model. Central to this model is the idea of agent causation, a kind of causation distinct from event causation. Usually, we think of causation as a relation between events, as when a bomb's exploding causes a building to collapse. The event of the bomb exploding is the cause and the event of the building collapsing is the effect. In contrast to event causation, in agent causation, the cause of an event can be an agent, a person.

On the agent causation version of the ultimate origination model of free   12.61
will, freedom of the will requires a special kind of causation, one that is
not a relation between two events but instead between an agent and an
event. Many reject this model as incoherent, for it is quite difficult to see
how an agent himself or herself can be a cause. According to critics of the
idea of agent causation, when an agent is involved in causation, some
change of state or condition of the agent must be the cause, that is,
some event involving the agent and not simply the agent himself or herself
must be the cause. One of the main criticisms, then, of the agent causation
model of free will, is that the very idea of agent causation, which is supposed to be distinct from event causation, doesn't make any sense.

Conclusion

Perhaps more than any other aspect of the mind, the will is especially sig-   12.62
nificant in assessments of moral responsibility. How can someone be
morally responsible for an act unless they freely choose it? Despite this
commonsense connection between freedom and responsibility, there are
many severe challenges to the idea that free will exists. The main challenges
have to do with determinism. Some philosophers view the challenges as so
severe that they conclude that free will doesn't exist. Others remain optimistic about the prospects of a viable compatibilism whereby free will can
exist in a deterministic universe.

Annotated Bibliography

Dennett, Daniel (1984) *Elbow Room: The Varieties of Free Will Worth Wanting*
(Cambridge, MA: MIT Press). Dennett defends a version of compatibilism.
Frankfurt, Harry (1969) "Alternate Possibilities and Moral Responsibility," *Journal
of Philosophy*, 66, 829–839. Frankfurt argues against the view that being
morally responsible requires that one could have done otherwise.
Frankfurt, Harry (1971) "Freedom of the Will and the Concept of a Person," *Journal
of Philosophy*, 68(1), 5–20. Frankfurt spells out a compatibilist account of free
will in terms of higher order desires—desires about desires.
Hume, David (1748) *An Enquiry Concerning Human Understanding*, full text
available at http://www.earlymoderntexts.com/he.html, accessed February
11, 2013. See especially chapter 8, where Hume defends his version of
compatibilism.

Reid, Thomas (1788) *Essays on the Active Powers of Man*, full text available at http://www.earlymoderntexts.com/reac.html, accessed February 11, 2013. Reid defends agent causation. See especially his chapter 4.

Strawson, Galen (2003) "On Free Will," *Richmond Journal of Philosophy*, 4, full text available at http://www.bookofparagon.com/Robots/FreeWill.pdf, accessed February 11, 2013. A highly accessible discussion of the philosophy of free will.

Stroud, Sarah (2008) "Weakness of Will," in Edward Zalta (ed.), *The Stanford Encyclopedia of Philosophy*, full text available at http://plato.stanford.edu/archives/fall2008/entries/weakness-will/, accessed February 11, 2013. Nice overview of the philosophical difficulties involved with the idea of a lack of willpower.

Wegner, Daniel (2002) *The Illusion of Conscious Will* (Cambridge, MA: MIT Press). Wegner is one of several scientists defending the view that neuroscience shows that free will does not exist.

13

INTENTIONALITY AND MENTAL REPRESENTATION

Introducing Intentionality

Many mental states have what philosophers call "aboutness" or *intentional- ity*. The belief that the sky is blue is *about* the sky. It is a belief that is directed at the sky or at the sky's being blue. "Intentionality" used in this context is a technical, philosophical term, and should not be confused with the more commonsensical notion of doing something *intentionally*, in the sense of doing it on purpose. Despite this difference between the technical term and the commonsense term, they do have a common origin having to do with *pointing*—"index," as in "index finger," has a similar origin. The core idea of the aboutness or intentionality of mental states is that of their *directed- ness*. Intentionality is the directedness of a mental state toward its contents. 13.1

Intentionality is the source of many difficult problems in the philosophy of mind. One such problem has to do with the way in which intentionality seems both to be relational and to involve things that do not exist. What's the problem here? Plausibly, you can think about or have beliefs about things that do not exist. I might have the mistaken belief that there is a man upstairs singing a song when there is no one upstairs at all. If intentionality is relational, then it is tempting to say that my belief in this example is something that relates me to some other man—the one that I think is singing. However, if it turns out that no such man exists, then there is no one that my thought thereby relates me to. 13.2

Another puzzling aspect about intentionality concerns the way in which we can have mental states directed at things that are so far away that we 13.3

This Is Philosophy of Mind: An Introduction, First Edition. Pete Mandik.
© 2014 John Wiley & Sons, Inc. Published 2014 by John Wiley & Sons, Inc.

couldn't possibly have had any causal interaction with them. Suppose I believe that there exists at least one galaxy that has exactly one trillion stars in it (not more and not less). Suppose further that there is such a galaxy. That would seem to make my belief true. However, the galaxy might be so far away that no causal interaction can transpire between its current state and mine. All causation in the universe must be mediated by exchanges of energy, and energy cannot be moved at a rate that exceeds the speed of light. That galaxy, let us suppose, is so far away that it would take a billion years for light from it to reach me. Nonetheless, there seems to be some relation between my belief and the current state of that galaxy.

13.4   One puzzle about intentionality concerns how something so mysterious can be consistent with a naturalistic or scientific view of reality. For example, if some version of physicalism is the most scientifically respectable view of the mind, how can intentionality possibly exist? The project of *naturalizing intentionality* is the project of showing how the existence of intentionality is consistent with the understanding of reality we have via the natural sciences.

13.5   In this chapter, we will examine some attempts to construct a naturalistic account of intentionality. But first we will further explore the puzzling aspects of intentionality.

The Inconsistent Triad of Intentionality

13.6   The heart of what is so puzzling about intentionality can be formulated as an inconsistent triad of propositions concerning intentionality, existence, and relations. The three propositions are:

Proposition 1: We can think about things that do not exist.
Proposition 2: Thinking about something is a relation between the thinker and the thing thought about.
Proposition 3: There can only be a relation between two things if both of the things exist.

Each proposition in the triad seems plausible when considered in isolation. However, when we consider all three propositions in conjunction, it is hard to see how they are mutually consistent. It becomes clear that at least one of them must be false. But which one?

13.7   Let's take a closer look at each individual proposition and see what makes each one separately plausible.

Defending each individual proposition

Proposition 1: We can think about things that do not exist. Do you believe 13.8
that Rudolph the red-nosed reindeer, a flying reindeer with a glowing nose,
really exists? Do you believe in the real existence of Zeus, the father of the
gods of Olympus, who throws lightning bolts down to Earth? Like many
people you are likely to answer "no" to both questions. Also, like many
people, you understand both questions perfectly well. You can demonstrate
such understanding by answering the following question: In answering
"no" to each question, who are you denying the existence of? Here the
answers seem clear, you are denying the existence of Rudolph the red-nosed
reindeer in the first case, and denying the existence of Zeus, the father of
the gods of Olympus, in the second case. When you think that Zeus doesn't
exist, who are you thinking about? Again, the answer seems clear. You are
thinking about Zeus. And since Zeus doesn't exist, in thinking about Zeus
you are thinking about something that doesn't exist.

Proposition 2: Thinking about something is a relation between the thinker 13.9
and the thing thought about. Consider the height of the youngest person
you know. Chances are, you are taller than that person. Being taller than
someone is a relation. So is being older than a person. Part of what makes
being taller or being older a relation is that it involves two things, one of
which is taller or older than the other.

Is thinking about something a relation borne toward that thing? Think 13.10
about the piece of furniture that is nearest to you right now. This seems to
be a relation as much as being near that piece of furniture is a relation. The
case of thinking about the piece of furniture looks like it involves two
things—there is you, the thinker, and then there is the nearby piece of
furniture, the thing that you are thinking about.

Proposition 3. There can only be a relation between two things if both things 13.11
exist. One way to talk about relations, such as the relation of being taller
than something, is to use variables like x and y, or blank spaces, in the following manner: "x is taller than y," "_ is taller than _." Consider the relation,
being filled with a liquid, that holds between a coffee cup and the coffee
inside of it. We can call this the "'x is filled by y'-relation" or the "'_ is filled
by _'-relation." Suppose there is some coffee cup that has absolutely nothing
in it. Is it filled by something? Is there some quantity of liquid or gas that
fills it? If, as we have stipulated, there is nothing in it, then there is nothing
that exists that fills it. Another way of putting the point is to say that
there exists no y such that the coffee cup is filled by it. Another way of put
this is to say that the coffee cup, being absolutely empty, does not bear the

"_is filled by _"-relation to anything. The relation of being filled requires two things. When no filler exists the container contains nothing. If this sort of thing is true of relations generally, then we can sum up by saying that relations can only take place between things that exist.

Spelling out the inconsistency

13.12 To help spell out the inconsistency of the triad, we can select a pair of propositions from the triad, assume for purposes of discussion that each member of the pair is true, and see that the remaining member of the triad must therefore be false.

13.13 *If 1 and 2 are true then 3 is false.* Suppose that we can think about things that do not exist and that thinking about something is a relation borne to the thing thought about. This would seem to entail that there is at least one relation that can be borne to nonexistent things, namely the thinking-about relation. But this contradicts proposition 3, which says that relations can only be borne toward existing things.

13.14 *If 1 and 3 are true then 2 is false.* Suppose that we can think about things that do not exist and that relations can only be borne toward existing things. This would seem to entail that thinking about something is not a relation between a thinker and a thing thought about. But that would contradict proposition 2, which says that thinking about something is a kind of relation borne to that thing.

13.15 *If 2 and 3 are true then 1 is false.* Suppose that thinking about something is a relation borne to that thing and that there can only be relations between existing things. This would seem to entail, then, that we cannot think about things that do not exist, thus contradicting proposition 1.

Internalism versus Externalism

13.16 One of the key ideas involved in the inconsistent triad of intentionality is the idea that intentionality might be a sort of relation. One line of thought *against* the idea that intentionality is a relation is the thought that I might have all the same ideas as I do now even though my mind or brain is the only thing that exists. The idea that intentionality does *not* depend on relations that your mind or brain bears to items in the external world is the philosophical position *internalism*. In opposition is the position *externalism*.

One way to think about the debate between internalists and externalists 13.17 is in terms of *supervenience*. "Supervenience" is a technical term referring to a kind of dependence between properties. Many philosophers of mind hold that mental properties depend on physical properties and they state their claims about that dependence in terms of supervenience. They say that mental properties "supervene" on physical properties. One sort of supervenience claim says that two individuals cannot differ in their mental properties without differing in their physical properties and that a single individual cannot change his or her mental properties without changing his or her physical properties.

An individual has two kinds of physical properties. The first kind is those 13.18 physical properties that are intrinsic or *internal* to the individual. The second kind is those physical properties that involve relations to entities *external* to the individual. An example of the first kind is the property of having more than a billion neurons in your brain. An example of the second kind is the property of being six miles away from the nearest sample of uranium.

The debate between internalists and externalists in the philosophy 13.19 of mind is a debate over which of an individual's physical properties their mental properties supervene on. According to internalists, an individual's mental properties supervene on only the intrinsic physical properties of an individual. One version of internalism holds that if the number and arrangements of particles in two people's nervous systems were exactly similar, then their mental states would be exactly similar. Internalists hold that external differences between two individuals are strictly irrelevant to what mental properties they each have.

In contrast, externalists hold that individuals who have intrinsically 13.20 similar brains can nonetheless differ in their mental properties if there are certain differences in the relations that the individuals bear to their respective physical environments. Where internalists say that mental properties supervene on physical properties that are internal to an individual, externalists say that mental properties supervene on external as well as internal physical properties. Where internalists say that mental properties have a "narrow" supervenience base, externalists say that mental properties have a "wide" supervenience base.

One of the most discussed versions of the internalism versus external- 13.21 ism debate focuses on intentionality. The opponents disagree about the answer to the following question: Could two intrinsically similar brains nonetheless differ in what they are thinking about in virtue of being related to different environments? Externalists, unlike internalists, say "yes." Externalists, unlike internalists, say things like "intentionality just ain't in the head."

For externalism: The Twin Earth thought experiment

13.22 One famous argument for externalism originates with the philosopher Hilary Putnam and features his famous Twin Earth thought experiment. To conduct the thought experiment yourself, you need to imagine the following situations. First, consider a stage in the history of the planet Earth wherein humans had not yet developed an understanding of chemistry that was sophisticated enough for them to know that the chemical composition of water is two parts hydrogen to one part oxygen. These are people living before anyone had discovered that water is H_2O. Imagine also that these people use the English word "water" to say things like "I am very thirsty and would enjoy a glass of water." They use the word "water" to refer to a liquid that, unbeknownst to them, happens to be the chemical H_2O.

13.23   Consider one such person. Call him "Oscar." Plausibly, since Oscar's "water" utterances refer to what happens to be H_2O, and since such utterances are expressions of thoughts, the thoughts thereby expressed are thoughts about H_2O. Despite being ignorant of the chemical composition of water, Oscar ends up thinking about H_2O in thinking the thoughts he expresses with his "water" utterances.

13.24   For the next stage of the thought experiment, imagine a planet that is extremely physically similar to Oscar's Earth, a planet that we can call "Twin Earth." Twin Earth is populated by beings similar to the beings populating Earth, including a counterpart to Oscar who we can call Twin Oscar. Just like Oscar, Twin Oscar uses the word "water" to say things like "I am very thirsty and would enjoy a glass of water." The main difference between Earth and Twin Earth is the chemical composition of the clear liquid referred to as "water." Instead of being H_2O, Twin Water is a wholly distinct chemical that we, in conducting the thought experiment, can just call "XYZ." Now, just like Oscar, Twin Oscar lives in a society wholly ignorant of the chemical composition of the stuff that they refer to as "water." However, despite their ignorance, and in virtue of having grown up on Twin Earth, the Twin Earthlings' "water" utterances refer to what happens to be XYZ, and such utterances are expressions of thoughts about XYZ.

13.25   The externalistic conclusion of the Twin Earth thought experiment is that Oscar's and Twin Oscar's thoughts each have a *wide supervenience base*.

In virtue of having been raised in different environments—an H_2O environment and an XYZ environment, respectively—Oscar and Twin Oscar have thoughts with distinct intentional contents. Oscar and Twin Oscar are different mentally in virtue of their external physical differences.

Against externalism: Swampman and the brain in the vat

Not all philosophers of mind have been convinced by the Twin Earth argument. Many philosophers have been swayed by a very strong intuition in favor of internalism. This is the intuition that what matters for mentality is wholly contained within the body of a person, and that perhaps all that really matters physically for mentality are physical facts about the structure and functioning of the central nervous system. One way to probe such intuitions is by contemplating certain thought experiments. Here we will take a look at the thought experiment of swampman and the thought experiment of the brain in the vat.   13.26

Imagine that there is a swamp thousands of miles away from me and that in this swamp there is a log that gets struck by lightning. This results, by amazing coincidence, in a being that is molecule-for-molecule a perfect physical copy of me. Down to the last particle, it has a microscopic physical arrangement exactly similar to mine. This swampman is a being we can call, for the purposes of the thought experiment, Swamp Pete, although if you asked him his name, he would simply reply, "Pete." Why would he say that? Because he is exactly internally physically similar to me, and that is precisely what I would utter in response to such a question.   13.27

Many philosophers express their allegiance to internalism by urging that my swamp counterpart would have precisely the same mental properties that I have. If I think that ice cream tastes great, then so does Swamp Pete, even though he has never actually tasted any ice cream yet—he was just formed in the swamp a few seconds ago and has not yet come into contact with any ice cream.   13.28

Serving a purpose similar to the swampman thought experiment is the brain in a vat thought experiment. Many philosophers have a very strong intuition that, for all they know, they could very well just be a brain in a vat, a brain that is not in a real body with real sense organs, but is instead hooked up to a virtual reality computer that simulates an external world and body, thus fooling the brain. In extreme versions of the brain in a vat thought experiment, the brain and virtual reality computer first formed in a swamp moments ago by a lightning strike. For all you know, according   13.29

to this thought experiment, you are a brain in a vat that just formed swamp-style only moments ago. If you and the swamp-formed brain in a vat think all the same things—if you both have thoughts with all the same intentionality or intentional content—then internalism must be true.

13.30   One question that arises in connection with the internalism versus externalism debates is the question of content determination. How does a state of the brain or mind come to represent what it does? What determines its intentionality or content? Further, how can this content be determined in a way that is consistent with a physicalist or naturalist world view? It is to such questions that we now turn.

Theories of Content Determination

13.31 Some philosophers have held that intentionality is one of the main obstacles to physicalism. In other words, because mental states exhibit intentionality, mental states cannot be wholly physical or wholly reducible to the sorts of properties studied by natural sciences such as physics, chemistry, and biology.

13.32   Other philosophers have resisted such a conclusion and have striven to construct theories consistent with physicalism or naturalism of how mental states can have intentional content. They have striven to *naturalize intentionality*. In the remainder of this chapter we will examine several of the main attempts to supply naturalistic accounts of what it would mean for a wholly physical system to have states with intentional content. These are attempts at spelling out a fully naturalistic *theory of content*.

13.33   Many such theories are spelled out in terms of a notion of *mental representation*. Mental representations are posits that are supposed to be the main bearers of intentionality or aboutness. In thinking a thought about something, one thereby has a mental representation that represents that thing. Many of the theories of intentional content that we will examine can be equally well described as theories of *representational* content or as theories of what *representing* consists in.

Resemblance theory

13.34 According to the resemblance theory of representational content, representation is a relation of *resemblance*—mental representations represent things in virtue of resembling those things. While the resemblance theory had many historical proponents (for example, both Aristotle and Berkeley sub-scribed to the view) contemporary thinkers tend not to be especially enthused about it.

One problem with the resemblance theory is that there are many things 13.35 we are able to think about without there being any plausible sense in which a state of our mind resembles the thing thought about. This is especially so on the physicalist assumption that mental states are brain states. I can think about something's being 60 feet tall and bright green without my brain state being either 60 feet tall or bright green.

Another key objection to the resemblance theory is that the resemblance 13.36 relation is symmetrical whereas the representation relation (if representa-tion *is* a relation) is not. If George resembles Larry, it follows that Larry resembles George. However, if a state of George's mind represents Larry, it does not follow that Larry represents a state of George's mind.

Other objections to the resemblance theory include points we already 13.37 discussed in chapter 11 in connection with arguments against picture-like representations (resemblance-based representations) serving to ground our general capacities for thinking. One such point is that resemblance seems ill suited to ground our ability to mentally represent negative states of affairs: There's a difference between thinking that there are no dogs in the room and that there are no cats in the room, but a representation such as a picture may not resemble one state of affairs any differently than the other. Another such point is that resemblance is ill suited to ground our ability to mentally represent abstract properties: The abstract property of being a triangle can be represented in thought, but anything resembling a triangle by being triangular is also a particular kind of triangle, for example, an equilateral triangle. Given that an equilateral triangle resembles other equilateral triangles more than nonequilateral triangles, what can suffice to make it a representation of triangles in general—an abstract representation that equally represents all kinds of triangles? Appeals to resemblance alone are insufficient to answer this question.

Interpretational semantics

The interpretational approach to mental representational content posits 13.38 that what makes a mental representation have its content is that it is *inter-preted* as having that content. The interpretational approach may be read as saying that mental representations and nonmental representations are similar in this regard. An example of a nonmental representation is the printed English sentence "Dogs are furry." It is a *nonmental* representation because it, the string of marks on a page or screen, is not a state of anyone's mind. Plausibly, what makes this string of marks represent dogs being furry as opposed to fish being slimy is that we, the speakers of the English language, interpret it that way. The meaning or content of those marks is thus *interpretation dependent.*

13.39   The philosopher Daniel Dennett has offered that there is an important analogy to be drawn between nonmental and mental representations. On his *intentional stance* theory of intentionality, a physical system comes to have states with certain representational contents just in case it is useful in predicting and explaining the behaviors of such a system to adopt the *intentional stance* toward it. The intentional stance is a point of view toward things wherein one interprets those things as having intentionality.

13.40   Many philosophers have rejected this intentional stance approach, and interpretational approaches generally, on the grounds that they lead to either circular or infinitely regressive accounts of intentional content. At the heart of the alleged problem is that interpretation is itself a kind of representation. So, if I interpret some string of marks or someone's brain state as representing *x*, then I myself am representing that string of marks or that brain state. So, in trying to explain representation in terms of interpretation, what the interpretational approach does is to try to explain representation in terms of representation. But this would seem to either lead to a circle or to an infinite regress.

Conceptual role semantics

13.41   The conceptual role approach tries to define a mental state's representational content in terms of relations it enters into with other mental states of the same mind. One way of viewing the conceptual role approach is as an application of functionalism to intentionality. Recall the functionalist idea, from chapter 8, that what makes a state a belief as opposed to a sensory impression or a desire is the set of causal relations it bears to the other states in the causal economy of an entire cognitive system. Analogously, the conceptual role approach says that what makes the belief a belief *that grass is green* as opposed to the belief *that the moon is round* is a set of relations to other cognitive states.

13.42   For example, on this proposal, the key relations to other mental states that help define a mental state as being a representation of grass are relations to mental states that represent plants, mental states that represent slender leaves, and mental states that represent the color green.

One of the main inspirations for the conceptual role account is a highly 13.43 plausible account of the source of the meaning of logical connective terms such as "and" and "or." Plausibly, in a logical system such as a logical algebra or a computer language, what defines the meaning of a symbol such as "and" is something like the following: If symbols "P" and "Q" are both true, then the symbol string "P and Q" is true. In such a symbol system, the meaning of "and" is constituted by the role that it plays in a system of symbols. A computer contains a symbol that means "and" if it is disposed to use that symbol to output "P and Q" upon receiving both of the inputs "P" and "Q."

Such an approach is highly plausible for the intentionality or content of 13.44 concepts like "and." This is because it is totally obscure what else the meaning of "and" might consist in. It is not like there is any plausible object or set of objects that can be regarded as the referent of "and" in the way that there are entities that "dog" refers to.

One of the advantages of conceptual role semantics is that it is plausibly 13.45 naturalizable. The sorts of relations posited between system states seem like the sorts of relations between states that a suitably programmed computer can realize. If a computer can do it, then there is little doubt that the thing done is something mechanical and fully consistent with a physicalistic and naturalistic view of reality.

However, even though conceptual role semantics can be seen as having 13.46 an advantage in accounting for the meaning of logical connective concepts like "and," many philosophers regard it as highly implausible as an account of the concepts that refer to real world entities the way that "dog" does. One oft discussed complaint against conceptual role semantics is that it leads to a kind of *meaning holism* that entails that distinct thinkers cannot have thoughts with shared contents.

Suppose that Xavier and Yvonne differ with respect to the things that 13.47 they believe about dogs. Suppose that Xavier believes that he was once bitten by a dog, but that Yvonne believes no such thing. It follows then that Xavier's dog concept is related to a different set of beliefs in his cognitive economy than Yvonne's dog concept is in hers. Conceptual role semantics seems to entail that Xavier and Yvonne are not thinking the same thing when they think the thoughts that each would express by uttering "the dog is on the mat." However, it is allegedly a truism of common sense that distinct thinkers with distinct sets of beliefs about dogs can nonetheless think thoughts about dogs with the same content. Distinct thinkers can each equally well think that the dog is on the mat. If so, then conceptual role semantics has a serious problem accounting for this.

13.48   However, maybe this objection is incorrect. Perhaps no two thinkers ever think exactly the same things. Instead, they think similar (but not identical) things—they have thoughts with similar contents. If so, then perhaps there's hope for conceptual role semantics after all.

Causal or informational theory

13.49 Motivated in part to avoid the sorts of problems seen to arise for conceptual role semantics, many philosophers have been attracted to views of intentionality whereby it is a kind of direct relation between a thinker and an object. On such a view, two thinkers can both think about one and the same dog despite holding wildly divergent beliefs about that dog or even wildly divergent beliefs about dogs in general. One attempt to ground intentionality as a kind of direct relation to real world objects is an approach that sees intentionality as grounded in a kind of *causal* relation between thinkers and the real world objects that they think about.

13.50   If intentionality is a causal interaction between a thinker and an object, what kind of causal relation is it? One sort of proposal is that it is, or is grounded in, perception—the relation between perceivers and perceived objects. That intentionality is grounded in perception is a philosophical view closely associated with the history of empiricism (as discussed in chapter 11).

13.51   One source of inspiration for the causal approach is a phenomenon occurring in the natural world that some philosophers have called "natural meaning." Natural meaning occurs when there is a causal relation between two phenomena such that one of them can be taken as a *sign* or *signal* indicating the presence of the other. Examples of uses of the words "mean" and "means" along the lines of this idea of natural meaning include "smoke means fire," "red spots on the face mean measles," and "a hundred tree rings in the cross-section of a tree trunk means that the tree was a hundred years old." The basic idea of natural meaning is that some naturally occurring phenomena *carry information* about other naturally occurring phenomena.

13.52   One way of applying this idea to the intentionality of mental states is to say that mental states represent the things that they are caused by or carry information about. Such a proposal has a certain amount of plausibility when applied to perceptual states. So, for instance, when you and I look at two different but highly similar umbrellas, what makes my perception a perception of one umbrella and not the other is that my perception is *caused by* the one umbrella and not the other.

Despite this plausibility when applied to perceptual states, the causal 13.53 approach seems to run into problems when applied to other mental states, especially such mental states as thoughts about future events and nonexistent entities. Future events can't be the causes of current thoughts, since (unless time travel is possible) things in the future cannot have effects on things in the present. Nonexistent entities can't have effects on actual thoughts, because . . . they don't exist! The problem of nonexistence is a very serious problem for the causal or informational theory of content.

Teleological evolutionary theory

At the heart of the teleological theory of content is the idea of *teleology*— 13.54 the idea of having an *aim* or a *purpose*. One way in which things have a purpose is if we assign a purpose to them. A wadded-up newspaper can become a door stop if I decide that that is its purpose. Another way in which things have a purpose, especially if those things are the traits and behaviors of living organisms, is if those things have *evolved*, that is, if those things have been selected for in the process of Darwinian evolution. The spots on an animal's fur have the purpose of acting as camouflage because this has conferred a survival advantage to that animal's ancestors.

What it means, on an evolutionary teleological view, to say that the eyes 13.55 are *for* seeing and that the heart is *for* pumping blood, is that seeing and pumping blood explains how those body parts got selected for in the process of evolution by natural selection. Extending this view to account for the intentionality of mental states involves spelling out what mental states are naturally selected for.

The teleological theory of content can be interpreted as an elaboration 13.56 of the causal theory of content. The elaboration is to combine the idea of *natural meaning* with the idea of *evolutionary purpose*. Mental states represent what they have been naturally selected to carry information about.

Such a combination shows promise of solving the problem of nonexist- 13.57 ence. Instead of saying, as the causal theory does, that a mental representation represents whatever causes it, the teleological theory says that a mental representation represents whatever it was selected for through evolution to be caused by. To illustrate, suppose that there is a state of a frog's brain that is activated whenever small dark things move in the frog's visual field. Plausibly, the evolutionary purpose of such a brain state is to indicate the presence of flies, since being able to detect flies (a source of food for a frog) conferred a survival advantage on the frog's ancestors. If a small ball bearing were dangled on a string in front of the frog's face, this would activate the frog's fly detectors. The states of these detectors would represent the frog's visual field as containing a fly, even if there doesn't currently exist any fly in the vicinity of the frog. This illustrates a way in which the teleological theory can be interpreted as offering a solution to the problem of nonexistence.

Conclusion

13.58 Intentionality is a pervasive aspect of our mental lives. It is so pervasive that some philosophers hold intentionality to be the *mark of the mental*—a state is a *mental* state if and only if it exhibits intentionality. However, despite the centrality of intentionality, it is a deeply weird phenomenon. And philosophers have struggled to show how the existence of intentionality can be consistent with a naturalistic worldview.

Annotated Bibliography

Cummins, Robert (1989) *Meaning and Mental Representation* (Cambridge, MA: MIT Press). An excellent overview of the main theories of content determination with an eye toward the issues that matter for cognitive science.

Frances, Bryan (2002) "Twin Earth," in Marco Nani and Massimo Marraffa (eds.), *A Field Guide to the Philosophy of Mind*, full text available at http://host. uniroma3.it/progetti/kant/field/tea.htm, accessed February 11, 2013. Fun overview of the discussions of externalism that grow out of Putnam's (1975) Twin Earth thought experiment.

Freeman, Walter (2007) "Intentionality," *Scholarpedia*, 2(2), 1337, full text available at http://www.scholarpedia.org/article/Intentionality, accessed February 11, 2013. A scientist's interesting though idiosyncratic overview of intentionality.

Haugeland, John (1990) "The Intentionality All-Stars," *Philosophical Perspectives*, 4, *Action Theory and Philosophy of Mind*, 383–427. Entertaining overview of some of the main positions concerning intentionality.

Jacob, Pierre (2010) "Intentionality," in Edward Zalta (ed.), *The Stanford Encyclopedia of Philosophy*, full text available at http://plato.stanford.edu/archives/fall2010/entries/intentionality/, accessed February 11, 2013. An absolutely top-notch overview of this difficult subject.

Pitt, David (2008) "Mental Representation," in Edward Zalta (ed.), *The Stanford Encyclopedia of Philosophy*, full text available at (http://plato.stanford.edu/archives/fall2008/entries/mental-representation/, accessed February 11, 2013. Terrific overview of the relevance of mental representation for different parts of philosophy of mind (e.g., consciousness, imagery, eliminativism).

Putnam, Hilary (1975) "The Meaning of 'Meaning'," *Minnesota Studies in the Philosophy of Science*, 7, 131–193, full text available at http://mcps.umn.edu/assets/pdf/7.3_Putnam.pdf, accessed February 11, 2013. Classic discussion of Twin Earth and externalism.

14

CONSCIOUSNESS AND QUALIA

Optimism about Explaining Consciousness

Consciousness and related topics such as qualia have figured quite a bit in 14.1
the philosophical discussions covered in this book. So far, the main theme
of such discussions has been a debate between pessimists and optimists
concerning whether consciousness and qualia can ever be explained, especially whether they can be explained in physicalistic terms. Dualists and
panpsychists have occupied the pessimistic position. Pessimism about ever
explaining consciousness has been central to their explanatory gap arguments against physicalism. Varieties of physicalism such as the mind–brain
identity theory and functionalism represent an optimistic stance on the
question of whether consciousness can ever be explained. What we haven't
seen yet, but will in the present chapter, are any real details on how the
optimists might propose to explain consciousness. In the present chapter
we will look at two such proposals. Both proposals reflect the general trend
in cognitive science-inspired philosophy of mind of being functionalistic
and representational. That is, they spell out explanations of consciousness
in terms of the roles that certain states play, roles that may very well be
played equally well by computers and biological systems. Further, there is
a significant role in each theory played by mental representations. Insofar
as these representational theories of consciousness are optimistic about
naturalizing consciousness, they are also optimistic about naturalizing representation, a major topic of the previous chapter.

This Is Philosophy of Mind: An Introduction, First Edition. Pete Mandik.
© 2014 John Wiley & Sons, Inc. Published 2014 by John Wiley & Sons, Inc.

14.2   Before turning to the theories, we will take a look at some basic ideas concerning what it is that needs explaining in offering an explanation of consciousness. The theories that we will examine strive to explain one or more of these various phenomena of consciousness. Further, they strive to explain the relations between these phenomena. One useful way to get a handle on consciousness is by examining different uses of the word "conscious" and related words.

Focusing on Several Different Uses of the Word "Conscious"

14.3   It is useful to investigate uses of such words as "conscious" and "consciousness," as well as such related words as "awareness." In this chapter, we will focus on four of the main uses of "conscious" that have attracted the interest of contemporary philosophers of mind. Each of these four uses of the word "conscious" arguably labels four distinct phenomena or four distinct kinds of consciousness (or, alternately, four distinct senses of the word "conscious") that a satisfying theory of consciousness should seek to explain. These four phenomena are (1) creature consciousness, (2) transitive consciousness, (3) state consciousness, and (4) phenomenal consciousness.

Creature consciousness

14.4   This first use of the word "conscious" is used to describe an entire organism, as opposed to a state of an organism, as being conscious. Near synonyms are "awake" and "aware." When we describe a person or a nonhuman animal as being unconscious—as when they are asleep or anesthetized—we are describing them as lacking *creature consciousness*. The main thing it seems to mean to distinguish a conscious creature from an unconscious creature is to say that the conscious creature is awake and responsive to stimuli whereas an unconscious creature is neither awake nor responsive.

Transitive consciousness

14.5   The transitive sense of the word "conscious" is marked by uses wherein we say that someone is conscious *of* something. In seeing something you become conscious of it. Hearing something is another way of being conscious of something. Arguably, another way of being conscious of something is by thinking about it. Unlike the creature use of the word "conscious," which is an adjective applied to a creature, the transitive use of the word "conscious" is used to refer to a relation between a creature and the thing that the creature is conscious of or aware of.

It should be noted that the relation of transitive consciousness may 14.6 simply be a relation in the grammatical sense without being a relation in the metaphysical sense. If thinking about something is not really a relation to a thing thought about (a hypothesis we discussed in the chapter 13), then in thinking about something one need not really, metaphysically, be related to an actual thing.

State consciousness

Like the creature use of the word "conscious," the state use of the word is 14.7 adjectival. However, instead of being used as an adjective that applies to an entire creature, in this use it is an adjective applied only to a state of a creature, in particular, a *mental* state of a creature.

If you are familiar with the basic idea of the Freudian unconscious, then 14.8 you may already be familiar with the basic idea of state consciousness. Sigmund Freud hypothesized that many of our behaviors were due to unconscious beliefs and unconscious desires. Since a belief or a desire is a mental state, in describing a belief or a desire as being conscious or unconscious, we are employing a concept of *state consciousness*.

The difference between conscious mental states and unconscious mental 14.9 states is important in understanding certain phenomena such as subliminal perception. In examples of subliminal perception, a stimulus is presented to a subject in such a manner that the subject does not report having seen it. However, there is still evidence that the subject did indeed see it. For example, if forced to guess about what they saw, they are better than chance in guessing the right answer. In such cases, then, it seems that the subjects have perceptual states that are *unconscious* perceptual states. Ordinarily, when we perceive something, we are able to report that we've perceived it. Arguably, in cases in which the perceptual states can be reported by the subject who has them, the perceptual states are *conscious* perceptual states.

Phenomenal consciousness

The notion of phenomenal consciousness is largely a technical notion that 14.10 has more to do with certain debates in philosophy than with an established usage of "conscious" in ordinary speech. The idea of phenomenal consciousness is an idea that encompasses such philosophical ideas as the idea of the *phenomenal character* of experiences, the idea of *qualia*, and the idea of *what it is like to be* certain beings or *what it is like to be* in certain states.

14.11   Arguably, the phrase "phenomenal consciousness" is either a technical way of talking about creature consciousness or a technical way of talking about state consciousness. The key to seeing this point has to do with the way that phenomenal consciousness is connected in the literature with the "what it is like" phrase. One use of the "what it is like" phrase has to do with creatures, as in Nagel's famous question about whether objective science can ever explain what it is like to be a bat. Another use of the "what it is like" phrase has to do with states of people, as in the question central to Jackson's knowledge argument, "Can someone who has never had a red experience know *what it is like* to have a red experience?" The question clearly concerns a kind of mental state, the state of having an experience of redness.

14.12   Despite being a technical usage without a clear connection to common-sense usages of the term "conscious," "phenomenal consciousness" is often used by philosophers to pick out what they consider to be the most philosophically important and vexing aspect of consciousness. The oft discussed "hard problem of consciousness" (to use the phrase widely associated with the philosopher David Chalmers) is a problem concerning whether any explanation can be given of *phenomenal consciousness*, especially explanations in terms of physical or functional properties.

14.13   We turn now to examine two theories of consciousness. The first is a version of a higher order representational theory of consciousness, David Rosenthal's *higher order thought theory* of consciousness. The second is the *first order representational theory* of consciousness, especially the version originating with the philosopher Michael Tye—his "PANIC" theory of consciousness.

Rosenthal's Higher Order Thought Theory of Consciousness

14.14   The gist of the higher order thought theory of consciousness, hereafter the HOT theory of consciousness, is that a state is conscious when one has a certain kind of thought, a higher order thought, about it. Recall our discussion of higher order mental states from chapter 13. What it means to say of a thought that it is "higher order" is that it is a thought about a mental state. A thought about something that is not a mental state, for example, a thought that there is a cat on the mat, is a first order thought. If you think to yourself, "I am thinking about a cat on a mat," then, in thinking that, you thereby have a higher order thought. In particular, you have a second order thought. A third order thought is a thought about a second order thought.

Of the four kinds of consciousness discussed earlier in this chapter— 14.15 creature consciousness, transitive consciousness, state consciousness, and phenomenal conscious—the kind that the HOT theory primarily seeks to explain is *state consciousness*. HOT theory seeks to explain what makes some mental states conscious, and what differentiates conscious mental states from unconscious mental states.

One of the main ideas that the HOT theory relies on is the commonsen- 14.16 sical idea that when you have a conscious mental state, you are conscious *of* that mental state. Recall that when someone is consciousness *of* something, this is *transitive consciousness*. Thus, in seeking to explain state consciousness in terms of being conscious of a mental state, HOT theory is seeking to explain state consciousness in terms of transitive consciousness. According to HOT theory, the crucial way in which we are conscious of our own mental states is by thinking about them. So, since a thought about another mental state is a higher order thought, the HOT theory is explaining state consciousness by reference to higher order thoughts.

It might seem, at least on the surface, that HOT theory is explaining 14.17 consciousness in terms of consciousness, and is thus offering a circular explanation. However, according to HOT theory, the explanation is not circular because it is explaining one kind of consciousness, *state* conscious- ness, in terms of a different kind of consciousness, *transitive* consciousness. Since it is not explaining one phenomenon in terms of itself, it is not a circular explanation.

One of the key features of the HOT theory that makes it noncircular can 14.18 be put this way: A state in virtue of which one is conscious of something need not itself be a conscious state. Take, for instance, a first order thought or perception that the cat is on the mat. Suppose that this first order state is unaccompanied by any higher order thought. According to HOT theory, in such a situation one would be transitively conscious of the cat on the mat without that state, the thought that the cat is on the mat, itself being a conscious state.

14.19   According to the HOT theory, you can be *unconsciously* conscious of things. For instance, you can be unconsciously conscious of the cat on the mat. Another way of putting this point is to say that, in cases of subliminal perception where one has a percept without being conscious *of* the percept, one is nonetheless conscious of whatever it is that one perceives. In such a case one is conscious of something without being *conscious of* being conscious of the fact that one is conscious of it.

14.20   So far we have seen how the main thing that HOT theory is trying to explain is state consciousness. But what about the three other kinds of consciousness that we mentioned—phenomenal consciousness, transitive consciousness, and creature consciousness? How are these kinds of consciousness to be explained? Though these have not been the main focus of HOT theory, HOT theory can nonetheless be interpreted as having something to say about the remaining three phenomena of consciousness.

14.21   Phenomenal consciousness is closely associated with the notion of *what it is like* and the notion of *there being something it's like* to be such-and-such a creature or to be in such-and-such a mental state. Arguably, what it is like is a matter of the *subjective appearance* of your mental states—that is, it is a matter of how your mental states appear to you. Also arguably, what it is like is fully determined by the content of a higher order thought. So, if I have a higher order thought the content of which is *I am seeing a red square*, then, what it is like to be me at that moment is, from my own point of view, just as if I was seeing a red square. Of course, I may not actually be seeing a red square—perhaps there is no red square to see. But if I *think* that I am seeing a red square, then this is how my mental life will *appear to me*. This higher order thought, then, determines *what it is like* to be me at that moment.

14.22   What about transitive consciousness? Implicit in the way we've described HOT theory so far is that transitive consciousness is explained in terms of certain kinds of representational states, such as thoughts and perceptions. So, if you have a thought or a perception of a cat being on a mat, you thereby are transitively conscious of the cat being on the mat. In short, transitive consciousness and intentionality are pretty much the same thing.

14.23   Regarding creature consciousness, if being creature conscious is simply a matter of being responsive to stimuli, and being responsive to stimuli just is a kind of disposition to be conscious *of* stimuli, then we have, at least implicitly, an explanation of creature consciousness in terms of transitive consciousness. However, as already mentioned, explaining aspects of con-

sciousness aside from state consciousness is not really the main concern of
HOT theory.

An objection to the HOT theory: Introspectively implausible

One objection to the HOT theory of consciousness is that it is introspec-   14.24
tively implausible. It is far more plausible, says the objection, that we often,
if not most of the time, have conscious states without being aware of those
states. Another way of putting this point is to say that (1) the core of the
HOT theory is the claim that all conscious states are occasions in which we
are self-conscious and (2) it is introspectively implausible that we are *self-
conscious* each and every time that we have a conscious state.

The HOT theory has a convincing response to this objection. According   14.25
to this response, the reason that we find the objection plausible is that we
seldom notice any higher order thoughts accompanying our conscious
states. Further, the higher order thought theory has an explanation of why
we seldom notice such higher order thoughts. In order to notice one of
your own second order thoughts, the noticing itself would constitute a
third order thought, a thought about the second order thought. However,
says this response, it is rare that we ever have thoughts of a higher order
than the second order. Therefore, it is to be expected on the higher
order theory that we seldom notice the presence of higher order thoughts.
That we seldom notice such thoughts, then, does not provide a strong
objection against the HOT theory. Let's turn to some other objections.

The next two objections hinge on versions of the claim that the HOT   14.26
theory is too intellectual—it focuses too much on the intellectual part of
the mind and, in so doing leaves out aspects of consciousness that are less
intellectually oriented and have more to do with, for example, nonintel-
lectual, sensory consciousness.

Another objection to the HOT theory: Too intellectual

One version of the "too intellectual" objection focuses on babies and non-   14.27
human animals. Both of these kinds of creatures plausibly have conscious
states. However, goes the objection, it is implausible that these creatures are
cognitively sophisticated enough to be able to have higher order thoughts.
Arguably, in order to think some thought you must grasp certain concepts—
concepts that need to be learned. For instance, in order to think that a cat

is on a mat, you must grasp a concept of cats as well as a concept of mats. Further, such concepts are implausibly concepts anyone is born grasping and thus must be learned. Even further, in the case of animals there are many concepts that they simply will not be able to learn. For example, a dog is unlikely to ever be able to learn the concept of an MP3 or grasp the concept of what Wednesdays are.

14.28   This objection continues by saying that, in order to have higher order thoughts, one must have a concept of mental states (how else could one think of mental states?). However, it is implausible that either babies or nonhuman animals grasp such a concept.

14.29   This version of the "too intellectual" objection says that (1) the HOT theory imposes concept possession requirements on babies and nonhumans that they can't satisfy even though (2) many babies and nonhumans clearly have conscious states. Stating the objection this way makes clear that the HOT theorist has two general ways to respond to the objection. The first way is to argue against (1), perhaps by arguing that babies and nonhumans can satisfy the conceptual requirements on having higher order thoughts. The second way is to argue against (2), perhaps by presenting reasons for thinking that babies and nonhumans don't actually have any conscious states.

14.30   Let's turn now to look at a second version of the "too intellectual" objection. This version does not focus on babies and nonhuman animals, but instead on full grown human beings. At the heart of this version is *nonconceptual content*. Arguably, there is more to the representational content of many of our mental states, especially sensory states, than can be captured by the concepts that we possess.

14.31   Consider all of the many colors that a normally sighted person can visually discriminate. Imagine that you are at a paint store looking at a hundred different varieties of paint samples. For each color sample that you can visually distinguish, you have a different visual state with a corresponding representational content.

14.32   Some philosophers argue that we do not have as many concepts as there are colors we can see. One line of evidence for the claim that we have very few color concepts concerns the fact that we cannot remember fine differences in color. For example, if you were looking at two very similar shades of blue and were shown a third sample a short time later, you would have a very difficult time remembering which of the first two was the same as the third one. Such a memory task is not difficult for colors that you clearly have concepts for, such as red and green. Suppose that the first two colors were as different as red and green, and that the third color is a shade of red. Upon seeing the third color you would have very little difficulty in remembering which of the first two it matched. Some philosophers conclude from such considerations that the content of our perceptions of colors is a nonconceptual content, a kind of content that is more fine grained than the contents of purely conceptual states such as beliefs and judgments.

If our conscious states do have the sort of fine-grained nonconceptual   14.33 contents that some philosophers have argued for, then this seems to pose a difficulty for the HOT theory of consciousness. The HOT theory says that the contents of consciousness are the contents of certain thoughts. Thoughts are assumed to have only conceptual contents—you can only think about what you have concepts of. The gist of this version of the "too intellectual" objection is that, since experience has fine-grained nonconceptual content, there are not enough concepts in our higher order thoughts to fully capture the true contents of our consciousness.

First Order Representation Theories of Consciousness

We turn now to look at a version of a first order representational theory of   14.34 conscious. We will focus mainly on Michael Tye's PANIC theory of consciousness. However, on a few occasions we will also mention a first order representational theory of consciousness originating with the philosopher Fred Dretske.

The main aim of Tye's PANIC theory is to explain phenomenal character.   14.35 "PANIC" is an acronym for *poised abstract nonconceptual intentional content*. The gist of the theory is to explain the phenomenal character of experience in terms of a kind of representational or intentional content, specifically, content that is poised, abstract, and nonconceptual. We've already seen what nonconceptual content is supposed to be (recall the "too intellectual" objection to the HOT theory). A little bit later we'll see what Tye has in mind by calling certain contents "poised" and "abstract."

PANIC theory mainly seeks to explain *phenomenal character*—that   14.36 aspect of conscious states in virtue of which there is *something it's like* to be in such states. First and foremost, then, PANIC theory seeks to explain phenomenal consciousness.

PANIC theory seeks to explain phenomenal character in terms of the   14.37 contents of first order representations, especially perceptual and perception-like representations of objects in the environment. According to PANIC theory, the phenomenal character of, for example, seeing an apple as red just is the first order representational content of that perceptual state. That perceptual state represents the apple as having the property of being red. The phenomenal character of the perceptual state is one and the same as the way it represents the apple as being. The represented redness of the apple is one and the same as the phenomenal character of the perceptual state.

14.38   A similar account applies to perception-like states such as afterimages and hallucinations (recall our discussions of perception-like states from chapter 11). In visually hallucinating a red apple, one has a mental representation with the first order content of an apple being red. Again, the represented redness of the apple is one and the same as the phenomenal character of the mental state.

14.39   Tye's PANIC theory puts two constraints on what is represented in experience. The first constraint is that what is represented is abstract. The second is that the representations are nonconceptual. What it means to say that a content is *abstract* is that it does not pertain to one particular object, but instead, pertains to properties that *many* objects can have in common. For example, two particular apples can both be red. Part of the representational content of an experience is the redness of an apple that one is seeing. One can have a similar content even if they are seeing a particular different apple. The content that is similar across two distinct experiences of two distinct apples is an abstract content. Tye's idea here is that phenomenal character—the *what it's like* aspect of experience—is abstract instead of particular. What it is like to see an apple can be the same as what it is like to see some numerically distinct apple.

14.40   Let us turn now to examine the main difference between first order and higher order approaches. The main difference concerns what they say about the relations between state consciousness and transitive consciousness. According to a higher order approach, in order for a state to be conscious one must be conscious *of* it. First order approaches, such as Tye's and Dretske's, deny this. Whereas the higher order approach says that a conscious state is one that you are conscious *of*, the first order theory says that a conscious state is one that you are conscious *with*. According to the first order theory, a state that makes you transitively conscious of something is itself a conscious state. A first order state need not be accompanied by a higher order state in order to be conscious.

14.41   Tye's account of phenomenal character can be interpreted as also supplying an account of state consciousness. We've already seen that, according to Tye, phenomenal character is a kind of representational content that is abstract and nonconceptual. Another aspect of his view is that the content must be poised—this is the "P" in PANIC theory. What it means for a content to be *poised* is for the content to be available for use by other mental systems, such as those involving belief, desire, and other states that are involved with intelligent or rational behavior, including verbal behavior.

The way that Tye's account may be read as providing conditions for state 14.42 consciousness is like this: A conscious state is a mental state that has representational contents that are poised, abstract, and nonconceptual.

The transparency argument for first order representationalism

One oft-discussed argument for first order representational theories of 14.43 consciousness is the *transparency argument*. The basic idea at the heart of the transparency argument is that conscious experiences are *transparent*, meaning that when you try to become aware of one of your experiences, all that you are capable of being aware of are the properties of the thing that the experience is an experience of. One cannot become aware of properties of the experience itself.

Consider, for example, your experience of the words you are reading 14.44 right now. In having that experience you are aware of the words—you are aware of the dark marks on a light background. Now attempt to become aware, not of the words, but of the *experience* of the words. Does this even make sense? Is there anything to be aware of besides what the experience is of, in this case, the words, the background, and their properties? First order representationalists answer "no."

The alleged transparency of experience is supposed to support first order 14.45 representationalism in the following way: If all one can be aware of in having an experience is what the experience is of, then the best explanation of this is to say that all there are to the contents of consciousness are the first order representational contents of the experiences. Note the way that this contrasts with higher order approaches. Higher order approaches assert that a conscious state is a state that one is conscious of. This would entail that a conscious experience is an experience that one is conscious of. But one way to read the transparency argument is as saying that it is difficult, and perhaps even impossible, to be conscious of one's experiences themselves as opposed to the worldly objects that the experiences are experiences of.

The "Spot" argument for first order representationalism

14.46 The "Spot" argument for first order representationalism is philosopher Fred Dretske's. Central to this argument is a phenomenon sometimes referred to as "change blindness" (although this label is perhaps misleading). In cases of so-called change blindness you can be presented with two scenes that differ in just one detail without noticing *which* detail is different.

14.47   Imagine that you are shown scene Alpha, which contains 15 small dark shapes, such as triangles, stars, circles, and hexagons. A few seconds later, scene Alpha is removed and scene Beta is shown. Scene Beta differs from Alpha in just one small detail. It has the presence of a 16th shape, a small spot in the lower right corner that we can call "Spot." Subjects shown the two scenes will have a very hard time noticing the difference. Some subjects can examine the two scenes very thoroughly without noticing the difference. (To find some interesting video demonstrations of this phenomenon, do an Internet search for "change blindness.")

14.48   A subject can be allowed to stare at each scene for several seconds, scanning the entirety of each scene with their eyes, and still not notice the difference between Alpha and Beta. Since the subject has looked at the entirety of Beta—visually scanned every part of it—it's plausible that the subject had a conscious experience of every part of it. This means that they've had a conscious experience even of Spot, since Spot is a part of Beta. However, the subject does not notice that their experience of Beta is different from their experience of Alpha. This can be interpreted as showing that the subject lacks a certain higher order awareness of their experiences. The subject is aware of Spot, but is not aware that their *experience* of Beta is different from their *experience* of Alpha.

14.49   Dretske urges that such considerations support the view that a mental state can be conscious without the subject of the state being conscious *of* the state. You have a conscious state, in this case, simply in virtue of being conscious of Spot. You need not be *self*-conscious—you need not be aware of your experience of Spot in order for it to be a *conscious* experience.

Conclusion

14.50 Consciousness and qualia have driven some philosophers to embrace dualism and despair at ever explaining phenomenal consciousness.

Nonetheless, many philosophers remain optimistic about the prospects of explaining consciousness. Especially interesting are projects that seek to explain consciousness in terms of intentionality, either along the lines laid out by the higher order approach or along the lines of the first order approach.

Annotated Bibliography

Chalmers, David (1995) "Facing Up to the Problem of Consciousness," *Journal of Consciousness Studies*, *2*(3), 200–219, full text available at http://consc. net/papers/facing.html, accessed February 12, 2013. Concise statement of Chalmers's notorious "hard problem" of consciousness.

Dennett, Daniel (1996) "Facing Backwards on the Problem of Consciousness," *Journal of Consciousness Studies*, *3*(1), 4–6, full text available at http:// imprint.co.uk/online/HP_dennett.html, accessed February 12, 2013. Dennett's reply to Chalmers (1995).

Dennett, Daniel and Akins, Kathleen (2008) "Multiple Drafts Model," *Scholarpedia*, *3*(4), 4321, full text available at http://www.scholarpedia.org/article/Multiple_ drafts_model, accessed February 12, 2013. Concise statement of Dennett's theory of consciousness—his "multiple drafts model" of consciousness.

Dretske, Fred (1993) "Conscious Experience," *Mind*, *102*(406), 263–283. The source of Dretske's "Spot" argument for first order representationalism about state consciousness.

Rosenthal, David and Weisberg, Josh (2008) "Higher-Order Theories of Con- sciousness," *Scholarpedia*, *3*(5), 4407, full text available at http://www. scholarpedia.org/article/Higher-order_theories_of_consciousness, accessed February 12, 2013. Nice overview by proponents of a higher order thought theory of consciousness.

Tye, Michael (1995) *Ten Problems of Consciousness* (Cambridge, MA: MIT Press). Very fun book serving as both an overview of the main philosophical prob- lems about consciousness and a defense of Tye's first order representationalism— his PANIC theory of consciousness.

15

IS THIS THE END?
PERSONAL IDENTITY, THE SELF, AND LIFE AFTER DEATH

Problems of Personal Identity

Most of this book has been, of course, about the mind, and we now turn 15.1
to what may possibly be a separate topic, the topic of persons. However,
for many philosophers these topics are not totally separate. For example,
one might hold that a person just is a mind. For others, the mind is an
aspect of a person, but a person is not just a mind. For some of these latter
philosophers, minds and mental phenomena may very well be important
in defining what a person is, even if it is not the whole story about personal
identity.

In this section, we will briefly look at four philosophical problems con- 15.2
cerning personal identity before moving on, in the rest of the chapter, to
focus mainly on one of them—the problem of persistence.

The first problem is the question of what sort of thing a person is. What 15.3
sort of thing am I? What is the self—is it a bundle of perceptions? Is the
self instead a *substance* in which various properties inhere? Perhaps the self
is nothing at all, and there really are no such things as persons. If so, then
who wrote this book, and who is reading it?

The empiricist philosopher David Hume offers an answer to this cluster 15.4
of questions, although it is somewhat open to interpretation exactly
what Hume has in mind. Hume suggests that when we go looking for a
thing that the self can be identical to, as when we introspect and look
for some sign of the thing that is having our various perceptions, we

This Is Philosophy of Mind: An Introduction, First Edition. Pete Mandik.
© 2014 John Wiley & Sons, Inc. Published 2014 by John Wiley & Sons, Inc.

are doomed to find nothing aside from our various perceptions. On one reading of Hume, what he is offering is something known as a "bundle theory" of the self—the self just is the collection of perceptions and there is no substantive thing that is *having* the perceptions. On a different reading of Hume, what he is offering is a "no-self" theory. On such a theory, which shares much in common with certain strains of Buddhist thought, the self is nothing at all, not even a bundle of perceptions. On such a view, words like "I," "me," "self," and "person" don't really refer to anything real and are more like names of fictional characters than terms signifying actual entities.

15.5   On a different view of what sort of thing a person is, a person is a kind of animal—a person is a member of the species *Homo sapiens*. On yet a different view, a person is just a *part* of a human animal—a person is one and the same as the brain of a human organism.

15.6   To get a feel for this brain theory of personal identity, imagine that you and some other person, George, are the subjects in a brain-swapping procedure. We take your brain and put it in George's body and vice versa. Suppose that your old body with George's brain in it is destroyed. Do you survive? If you are a person, and you have survived this event, then it seems that what you are is a brain.

15.7   The second problem of personal identity concerns the question, "What does it take to count as a person?" Could a suitably programmed computer, perhaps in a robot body, count as a person? How about a fertilized human egg—is that already a person? Could a sufficiently intelligent nonhuman—perhaps a chimpanzee or a dolphin—count as a person? What about a human being who has had significant portions of their brain irreparably damaged so that they can no longer think or feel, but still are able to breathe and maintain a heartbeat. Is such an entity still a person?

15.8   The third problem concerns the question of what determines how many people there are at a given time. Could there be more people than bodies—as in a hypothetical case of two people in a single human body? Could two distinct bodies be (or be the bodies of) only one person (as perhaps might be the case in certain hypothetical "fission" cases, which we will discuss later in this chapter)?

15.9   The fourth problem is the problem of persistence. Do you remain one and the same person over time despite changing in various ways? If so, how? If not, why not? The problem of persistence is the problem that will be the primary focus of the rest of the chapter, so let us dive more deeply into it now.

The Problem of Persistence

Recall our discussion of Leibniz's law from previous chapters, especially chapter 2. Leibniz's law is a logical principle governing the concept of identity. One way of putting the core idea of Leibniz's law is to say that if x has some property that y lacks, then x and y are not identical—they are not one and the same entity but are instead two distinct entities. The problem of persistence arises when we try to reconcile Leibniz's law with the commonsense view that one and the same person can have different properties at different times.　15.10

Suppose that Melissa gets a haircut. At a time previous to her haircut, time t_1, Melissa has long hair. At a later time, time t_2, Melissa does not have long hair. We can plug these facts about Melissa into Leibniz's law in the following way: Let x be Melissa at t_1, and let y be Melissa at t_2. Melissa at t_1 has a property that Melissa at t_2 lacks—x has long hair, and y does not have long hair. According to Leibniz's law, x and y cannot be one and the same entity. But this would mean, then, that one and the same entity did not persist through the process of getting a haircut. Melissa with long hair and Melissa with short hair are two distinct people.　15.11

The conclusion of this line of thinking might be summed by saying that if a person changes in any of their properties, they stop existing and a numerically distinct person comes into existence. But this violates the commonsense proposition that persons can persist despite undergoing changes. Common sense seems to allow that one and the same person can have long hair on one day and short hair on the next. If the commonsense thinking on personal persistence is correct, then persons can survive all sorts of changes. Not only can a person survive getting a haircut, they can, for example, survive gaining weight and height, as is typical in the transition from childhood to adulthood. Further, the material in your body is constantly being replenished and it is unlikely that any of the particular molecules in your body right now were there seven years ago.　15.12

The philosophical problem of persistence, then, is the problem of explaining either (1) how it is possible for people to persist through change or, (2) if it is not possible, then why it is not possible.　15.13

Approaches to the Problem of Persistence

15.14 We turn now to look at four philosophical approaches to dealing with the problem of persistence. They are (1) the psychological approach, (2) the bodily approach, (3) the temporal parts theory, and (4) the no-self view.

The psychological approach

15.15 One of the earliest and most discussed advocates of the psychological approach to the problem of persistence is the philosopher John Locke. Locke holds that *consciousness* determines personal identity—the persistence of one and the same person over time is due to the continuity of that person's conscious memories of previous times in their life. Locke's theory allows for personal persistence even when a person undergoes a complete change of the molecules out of which they are made. The crucial factor for a person's persisting is their consciously remembering earlier times in their life. This continuity of conscious memory is what makes a person at time t_1 one and the same as a person at time t_2.

15.16 Locke illustrated the importance of psychological factors in determining personal identity with his thought experiment of the prince and the cobbler. Locke invites us to imagine a prince's soul, containing the conscious memory of the prince's history, trading places with the soul of a cobbler so that each soul now inhabits a new body. When you imagine this hypothetical soul swapping, where do you imagine the prince to wind up? Is the prince located in one and the same place as the prince's original body? Or does the prince go along with the soul, a soul now inhabiting and controlling the body formerly inhabited by the soul of a cobbler? The conclusion urged by proponents of the psychological approach is that the person goes with the soul—the prince now has a new body, but is still the prince.

15.17 Locke's thought experiment seems to presuppose substance dualism in its talk of souls, but even a physicalist can agree with the main point here. If whatever is responsible for consciousness and memory has been transferred from the body of the prince to the body of the pauper, then the prince himself now occupies the body of the cobbler.

15.18 A more explicitly physicalistic version of Locke's prince and cobbler thought experiment is the thought experiment of the brain transplant. Suppose that your brain was transplanted into someone else's body, a body that had its brain removed and destroyed. The transplantation procedure is done in such a way that your brain and its new body are kept alive throughout, and after the procedure, are able to interact—brain interacting with body—in normal ways. After the procedure, information coming in through the body's eyes and ears are sent to the sensory areas of your brain. And motor commands from your brain activate the muscles of the new body.

Here is a key question concerning personal identity in relation to the 15.19 brain transplant thought experiment: Do you survive the procedure? Many people would be inclined to answer "yes" to such a question.

On the supposition that you are a person and that you survive the pro- 15.20 cedure, it seems that personal identity is determined by factors that go along with the brain. And this can be seen as a point in favor of the psychological approach because, plausibly, the main reason that personal identity would go along with the brain instead of say, the foot or the liver, is because the brain is the main organ responsible for our psychological properties. It is the main organ responsible for our consciousness and memory.

Suppose that Alice's brain is put in Betty's body, forming an entity that 15.21 we can call, for discussion's sake, "Carla." Suppose also that Alice's old body and Betty's old brain are destroyed. One key question regarding personal persistence can be posed like this: Is Alice numerically identical to Carla? Are they one and the same person?

Quite plausibly, memories are stored in brains. So, if we asked Carla what 15.22 her name was, she would say "Alice." If we presented Carla with questions about the past events of the lives of Alice and Betty and asked Carla which events were from *her* life, she would say that her memories are of living Alice's life. Advocates of the psychological approach would see these points as favoring their own view of personal persistence. They would say that Carla is Alice—they are the same person. Alice got a new body, but she is still Alice.

The fission problem for the psychological approach

There is a set of problems posed in philosophical discussions of personal 15.23 identity known as *fission problems*. One such fission problem is posed as a problem for the psychological approach.

Suppose that Alan's brain is split into halves—the left half and the right 15.24 half. Alan's brain halves are kept alive and transplanted into two bodies that had their brains removed and destroyed—body 1 and body 2. Call the entity formed by implanting the left half of Alan's brain into body 1 "Lefty," and call the entity formed by implanting the right half of Alan's brain into body 2 "Righty." All of Alan's memories survive, but they are distributed across the two brain halves. Both Lefty and Righty seem like living normal human beings, and each one demonstrates evidence of thinking of itself as Alan.

15.25   So, what is the problem that is posed for the psychological approach? To see the problem, it helps to keep in mind a logical principle about identity that we can call *the transitivity of identity*. One way of describing the transitivity of identity is to say that, for all x, y, and z, if x is identical to y and y is identical to z, then x is identical to z. Closely related is the idea that if x is not identical to y, then if z is identical to x, z cannot be identical to y.

15.26   With these ideas about the transitivity of identity in mind, let's examine the case of Alan, Lefty, and Righty. If Lefty and Righty stood on a scale together, the scale would indicate a weight about twice that of just Lefty or just Righty on the scale. Many people would say that this is because Lefty and Righty are two distinct people. If we accept the nonidentity of Lefty and Righty, and also the transitivity of identity, then it becomes deeply puzzling what we should say about Alan. If Alan is identical to Lefty, then he cannot be identical to Righty. And if Alan is identical to Righty, then he cannot be identical to Lefty.

15.27   One way of applying the psychological approach to this case is to say that Alan is identical to *both* Lefty and to Righty, since both Lefty and Righty are psychologically contiguous with Alan—they carry the memories of living Alan's life. However, by the transitivity of identity, if Alan is identical to Lefty, and Alan is identical to Righty, then Lefty and Righty must be identical to each other. Even though they have qualitatively distinct bodies and occupy distinct spatial locations, Lefty and Righty would have to be, on this line of thinking, numerically identical, that is, one and the same person. This is puzzling indeed and may be regarded by some philosophers as an intolerable consequence of the psychological approach.

The somatic or bodily approach

15.28   Despite having a certain appeal, the psychological approach has not been universally accepted by philosophers. An alternative approach is one that ties personal identity to bodily or organismic factors. On one version of the somatic approach, a person is an entire living body, not just the organ that supports psychological functioning. On one view of the somatic approach, it would interpret of the fission case of Alan, Lefty, and Righty in the following way: Alan does not survive the brain splitting and implantation procedures because neither of the resultant entities, Lefty nor Righty, is the same biological organism as Alan was.

The somatic approach may be seen as more plausible than the psycho- 15.29
logical approach in the face of the brain splitting fission case. However, there is another sort of fission case that seems to pose trouble for the somatic approach as well as the psychological approach.

This second fission case has at its heart a thought experiment concerning 15.30
a matter teletransportation device. Imagine a device that can take a precise measurement of the exact location of every molecule in a physical object at a particular time. This device then transmits a radio signal containing the information from this measurement to a receiver device. The receiver device takes the information and makes an exact physical duplicate of the physical object that was measured at the sending station. Such a system would be like a fax machine for three-dimensional physical objects. Imagine that, in the future, even a human body can be "faxed" using such a matter teletransportation system.

On one version of the matter teletransportation thought experiment, we 15.31
are to imagine that when an object undergoes the measurement procedure at the sending station, the original object is destroyed—all of its molecules are taken apart and stored for future use. What is transmitted from the sending station to the receiving station is simply a radio transmission containing information about the molecules. No actual molecules are sent from the sending station to the receiving station. At the receiving station, a holding tank stores spare molecules so that any received information can be used to create a physical object out of the molecules.

To continue the thought experiment, imagine that in the far future, 15.32
Antoine goes into the sending station, has his molecules disassembled and his information sent to a receiving station on Mars. A technician at the receiving station accidentally presses the "receive" button twice, resulting in two perfect molecular duplicates of Antoine's body, including his brain. Call these two resulting entities "Bruce" and "Colin." Bruce and Colin are, at time t_2, intrinsically physically exactly similar to both each other and to Antoine at time t_1.

There are two crucial questions to ask about this thought experiment. 15.33
The first is, did Antoine survive the teletransportation procedure? The second is, if Antoine did survive, is he identical to Bruce, or to Colin, or to both Bruce and Colin?

15.34   One way of reading the somatic view is that it must answer "yes" to the first question: Since at least one of the entities at time t_2 share all of their bodily properties with Antoine, it would seem that Antoine did survive. However, things get especially puzzling when we contemplate the second question. Since Antoine shares bodily properties with both Bruce and Colin, this would push the somatic approach to saying that Antoine is identical to both of them. However, assuming that identity is transitive, this would seem to mean that Bruce and Colin are numerically identical. But this will strike many as an intolerable conclusion, since it will seem obvious to them that Bruce and Colin are, despite their similarities, two distinct people and not one and the same.

Temporal parts theory aka perdurantism aka four-dimensionalism

15.35   On the temporal parts theory, objects have temporal parts—parts that are located at different times. This is analogous to the way in which objects have such spatial parts as the left half and right half.

15.36   The temporal parts theory sees time as a fourth dimension, a dimension in addition to the three spatial dimensions of up–down, left–right, and forward–back. Following contemporary physics, the temporal parts theory sees space and time united as a single manifold—spacetime. Spacetime contains four-dimensional entities that can be spread out across the three spatial dimensions and the one temporal dimension. The entire life of an entity can be visualized as a four-dimensional spacetime "worm" whose length is stretched out through time from the moment of the entity's birth to the moment of its death. The spatial thickness of the worm is defined by how much of the three spatial dimensions it occupies at some point in time.

15.37   On the temporal parts theory of personal identity, you are a spacetime worm, and different moments of your life are different temporal parts of that worm. The version of you on your ninth birthday is just one "time slice" of this four-dimensional worm. The version of you reading this book is another such time slice. Those two time slices are two different temporal parts of one and the same "worm."

15.38   On the temporal parts theory, the solution to the problem of persistence, the problem of understanding how a person can survive undergoing changes, is to see how a person is *not* a three-dimensional entity that has one set of properties at one time and a different set of properties at a different time. Instead, a person is a four-dimensional spacetime worm that has different parts located both at different spatial locations and different times. So, for example, the 9-year-old version of me, the 27-year-old version of me, and the present, 42-year-old version of me are three different temporal parts of one and the same entity. Strictly speaking, a person does not change, since a person is an entity that exists across multiple times "all at once."

Some philosophers have resisted this view because it seems to imply   15.39
that the past and the future are as equally real as the present. One unappealing feature of such a view is that, if the future is as set and as real as the past, then this would seem to imply a kind of determinism, a determinism that is incompatible with many conceptions of free will. Of course, the ins and outs of various arguments about free will were discussed in chapter 12.

The no-self view

One reaction to the philosophical problem of personal persistence, a reac-   15.40
tion that can be applied to other problems of personal identity as well, is to simply deny that there are any such things as persons. Similarly, such a reaction is to deny the existence of the self. This view, which we can call the *no-self view* or *personal nihilism*, is reminiscent of the Buddhist doctrine of *anatman*—the doctrine that there is no persistent entity, no soul and no self, that comprises a person.

Some materialist versions of the no-self view can be seen as versions of   15.41
eliminativism or eliminative materialism, the main topic of chapter 10. Recall that eliminativism affirms the existence of physical things such as human bodies and their brains, but denies that such things have mental states such as beliefs or mental properties such as qualia or phenomenal character. A materialist version of the no-self view of personal identity would similarly affirm the existence of human bodies, or, at least, some kinds of physical objects, but would deny that they, or anything, should be regarded as selves or persons.

Note, however, that materialist versions of the no-self view do not need   15.42
to embrace all versions of eliminativism. The no-self theorist can affirm the existence of such mental states as beliefs and perceptions while at the same time denying that there are any such entities as selves or persons that *have* the mental states.

Why would anyone believe the no-self view? One line of thought is based   15.43
on the claim that the other theories do an overwhelmingly a poor job in trying to solve the problem of persistence and such related problems as the

fission problems. The various problems that arise show the very concept of a person to be an inherently confused and nonsensical concept.

15.44   Another line of thought is the *problem-of-the-many argument* against the existence of persons. If persons do exist and they are material things, then a person is a collection of physical particles, molecules, and atoms, which are themselves collections of even smaller particles (neutrons, protons, etc). However, for any alleged person, there are *many* distinct collections of particles that are equally plausible candidates for being that person.

15.45   To see this main point, consider a collection of particles that might constitute our friend George. For example, consider a collection of particles in George's body, and call that collection "$George_1$." Now consider the collection of particles that is $George_1$ minus one of the particles. Call that collection "$George_2$." Now consider the collection which is just like "$George_1$" minus one of the other particles, that is, minus one of the particles other than the one we excluded in defining $George_2$. Call this most recent collection "$George_3$."

15.46   Now, let's go back to thinking about which collection of particles George is identical to. If George is made of any particles at all, George is made of trillions of them. One estimate of how many atoms are in the body of an average adult human is *7 billion billion billion*—that's a 7 followed by 27 zeros. (Wow!) There are thus trillions of candidate collections of particles that George might be identical to—George might be identical to $George_1$, or $George_2$ ... or $George_{100}$ ... or $George_{1,000,000,000,000}$.

15.47   As if there weren't already too many choices, we can identify additional collections besides the ones just mentioned. There are, in addition to the collections that are just like $George_1$ with the exclusion of just *one* particle, the collections that are just like $George_1$ with the exclusion of just *two*. Also, there are the collections that are just like $George_1$ with the exclusion of *three* particles, and so on, up to some unspecified yet very large number. There are more candidate collections than there are individual particles in George's body. Anyway, at this point, you get the basic idea—there are a lot of different collections of particles within your body that are candidates for the collection that makes up the material object that you are identical to. The same goes for me: There are trillions of candidate collections of particles that I might be identical to.

15.48   Let us continue, now, with this argument against the existence of persons.

15.49   According to this argument, if "I" refers to anything, it either refers to just one thing or it refers to many. However, the proposal that "I," when uttered by me, refers to more than one thing, goes against common sense.

Grammatically, "I" is a singular term, not a plural term. The commonsense presupposition seems to be that, if I am any person at all, I am just one person. So, if I am a material thing, then I am a collection of particles, and further, I am just *one* collection of particles. However, selecting just one collection out of the many (the *trillions!*) as the one collection that I am identical to seems *totally* arbitrary. We have no reason for picking one at the exclusion of any other. So, since "I" refers to neither just one collection nor to many collections, it must refer to none of them. It therefore refers to nothing at all. The same line of thinking can be applied for other personal words like "me" and "person." Conclusion: Persons don't exist— there's no such thing as a person.

The way we've discussed the argument so far has been in terms of *spatial*   15.50
parts. In particular, the spatial parts were different particles in a collection. A similar problem-of-the-many argument can be given against temporal parts views of persons. Instead of using "George$_1$" to refer to a collection of particles, use it instead to refer to a collection of time slices of a spacetime worm. Let "George$_2$" refer to that collection minus a slice at the beginning of the worm. Let "George$_3$" refer to that collection minus two slices, and so on for some unspecified but large number of slices, etc. Just like in the previous version of the argument, there seems to be no principled reason for picking one of the collections over the other as the one thing that a word like "person" or "I" refers to.

Life after Death

Many religious traditions subscribe to a doctrine of life after death. This is   15.51
a topic of philosophical interest as well. The question of whether there is indeed a life beyond the death of the body, or whether it is even possible, can be seen as closely related to the problem of persistence. What criteria of personal persistence, if any, would be consistent with a person surviving the death of their body?

Religion aside, there are nonreligious reasons for contemplating the pos-   15.52
sibility of life after death. Obviously, the question of life after death overlaps somewhat with the mind–body problem. For example, physicalism and substance dualism seem to impose different constraints on the possibility of survival beyond the death of the body. If minds are distinct substances from bodies, surviving the death of the body should be a pretty easy thing for the mind to do.

15.53   Things might not be so easy, however, if physicalism is true. But there may still be hope for post-bodily survival. Some scientists and philosophers have even proposed a possible *technological* implementation of life after death in the form of "mind uploading." If certain versions of functionalism (chapter 8) are correct, then perhaps the mind is the software of the brain. As such, perhaps this software could be run on a computer after the brain and the rest of a human's organic body have died.

15.54   In the remaining parts of this chapter, we will further explore philosophical accounts of how it might be possible to survive death.

Substance dualism and the afterlife

15.55   Recall the varieties of substance dualism that we discussed in chapter 2. The core idea of substance dualism is that the mind or soul is a thing distinct from any physical body. Part of what this distinctness consists in is that the mind can exist without any physical body existing. It is clear, then, that whatever other problems substance dualism may have, *if* substance dualism were true, there wouldn't be any additional philosophical problem concerning the afterlife. One's physical body may come to be destroyed at death, and the nonphysical substance which is the human mind can go on existing. The continued mental life of the thinking substance would indeed be, then, a life after death.

15.56   One possibility left open on substance dualism is that the afterlife is wholly spiritual or wholly mental. Yet another possibility, also left open on substance dualism, is that the thinking substance be rejoined with a physical body, perhaps a reconstituted version of your old body, or perhaps, as in many reincarnation scenarios, joined with an entirely new and different body.

15.57   While the possibility of an afterlife doesn't raise any *special* problems for substance dualism, it of course remains that substance dualism has many problems anyway. As we saw in chapter 2, such problems include the problem of interaction. Perhaps, then, we should be looking for a different solution to the mind–body problem, as well as a different solution to the problem of life after death. Fortunately, substance dualism isn't the only way in which the afterlife might be achieved. There are physicalistic versions of life after death as well.

Mind–brain identity theory and the afterlife

15.58   If the mind is identical to the brain, and the brain dies, how could it be possible for mind to survive death? One possibility depends on viewing the brain as a collection of particles in a certain configuration. If the pre-death configuration of particles could be restored after death, then a psychologically similar mind would thereby be brought into existence. Perhaps this reconfiguration of the particles could be brought about by advanced technologies, or perhaps it would require the intervention of a super-powerful supernatural being. But, either way, if mind–brain identity theory is true, it seems that a mind very similar to the one you have now could be brought about even after your brain has died.

Of course, there remains the personal identity question of whether that mind would be one and the same person as the person you are now. There are, of course, different philosophical answers to such a problem of personal persistence. One special wrinkle brought about by the fact of death is the question of whether one and the same person could exist at different times if there is a period of brain death between those two times. Presumably, during the period in which the brain is dead (perhaps a period in which its particles are widely scattered because the death was due to a violent explosion) it is clear that the mind previously supported by the brain no longer exists. So, there is a bit of a puzzle about whether the mind that is brought into existence after the particles are retrieved and reassembled into a living brain would be one and the same mind, that is, one and the same person as before death. 15.59

Functionalism and the afterlife

If the proper solution to the mind–body problem is a version of functionalism, then this opens up further possibilities for what an afterlife might be. On one possibility, post-death life could be technologically accomplished via a process of mind uploading—a living brain is scanned and then its activities are simulated in a highly detailed computer simulation. According to at least one version of functionalism, such a computer simulation of a brain would suffice to give rise to an actual—not merely simulated—mind. After the brain is scanned, it could be destroyed and disposed of without any real loss suffered by the surviving mind. There is, however, the remaining question of personal persistence: Would the mind that survives be one and the same person as the person whose brain was scanned? 15.60

Temporal parts and the afterlife

The temporal parts view of personal persistence can also be applied to the question of the afterlife. On the temporal parts view, if a person can indeed 15.61

survive bodily death, then a person is a four-dimensional entity that has a dead temporal part surrounded by living temporal parts. A resurrected person is a spacetime worm with a dead time slice surrounded by earlier and later time slices that are alive.

No-self and the afterlife

15.62   On the no-self view, there are, strictly speaking, no persons. Strictly speaking then, no person survives bodily death. Even though the no-self view doesn't offer a positive answer to the question of how the afterlife may be achieved, it does offer an interesting view to contemplate in connection with the topic of death. If, as the no-self view holds, there is no real continuity of personal existence from each changing moment to the next, then there is no *real* difference between a change from one moment of life to the next and a change from being alive to being dead. For any two moments in the existence of a human body, there is no single person that survives from one moment to the next. This is equally true for two moments in which the body is alive and two moments in which the body is alive at one moment and dead at the next. Bodies may die, but persons do not, on this view, because no person ever existed in the first place.

Conclusion

15.63   Most readers of this book are persons. Unless, of course, there just is no such thing as a person. If there is no such thing as a person, then the belief that you are one is a kind of illusion. But who or what is suffering the illusion? How can there be illusions without persons? Such questions are absolutely central to understanding who or what we are, and where we are going. However, philosophers of mind, as well as other investigators, may very well be at only the earliest stages of understanding these deepest of mysteries.

Annotated Bibliography

Dennett, Daniel (1978) "Where Am I?," in Daniel Dennett, *Brainstorms: Philosophical Essays on Mind and Psychology* (Cambridge, MA: MIT Press), full text available at http://www.newbanner.com/SecHumSCM/WhereAmI.html, accessed February 13, 2013. Philosophical reflections on the nature of the self, packaged as a fun science fiction story about—spoiler alert—Dennett getting his brain removed to control his body remotely.

Flanagan, Owen (2011) *The Bodhisattva's Brain: Buddhism Naturalized* (Cambridge, MA: MIT Press). Chapters 4 and 5—"Selfless Persons" and "Being No-Self and Being Nice"—contain accessible discussions of the Buddhist no-self doctrine, *anatman*.

Hasker, William (2010) "Afterlife," in Edward Zalta (ed.), *The Stanford Encyclopedia of Philosophy*, full text available at http://plato.stanford.edu/archives/fall2010/entries/afterlife/, accessed February 13, 2013. Not simply a religious issue, there are philosophical questions raised by the possibility of the afterlife. These issues are well covered here.

Hume, David (1739) *A Treatise of Human Nature, Book 1*, full text available at http://www.earlymoderntexts.com/htb.html, accessed February 13, 2013. Hume's view of the self is highly influential, though it's controversial whether he has a no-self view or a bundle view. Check out part 4, section 6 and decide for yourself.

Locke, John (1690) *An Essay Concerning Human Understanding*, full text available at http://www.earlymoderntexts.com/loess.html, accessed February 13, 2013. This is the classic presentation of the psychological approach to personal identity and the problem of persistence. See especially book 2, chapter 27.

Unger, Peter (1979) "Why There Are No People," *Midwest Studies in Philosophy*, 4(1), 177–222. For the problem-of-the-many argument against the existence of persons, see especially section 7, "The Inconsistency of 'Person.'"

INDEX

This Is Philosophy of Mind: An Introduction, First Edition. Pete Mandik.
© 2014 John Wiley & Sons, Inc. Published 2014 by John Wiley & Sons, Inc.

236   Index

Printed and bound by CPI Group (UK) Ltd, Croydon, CR0 4YY